ABORTION RIGHTS
AS
RELIGIOUS FREEDOM

In the series

Ethics and Action, edited by Tom Regan

ABORTION RIGHTS
AS
RELIGIOUS FREEDOM

PETER S. WENZ

TEMPLE UNIVERSITY PRESS
Philadelphia

Temple University Press, Philadelphia 19122
Copyright © 1992 by Temple University. All rights reserved
Published 1992
Printed in the United States of America

♾ The paper used in this publication meets the minimum
requirements of American National Standard for Information
Sciences—Permanence of Paper for Printed Library Materials,
ANSI Z39.48-1984

Library of Congress Cataloging-in-Publication Data

Wenz, Peter S.
    Abortion rights as religious freedom / Peter S. Wenz.
        p.   cm. — (Ethics and action)
    Includes bibliographical references and index.
    ISBN 0-87722-857-4 (cloth : alk. paper)
    ISBN 0-87722-858-2 (paper : alk. paper)
    1. Abortion—Religious aspects.   2. Women—Civil rights—United
States.   3. Abortion—Law and legislation—United States.
4. Religious liberty—United States.   I. Title.   II. Series.
HQ767.2.W46   1992
363.4'6'0973—dc20   91-11610

To my mother, Alberta Delia Wenz, who has maintained all her adult life that a woman's abortion "is nobody else's (d____) business."

Contents

Preface

THE SUPREME COURT'S DECISIONS regarding abortion remind me of a story about a novice judge who was anxious about judging correctly. Her anxiety was allayed somewhat by an older colleague's confidence that her decisions would probably be correct, even though her reasons for those decisions would probably be mistaken. Render a decision without giving reasons, the veteran advised. In view of the Supreme Court's role in our government and society, its justices seldom have the luxury in important cases of rendering decisions without reasons. Of course, Supreme Court justices are not novices. Nevertheless, their reasons are often less persuasive than their decisions are acceptable. I maintain in this work that the abortion decisions, especially *Roe v. Wade*, suffer from this defect. The reasoning provided is poor, while the result is largely justifiable.

I have two goals: to assist lay people in understanding constitutional issues regarding abortion, and to provide a new, better foundation in the Constitution for a woman's right to terminate her pregnancy. I pursue the first goal by explaining all legal terms and including them in a glossary. I achieve the second goal, to provide a more secure constitutional justification for abortion rights, in two stages. I criticize the Court's reliance on a right of privacy and then argue that during at least the first twenty weeks of pregnancy, the issue is inherently religious. Abortion rights are a species of the right to religious freedom.

I judge rival interpretations of the Constitution according to two basic criteria: congruence with appropriate written documents, and conformity with moral and political ideals. Other things being equal, an interpretation is better that is confined to specific rights explicitly protected in the Constitution, and that accords with more Supreme Court precedents. On many matters, including abortion, there is no perfect irrefutable interpretation of the Constitution because the relevant words and phrases in the Constitution are general, and their limits are inherently imprecise. Such terms include "liberty," "due process of law," and "religion," to name but a few. Constitutional interpretations remain problematic also because they are judged in part by their compatibility with past decisions of the Supreme Court. Since those decisions span two hundred years and were made by people with different life experiences and values, it is often impossible for an interpretation to agree with all Supreme Court decisions on a topic. Those decisions do not always agree with one another. Preference is usually given to interpretations in better accord with Court opinions that are more recent and that better express our moral and political ideals.

Conformity with our moral and political ideals, the second criterion for the acceptability of constitutional interpretations, is an application of what is often called the principle of charity. Other things being equal, interpretations are preferred that place what is being interpreted in a better light. Constitutional interpretations are better when they place the Constitution in a favorable light by implying that it furthers what we currently consider to be the highest and best moral and political values.

Constitutional interpretations are often problematic as a result of tensions between these two criteria. An interpretation that accords best with our current highest moral and political ideals may not conform best to the words of the Constitution or to past decisions of the Supreme Court. Controversy can stem also from conflicts among our moral and political ideals.

The goal of the present work, then, is to find an inexplicit, underlying rationale for the Supreme Court's abortion-related decisions. I maintain that a rationale featuring the moral and political ideal of religious freedom accords best with the words of the Constitution and with Supreme Court decisions in a variety of areas. This rationale best expresses our contemporary ideals regarding religious freedom and gives due weight to two additional ideals: majority rule and individual rights. Because I disagree with the rationale given by the Court in *Roe v. Wade*, I hope to vindicate the critics who point out the weakness of that rationale. At the same time, however, because my interpretation of the Constitution shows the decisions in *Roe* and in other abortion-related cases to be justified, I vindicate the view of those who defend a woman's constitutional right to terminate her pregnancy.

The present work was facilitated greatly by the Center for Legal Studies at Sangamon State University, especially Director Nancy Ford and Assistant Director Rebecca Wilkin. Typing and other secretarial support was provided by Kathy Barnhart, who not only managed the office but typed on weekends to complete the project on time. Other Center typists are, principally, Marilyn Beveridge, as well as Shawnelle Kapper. I thank also Joel Johnson, a Center graduate assistant, for his help in proofreading the manuscript and page proofs, and Delores Bandow, a recent journalism graduate and my sister-in-law, for teaching me to write more concisely.

Colleagues whom I thank for reading and making helpful comments on the manuscript are George Agich, Ed Cell, Larry Golden, Gershon Grunfeld, Richard Palmer, and Eric Springsted. I thank especially Ed Cell, who read everything at least once and applied unstintingly to this project his keen analytic mind and superb rhetorical skill. He noted omissions and errors in many arguments and often could see and articulate more clearly than I the point at issue and the appropriate manner of addressing it. I am embarrassed to think what this book would have been like without his help.

I thank my wife, Patricia Wenz, and scholars Ray Frey and Tom Regan for their encouragement and advice on this project and others.

Finally, I thank members of the judiciary, principally justices of the Supreme Court, whose thought has been my guide. I have learned no less from, for example, Justices William Rehnquist and Byron White, who generally oppose the results that I advocate, than from Justices Harry Blackmun, William Brennan, Thurgood Marshall, and Lewis Powell, who generally support those results. My criticism of judicial opinions most often reflect reasoning articulated first by members of the Court. Justice Sandra Day O'Connor's criticisms of the trimester framework, Justice John Paul Stevens's appeal to the Establishment Clause, and Justices Oliver Wendell Holmes, Hugo Black, and Byron White's objections to substantive due process are particularly noteworthy. I must thank also Justices William Brennan, Warren Burger, and Sandra Day O'Connor for their thoughts on the Religion Clauses. In sum, I have relied on a variety of judicial opinions and especially on the interplay among them. The result is my partial agreement with everyone, my complete agreement with no one, and my increased appreciation for the Court as an institution.

ABORTION RIGHTS
AS
RELIGIOUS FREEDOM

Introduction

Roe v. Wade *under Attack*

THE SUPREME COURT DECISIONS in *Roe v. Wade*[1] (1973) and its companion case, *Doe v. Bolton*,[2] increased enormously the availability in the United States of legal abortions. Since those decisions, people on opposite sides of the abortion issue have often focused on *Roe v. Wade*. Those (generally) opposed to abortions have called for the reversal of that decision, whether through constitutional amendment, congressional action, or judicial overturn. In contrast, people favorable to legal abortions have tended to rally round the *Roe v. Wade* decision as a judicial precedent that should remain in force. An examination of the rationale and decision in that case is thus a good place to begin a discussion of the constitutional status of abortion.

An understanding of the constitutional status of abortion requires a reexamination of *Roe v. Wade* also because the majority that decided the case has been eroded by retirement.[3] Some of their replacements have openly criticized the decision. One example is Justice O'Connor's dissent in *City of Akron v. Akron Center for Reproductive Health* (1983). She writes, "There is no justification in law or logic for the trimester framework adopted in *Roe* and employed by the Court today on the basis of *stare decisis*."[4] *Stare decisis* is the principle that present and future decisions should follow the precedents established by prior judicial decisions. No one doubts that *stare decisis* should be adhered to most of the time, as it enables people to use past judicial opinions to predict the Court's response in similar cases. Without *stare decisis*, it would often be impossible for people to predict accurately how the

1

Court might interpret a statute or constitutional clause. People would then lack the information necessary to assure their compliance with statutory and constitutional legal requirements. So general adherence to *stare decisis* is a precondition of the security that comes from knowing that one's behavior is law abiding. For these reasons, a judge rarely finds a prior decision so repugnant that she is willing to sacrifice *stare decisis*. Yet O'Connor is willing to make an exception where *Roe v. Wade* is concerned.

Joining O'Connor in this negative attitude toward *Roe v. Wade* is Justice Antonin Scalia, another member who joined the Court in the 1980s. He writes in *Webster v. Reproductive Health Services* (1989) concerning Justice Blackmun's worry that *Roe v. Wade* may be overruled: "I think that should be done."[5]

The two justices who originally dissented from the 7 to 2 decision in *Roe v. Wade*, Justices Rehnquist and White, show no signs of having changed their minds about the propriety of that decision. In *Thornburgh v. American College of Obstetricians and Gynecologists*[6] (1986) Justice White seconded O'Connor's willingness to depart from the *Roe v. Wade* precedent. Rehnquist, now chief justice, maintained in his *Webster* opinion that "the rigid *Roe* framework is hardly consistent with the notion of a Constitution cast in general terms, as ours is, and usually speaking in general principles, as ours does."[7] He, too, referred in this context to the limits of *stare decisis*.

Since the votes of only four justices are needed for a writ of certiorari, which brings a case before the Supreme Court, it seems almost certain that Justices Rehnquist, White, O'Connor and Scalia will mandate consideration of one or more cases that provide the opportunity for a major revision or wholesale reversal of *Roe v. Wade*. So an examination of the constitutionality of abortion rights cannot reasonably be premised on *Roe* as a precedent that the Court will continue to follow. Instead, the rationale behind *Roe* must be explored and, if it is found wanting, a constitutionally acceptable substitute must be developed if the Constitution is to continue protecting abortion rights. Developing a substitute rationale is a major goal of the present work.

Individual Rights and Majority Rule

The present work concentrates on issues of constitutional law. Embodied in our Constitution is the democratic ideal of majority rule. Through their representatives, people are supposed to be able to govern themselves by passing legislation. This is representative democracy, which is also called "indirect democracy" and "a republican form of government." The majority does not (usually) govern directly by passing legislation, but indirectly by electing those who are thereby authorized to legislate. In addition to the indirectness of the majority rule that it institutes, the Constitution further limits majority rule so as to protect individual rights. The tension between these two ideals, majority rule and individual rights, forms the background of many constitutional debates, including debates about abortion rights. Do women have constitutional rights as individuals to terminate their pregnancies, or can majorities, acting through their legislatures, legitimately curtail or prohibit the abortion procedure? In the present section I explore in general terms the tension between majority rule and individual rights in order to set the stage for an understanding of abortion as a constitutional issue.

The Framers of the Constitution believed that majority rule must be limited in several ways. First, they believed that some individual rights are so important that they should be denied, if at all, only for extraordinarily powerful reasons. These are constitutionally fundamental rights (or fundamental rights, for short). Adoption of the Bill of Rights in 1791 was designed to give voice and constitutional force to demands of individual rights. The First Amendment, for example, specifies that regardless of the will of the majority, "Congress shall make no law respecting an establishment of religion, or prohibiting the free exercise thereof; or abridging the freedom of speech, or of the press." Similarly, regardless of how eager the majority may be to fight crime, the Fourth Amendment protects everyone against "unreasonable searches and seizures," the Fifth Amendment outlaws double jeopardy in criminal cases as well as forced self-incrimination, and the Eighth Amendment prohibits "cruel and unusual punishments."

When originally adopted, the Bill of Rights guaranteed these and other individual rights only against the tyranny of the majority at the federal level. Only the federal government was debarred from establishing a religion, curtailing freedom of the press or imposing cruel and unusual punishments. But the slavery issue of the mid-nineteenth century focused attention on the denial of individual rights by many states. So in 1868, in the wake of the Civil War, the Fourteenth Amendment was adopted. Like the other two post Civil War amendments, the Thirteenth (1865) and the Fifteenth (1870), the Fourteenth Amendment is directed at protecting citizens against at least some abuses by democratic *state* majorities. It provides, among other things, that no state shall "deprive any person of life, liberty, or property, without due process of law; nor deny to any person within its jurisdiction the equal protection of the laws." Besides guaranteeing due process and equal protection, the Fourteenth Amendment has over the past one hundred years been interpreted to apply to state action an increasing number of the guarantees contained in the Bill of Rights. Under its current interpretation, the states, like the federal government, are prohibited from establishing a religion, abridging the freedom of speech, and imposing cruel and unusual punishments.

Fundamental constitutional rights are the corollaries of these prohibitions. What is constitutionally prohibited to the federal and state legislatures is retained as a constitutional right by individual citizens. Thus, citizens have fundamental rights to freedom of speech, freedom of the press, equal protection of the laws, and due process of law.

But a fundamental right is not an absolute right. In the classic illustration, freedom of speech does not include the right to shout "Fire!" in a crowded theater (in which one does not believe there is a fire) because doing so could lead to unnecessary and grave harm to others. Even if there is a fundamental right to terminate one's pregnancy, then, it does not follow that one can do so whenever and however one chooses.

Majority rule, the other end of the tension that we are exploring, is expressed primarily in legislation. Typically, legislation defines different classes among people and permits to (or imposes on) members of some classes what is not permitted to (or imposed on) members of other classes. People over twenty-one years of age, for example, may legally buy hard liquor in most states, whereas people under twenty-one may not. Most people may legally borrow money from a given bank, but not those who own the bank. Young men must register with the federal government upon turning eighteen; young women need not. Of course, many criminal statutes apply to everyone. No one may simultaneously have more than one spouse.

As these examples illustrate, legislation typically limits people's freedom and alters their legal rights and responsibilities. With different legislation, people would have a legal right to have more than one spouse at a time, young people would be able to buy hard liquor at age sixteen instead of having to wait until they are twenty-one, and neither males nor females would have to register with the federal government at age eighteen. In these and myriad other cases, the legislation, notwithstanding the fact that it alters and limits people's legal rights, is presumed by the Supreme Court to be constitutionally valid. This presumption of validity reflects the value attached to majority rule in our republican form of government. Majority rule, as reflected indirectly in the decisions of elected representatives, should prevail unless the contervailing considerations are particularly strong.

As we have seen, among the strongest countervailing considerations are individuals' fundamental constitutional rights. Additional tests that legislation must pass to be held constitutional concern the procedure of its enactment, the specificity of its requirements, the relationship it bears to a legitimate public purpose, and the nature of the classifications it creates. I deal with these in turn before returning for additional consideration of fundamental rights.

Governmental restrictions of people's liberty must be properly enacted. This is primarily a protection of people's liberty against administrative regulations and decisions that lack appropriate authorization. For example, Congress has authorized the Food and Drug Administration (FDA) to determine the safety and efficacy of all new medications offered for sale in the United States. If the FDA were to issue regulations concerning the safety of children's toys, it would exceed its authority. The regulations would be unauthorized attempts to limit people's liberty, and this would violate the Fourteenth Amendment's Due Process Clause. As we have seen, the Fourteenth Amendment guarantees that no one be deprived of "life, liberty, or property, without due process of law." Since laws most often interfere with people's liberty or property, one aspect of due process is that these restrictions represent the will of the majority as the political system has seen fit to represent that will in actions of democratically elected legislatures operating in accordance with some form of majority rule. This due process requirement would not be met were the FDA to issue regulations outside the areas of its congressional mandate. The regulations would lack the indirect authorization of the majority that we require in our form of government. The regulations would violate *procedural* due process because the focus is on the procedures employed in the creation of legal restrictions and requirements. The background value is that of representative democracy. Appeals to procedural due process, then, do not call into question the ideal of majority rule. Instead, appeals to procedural due process are designed to ensure that legal rules embody the indirect majority rule that characterize our republican form of government.

Another requirement of due process where fundamental rights are not at issue concerns clarity. Vague legislation makes it impossible for people to know what behaviors are forbidden or required. When limiting people's liberty, the government must specify with reasonable clarity the nature of those limitations so that people can know how to conform their behavior to the law, and so that they will not be subject to unpredictable or arbitrary governmental interference in their lives. The underlying value here is the individual's right to self-determination within the limits of public acceptability.

It is also required by due process that a statute "rationally furthers some legitimate, articulated state purpose."[8] There are two aspects to this. First, there must be a legitimate state (or federal) purpose. For example, protecting the health and welfare of young people, reducing the probability of fraud or mismanagement in the banking industry, and preparing for the nation's defense are legitimate purposes of legislation. Given such a purpose, the legislation must be rationally related to the furtherance of that goal. That is, there must be some plausible understanding of the relevant facts and of how things work in the world that would make a reasonable individual think that the legislation in question could further the goal. For example, requiring people to be twenty-one years of age before they can buy hard liquor can plausibly further the goal of protecting the health and welfare of young people. Making it illegal to borrow money from the bank that one owns is rationally related to the goal of reducing the incidence of fraud and mismanagement in the banking industry, as is requiring young men to register with the government related to the goal of providing national defense.

The requirement of a rational relationship is in our era usually interpreted to exclude as unconstitutional only patently absurd, not merely unwise, legislation. In declaring legislation to be valid, the Supreme Court is not endorsing the means chosen by the legislature to effect its purpose. It may deem those means entirely unsuitable and may still find the legislation valid because the value of representative democracy is usually best served when democratically elected legislatures, rather than appointed judges, make determinations of the best means to serve a given end. This judicial deference to legislative judgments is called judicial restraint. As a result of such restraint, legislation that does not involve fundamental rights is not usually judged invalid unless, in the Court's judgment, no plausible reading of the factual situation would allow reasonable people to think that the means chosen in the legislation would further any relevant state objective.[9] When legislators adopt unhelpful means to reach public goals, but no fundamental rights are at issue, the Court usually maintains, as Chief Justice Morrison Waite did long ago in *Munn v. Illinois*, that "for protection against abuses by legislatures the people must resort to the polls, not the courts."[10]

Where fundamental rights are concerned, however, the situation is entirely different. One such right, guaranteed by the Fourteenth Amendment, is the right to "the equal protection of the laws." Consideration of this right has led the Court to view with suspicion certain kinds of legislative classifications. I turn now to a consideration of such *suspect classifications*.

We have seen that legislation typically classifies people and allows to (or imposes on) some people what is not allowed to (or imposed on) others. Nevertheless, some of these classifications, for example, those by race or national origin, are suspected by the Court of unfairly denying individual rights to members of minority groups. A group that is insular or politically weak may not be well enough represented in the legislature to assure that its members' rights are adequately protected by a political process geared to the creation and maintenance of majority coalitions.[11] Blacks, for instance, suffered legal liabilities, especially in the South, regarding education and transportation (to name but two). Redress through normal political processes was impossible because blacks were a minority who first were denied the right to vote and then could never beat the majority at the ballot box. The Court maintained that blacks were thus denied "the equal protection of the laws" promised by the Fourteenth Amendment. The Court's decisions in this area did not rest on the belief that blacks, or others, have fundamental (constitutional) rights to education or transportation. Instead, the underlying value was equality before the law. People have a fundamental right to be treated by the law equally, regardless of the legislation's subject matter. The normal presumption that such equality is being respected by the state does not apply in the case of legislation containing suspect classifications.

The Court now addresses the problem of equal protection of the laws by applying strict scrutiny to suspect classifications. Strict scrutiny often results in a reduction of judicial restraint. "Strict scrutiny means that the state system is not entitled to the usual presumption of validity, that the state rather than the complainants must carry a 'heavy burden of justification.'"[12] In these cases the state must show that its legislation is not merely rationally related to a legitimate state goal, but that it is *necessary* to meet a *compelling* public need.

Both sides in the abortion debate have raised the issue of suspect classifications. Pro-choice advocates have claimed that because women as a group are much less politically powerful than men, and legislation restricting abortion rights primarily affects women only, the Court should subject such legislation to strict scrutiny. According to this view, such legislation is constitutional only if the state can show that it serves some goal of unusual importance that can be reached in no other way than by restricting or forbidding abortions. Pro-life advocates, in contrast, have maintained that fetuses as a group are even less able than women to speak for themselves politically. So legislation that allows abortions should be subjected by the Court to strict scrutiny. Both claims are discussed in Chapter 2.

Strict scrutiny is applied by the Court whenever fundamental rights are at issue. The right to "equal protection of the laws" is only one example. The same strict scrutiny would apply if a woman has a fundamental right to terminate her pregnancy. In that case, too, the state may significantly limit that right only if it shows that the limitation is really necessary to meet a compelling public interest. If the state has a goal it wishes to serve by the limitation of a woman's right to terminate her pregnancy, then, if that right is fundamental, the goal will have to be unusually important (compellingly so) for the statute to be valid. Also, even if the goal is compelling, the statute is still invalid if the means chosen by the state limit the woman's right more than is necessary to reach the goal. Thus, even though fundamental rights are not absolute rights, the designation of a right as fundamental makes legislative limitations of it much harder to justify.[13]

Constitutional Interpretation

How does one know which rights are fundamental? Since by "fundamental" we mean fundamental according to the Constitution, it is all a matter of constitutional interpretation. Disparate constitutional interpretations arise in part from different views about how the Constitution should be approached. In this section I explain opposite, extreme positions on this matter; then I discuss and critique these extremes and some positions in between. No one's approach to the Constitution conforms to either of the extremes, but their elaboration helps clarify the issues that separate those who occupy different positions on the continuum between them. I conclude by indicating the position taken in this work.

Two matters of principal contention are these: First, to what extent should the Constitution be interpreted to guarantee only those rights mentioned *explicitly* in the text? Freedoms of religion and speech, for example, are mentioned explicitly in the Bill of Rights, but freedoms of association and procreation are not. The latter are constitutionally guaranteed only if the Constitution is interpreted to include *implicit,* as well as explicit, guarantees. The inclusion of implicit guarantees is controversial.

Also controversial are interpretations that rely on very *general*, as opposed to more *specific*, guarantees. Guarantees concerning "unreasonable searches and seizures" (Fourth Amendment) and self-incrimination (Fifth Amendment) are relatively specific when compared to the guarantee of "liberty" contained in the provision that no state shall "deprive any person of life, liberty, or property, without due process of law" (Fourteenth Amendment). Some interpreters favor reliance on the more specific guarantees, whereas others rely equally on relatively general guarantees.

These two dichotomies—explicit/implicit and specific/general—help clarify the differences among competing approaches to the Constitution. One extreme view is that the Constitution guarantees only those relatively specific rights explicitly mentioned therein and that the meaning, extent and implications of these rights are just what the original authors believed them to be. I will call this the Conservative view. Thus, for example, if the Framers of the First Amendment intended the guarantee of free speech to extend only to speech used in the process of political debate, such speech would forever be all that the First Amendment guarantees.[14] If the authors of the Eighth Amendment believed that capital punishment is not "cruel and unusual punishment," then all statutes providing for capital punishment are forever protected from constitutional challenge on Eighth Amendment grounds. If the authors of the Fourteenth Amendment did not view state legislation requiring racial segregation to violate that amendment's guarantee of "the equal protection of the laws," then legislated segregation can never be found inconsistent with equal protection.

This view minimizes the constitutional requirements that legislation must meet. Because it affords maximum latitude to legislative majorities, it reflects greater respect for the value of majority rule than for the value of individual rights. I call this the Conservative view, though it does not invariably support politically conservative causes.

No one endorses this view in its pure form because its implications are too radical. It would deny constitutional protection to individual rights where we have come to expect it. For example, the authors of the Fourteenth Amendment did not intend it to disallow racial segregation, so state laws requiring racial segregation in schools would be perfectly constitutional as long as their enactment was procedurally correct. Similarly, it is unlikely that the authors of the Fourteenth Amendment intended it to require application to the states of the guarantees contained in the Bill of Rights. If the authors' intent were to prevail, then, the states could pass constitutionally unobjectionable laws allowing officials to conduct unreasonable searches and seizures, institute cruel and unusual punishments, and limit in any ways they chose the freedoms of speech, assembly, and religion. The restrictions and denials of individual rights that would be allowed on this approach to the Constitution are legion. Too many rights that we have come to regard as (constitutionally) fundamental would be denied for the Conservative view to be accepted in its pure form.

I pointed out in the Preface that the first criterion of success for interpretations of the Constitution is their congruence with the words of the Constitution and with Supreme Court interpretations of those words. The basic approaches to the Constitution being discussed in this section are guidelines to be used in arriving at such constitutional interpretations. We have just seen that the extreme Conservative view would lead to interpretations that diverge widely from those accepted by the Court. So these interpretations, and the basic approach that leads to them, fare poorly on the first criterion of success.

The second criterion of success is conformity with our moral and political ideals. The extreme Conservative view fares poorly on this measure as well. Our current political ideals include, I think, the belief that individuals should be protected by the federal Constitution from state denials of free speech, freedom of religion, and freedom of the press. We have such a moral and political commitment to equality before the law that we expect our Constitution to protect individuals against laws that discriminate on the bases of race, religion, or national origin. The extreme Conservative view fails adequately to portray the Constitution as reflecting the ideals that we expect it to embody. It casts the Constitution in a relatively unfavorable light by making it appear less responsive than we would wish to individual rights.

Finally, the extreme Conservative view is not coherent.[15] It endeavors to enhance the power of majority rule by limiting the scope of legitimate constitutional objections to the will of legislative majorities. Constitutional objections are supposed to be limited by interpreting the Constitution according to the Framers' original intent. But to the best of our knowledge, the Framers' original intent was that the Constitution severely limit majority rule. Distrust of the majority was reflected in the fact that blacks and women were not allowed to vote, and that states were allowed to refuse the franchise to those who lacked property. Even those who could vote were not permitted to elect directly either senators or the president; senators were elected by state legislatures and the president by the electoral college. Members of the Supreme Court were appointed and confirmed for life by the indirectly elected president and Senate.

These are not accidental departures from the ideal of majority rule. They were calculated to reduce the extent of majority rule in order to protect individual rights from encroachments by democratically elected legislatures. James Madison wrote to Thomas Jefferson, "The invasion of private rights is chiefly to be apprehended, not from acts of government contrary to the sense of its constituents, but from acts in which the Government is the mere instrument of the majority number of the Constituents."[16] John Adams also was convinced that majority rule was incompatible with proper respect for individual rights. Because democrats do not respect individual rights, "democracy never lasts long. It soon wastes, exhausts, and murders itself."[17] The intent of the Founding Fathers, then, was to provide in the Constitution checks against the excesses of majority rule. Original intent cannot be invoked to minimize judicial interference with majority rule, since the Founding Fathers intended majority rule to be limited substantially.

In sum, the extreme Conservative view lacks coherence, and it leads to interpretations that conflict sharply with a great many Supreme Court decisions and with some of our most cherished moral and political ideals. Any relatively Conservative view contains these defects in greater degree as it approaches the extreme.

The opposite extreme affords maximum protection to individual rights at the expense of respect for the role of majority rule in our republican form of government.[18] According to this approach, the Constitution embodies universal principles of natural law and natural rights. These are principles, discoverable by reason alone, that specify the rights that individuals have by nature. Because the Constitution is believed, according to the extreme Liberal view, to protect all the rights individuals have by nature, it is unnecessary in establishing constitutional protection for a right that explicit mention of the right be found in the Constitution. So if there is (believed to be) a natural right to the free expression of sexuality among consenting adults, any legislation that significantly limits this right is unconstitutional unless the restrictions it imposes are the minimum necessary to meet a compelling public need. This result obtains whether or not a right to sexual preference is explicitly mentioned in the Constitution or is clearly implied by a right that is explicitly mentioned. Similarly, if it is believed on grounds of natural law that women have a natural right to terminate their pregnancies, then no textual support from the Constitution is needed to declare unconstitutional any and all statutes that restrict this right more than is necessary to meet a compelling public need. I call this the Liberal view, in honor of the nineteenth century liberals' zeal for individual rights, even though the view does not invariably support what we today call liberal political causes.

In its extreme form the Liberal view fails adequately to satisfy the criterion of congruence with the Constitution and with its interpretation by the Supreme Court. It is inherent in the view that the words of the Constitution are to be given little weight when individual rights are at issue. This generates conflict not only with the Constitution but with most of the history of Supreme Court interpretations, as the Court has for the most part taken pains to tie its interpretations to the words of the document it is interpreting.

The extreme Liberal view might seem at first to satisfy much more adequately the second criterion. One might expect it to endorse interpretations of the Constitution that reflect current moral and political ideals. This is not entirely the case. First, many Supreme Court decisions of the past that employed the extreme Liberal view did not reflect what we would consider the most enlightened moral views of their time. For example, when slavery was an issue, the Court's *Dred Scott* decision supported slavery against abolition. As we see in Chapter 1, the Court also blocked legislation early in this century that many at the time, and we today, believe necessary to protect workers' health and safety.[19] More generally, the Supreme Court is sometimes called on to make decisions that are important precisely because contemporary moral and political ideals come into conflict with one another. The abortion issue featured in the present work is a case in point. Because there are current moral and political ideals supporting opposite decisions by the Supreme Court, the decision reached, even if guided by the extreme Liberal view, cannot possibly correspond uniquely to relevant ideals.

The extreme Liberal view suffers also on the criterion of correspondence with current moral and political ideals because one of our principal ideals is majority rule. The extreme Liberal view justifies the substitution by unelected judges of their moral and political opinions for those of democratically elected legislatures. Because Americans are currently less suspicious of majority rule than were James Madison and John Adams, the extreme Liberal view suffers from a failure of correspondence with this central political ideal. In sum, the extreme Liberal view, like the extreme Conservative view, leads to interpretations that conflict sharply with a great many Supreme Court decisions and with some of our most cherished moral and political ideals. Any relatively

Liberal view, like any relatively Conservative view, suffers from these defects in greater degree as it approaches the extreme.

Positions taken between the extremes include the following: Leaning toward the Conservative extreme is the view that the Constitution protects only those specific rights explicitly mentioned as protected, but the nature, extent, and implications of these rights can be understood in ways that differ somewhat from the Framers' understanding. The smaller the difference allowed between the current and the original understanding of these rights, the more latitude is given to majority rule and the less constitutional protection is afforded to individual rights.

Leaning toward the Liberal extreme (of protecting all manner of individual rights) is an approach that finds implicit in the Constitution guarantees of rights not mentioned explicitly but arguably implied by those that are mentioned explicitly. Farther from the extreme is an approach that is confined to rights mentioned explicitly in the Constitution but that concentrates on those rights in their most general form. The right to "liberty" guaranteed in the Fourteenth Amendment is such a general right. All the Liberal approaches are illustrated in Chapter 1. The Conservative view is discussed further in Chapter 3.

I adopt a view that I believe to be closer than any of those so far mentioned to the midpoint between the extremes of total deference to majority rule and complete protection of individual rights. I call this the Moderate view. I would confine the constitutional protection of individual rights to rights explicitly mentioned in the Constitution. I would further confine constitutional protection to those rights in their relatively specific, rather than general, form. But I would allow broad scope to the development of the meaning of the specific concept in question. Thus, the meaning of the Equal Protection Clause can legitimately evolve to render suspect any classifications based on race, since the clause appears in the Fourteenth Amendment, whose original goal was to guarantee equal citizenship to blacks. In Chapters 3, 4, 5, and 6 I argue similarly that the concept of religion in the First Amendment has legitimately evolved to include many matters concerning abortion. In Chapter 1, in contrast, I show why the general right to liberty should not be invoked to grant constitutional protection to specific rights not mentioned in the Constitution. The term "liberty" is too general and broad for the Court to gain specific guidance from it. (Almost) every law limits (someone's) liberty, so appeals to a general right to liberty cannot, by themselves, tell us which laws are, and which are not, constitutional. Without more specific guidance, the Court's interpretations of the Constitution are liable to give insufficient weight to the principle of majority rule and excessive weight to unelected judges' particular, and possibly idiosyncratic, opinions about morality, politics, and economics. This is the vice of the Liberal view.

I favor the Moderate view because I believe it fares best on the criteria of congruence with written documents and correspondence with moral and political ideals. Congruence with the Constitution itself is guaranteed by the fact that the Moderate view endorses extending constitutional protection to all and only those relatively specific rights that are explicitly mentioned therein.

On the criterion of correspondence with moral and political ideals, no view can endorse decisions that correspond to all relevant ideals when the opposite sides of a legal dispute feature different ideals. But any acceptable view must strike a reasonable balance between the master political ideals of majority rule and individual rights. We have seen that in their extreme forms the Conservative view slights individual rights in favor of majority rule, and the Liberal view slights majority rule in favor of individual rights. The Moderate view does a better job of giving due weight to each of these central political ideals.

One's view of the proper approach to constitutional interpretation affects one's evaluation of arguments in constitutional law. Thus, I offer arguments that accord with my Moderate view and criticize the arguments of others as too conservative or too liberal. I also argue that the Moderate view is the best approach to the Constitution. In addition, I argue that only on the Moderate view, especially as applied to the First Amendment guarantees regarding religion, can the Supreme Court's various decisions regarding abortion be understood to express a consistent, and constitutionally appropriate, approach to the matter.

Preview of Chapters

I begin by investigating (constitutional) justifications for the concerns of those four Supreme Court justices who have indicated their desire to reconsider *Roe v. Wade.* I do this by addressing the controversy surrounding *Roe*'s derivation and specification of the fundamental right, proclaimed there for the first time, of a woman to terminate her pregnancy. Chapter 1 reviews the precedents on which Justice Blackmun relied when deriving that right from others mentioned explicitly in the Constitution. I argue that crucial precedents are not themselves well-grounded in the Constitution and that *Roe* may not be a logical extension of them anyway. I further argue that Justice Stewart's alternative justification, though better, is still weak.

Chapter 2 discusses the limitations placed by the Court in *Roe* and in later, related decisions, on a woman's right to terminate her pregnancy. Criticism centers on the meaning and importance of fetal viability.

All of this is preliminary to justifying on entirely different constitutional grounds a result substantially similar to that reached in *Roe v. Wade.* Chapters 3, 4, 5, and 6 argue that a woman must have a right to terminate her pregnancy at least during its first twenty weeks. I reach this result by analyzing the meaning of "religion" as it appears in the First Amendment, where it says "Congress shall make no law respecting an establishment of religion, or prohibiting the free exercise thereof." I find that according to the Supreme Court, this amendment prohibits laws whose sole purpose or principal effect is support for a religious belief. I find also in the Court's interpretations of the Religion Clauses the view that religious beliefs are those that one cannot establish with arguments employing secular premises alone. Secular premises reflect the agreements in belief, thought and practice that are integral to our society's common way of life. Religious beliefs, by contrast, are those that the Court considers to constitute, or rest at least partly on, beliefs that are optional in our society. People in our society can agree to disagree about religious beliefs because our common way of life is not jeopardized by disagreement. The paradigm case is belief in the existence of God. I argue that believing a human fetus to be a human person before it has completed twenty weeks of gestation is similarly a religious belief. So laws restricting abortions during the first twenty weeks of pregnancy are unconstitutional violations of the First Amendment religion guarantees, unless they can be justified on grounds other than those which presuppose that fetuses are human persons during the first twenty weeks of gestation.

These First Amendment arguments illustrate the Moderate view of constitutional interpretation. Freedom of religion is explicitly mentioned in the Constitution and is relatively specific. But the meaning that the Court attaches to the word "religion" has expanded, especially during the past fifty years, and the arguments offered in the present work employ this newer, expanded meaning.

Chapters 7 and 8 apply the foregoing reasoning to cases concerning such issues as the public funding of abortions, the use of public facilities for abortions, the rights of minors to have abortions without parental consent or notification, and state requirements that certain information be supplied before an abortion can be performed. I find the Supreme Court's decisions on these issues to be largely justified, but their rationales to be largely deficient.

CHAPTER 1

The Derivation of Roe v. Wade

THE DECISION in *Roe v. Wade* rests largely on the claim that the Constitution gives a woman a fundamental right to terminate her pregnancy. This right was derived in two different ways from the text of the Constitution as that text has been interpreted in previous Supreme Court decisions. Justice Blackmun, writing for the Court, cites a line of precedents that establishes the existence of a fundamental, constitutional right of privacy. He maintains that a woman's right to terminate her pregnancy is one of these rights of privacy. But some of the precedents relied on by Blackmun are themselves poorly grounded in the Constitution, and even if a constitutional right of privacy is constitutionally well grounded, it cannot plausibly be extended to include a right to have an abortion.

Justice Potter Stewart, concurring in the decision of the majority, offers a different justification. He appeals to a fundamental right to liberty guaranteed by the Fourteenth Amendment's Due Process Clause. Though better than Blackmun's, Stewart's rationale is also weak because it relies on a very general right to liberty. This use of general rights is dangerously close to an extreme Liberal view of constitutional interpretation.

The present chapter explains both rationales and exposes their defects. The judicial precedents employed by Blackmun and Stewart are historically intertwined. I consider the precedents in chronological order and unweave the strands of privacy and due process to clarify their use by Blackmun and Stewart in *Roe v. Wade*.

I first explain the doctrine of substantive due process as it was originally applied in the economic sphere. Then I trace the transfer of its use

17

from economic to personal contexts, especially those of family life. I
discuss *Griswold v. Connecticut* next, concentrating on the privacy rationale given there for the right of married couples to use contraceptives. The section that follows explains why the privacy rationale is
strained beyond recognition when applied to the right of unmarried
people to have access to contraceptives. These same considerations apply to *Roe v. Wade*, nullifying Justice Blackmun's contention that
women have a *privacy* right to terminate their pregnancies. Instead of
deriving a fundamental right from a right of privacy, Blackmun derives
what he calls a right of privacy from what he has (on other grounds,
one must suppose) already come to regard as a fundamental right. Section I then return to the doctrine of substantive due process because
that is the only rationale mentioned by any of the justices that promises
to tie abortion rights to the Constitution so as to make them constitutional rights. But appeals to substantive due process in any area of human activity are in principle antidemocratic, antiseparation of powers,
and not susceptible of reliable limitation. They reflect an excessively
Liberal view of constitutional interpretation. The next section reviews
and rejects Laurence Tribe's arguments for substantive due process and
the extreme Liberal view. I conclude that appeals to substantive due
process should be replaced wherever possible by considerations that
gain for a right more secure moorings in the Constitution. Later chapters are devoted to this task.

Economic Substantive Due Process

As I explained in the introductory chapter, the Constitution prescribes a
system of representative democracy but limits its application in order to
protect the rights of individuals against the tyranny of the majority.
Among the provisions designed to protect individual rights is the Due
Process Clause of the Fourteenth Amendment, which declares that "no
state shall . . . deprive any person of life, liberty, or property, without
due process of law." As we have seen, this is interpreted to mean that
legislation must be duly enacted by an appropriately authorized legislative body and that it must be rationally related to a legitimate public
purpose. This is called procedural due process because the Court's primary concerns are with the procedures of the statute's enactment and
with the formal relationship of the statute to work that is within the
legislative province.

Around the turn of the century, another meaning was given to the

Due Process Clause. Concentrating on the clause's guarantees regarding liberty and property, the Court began treating rights to property and to economic liberty as fundamental constitutional rights. State economic regulations (of working hours, working conditions, and so forth) were invalidated as unconstitutional. Since fundamental rights were at issue, the state statutes were presumed invalid, and the Supreme Court was often unconvinced that the states had shown them to be really necessary for the public good. Because the Court's concerns in these decisions focused on the substance of the legislation, and because the Court gave substance through these decisions to certain rights (to property and to economic liberty), this use of the Due Process Clause is known as *substantive* due process. It is called substantive *due process* merely because the rights to liberty and property that are given substantive weight just happen to appear in the Due Process Clause.

The most famous, and infamous, judicial appeal to substantive due process was made by Justice Rufus Peckham in *Lochner v. New York* (1905). Referring to "the right of the individual to his personal liberty" and "to enter into those contracts in relation to labor which may seem to him appropriate or necessary for the support of himself and his family," Peckham declared unconstitutional a New York statute forbidding employment in a bakery for more than sixty hours a week or ten hours a day. "We think," he wrote, "that a law like the one before us involves neither the safety, the morals, nor the welfare, of the public." "The law must be upheld, if at all, as a law pertaining to the health of the individual engaged in the occupation of a baker." But if "neither the safety, the morals, nor the welfare, of the public" is affected by the baker's decision, why should his exercise of liberty be curtailed by the state? The law is "an unreasonable, unnecessary, and arbitrary interference with the right of the individual to his personal liberty"[1] and, therefore, is a deprivation of liberty "without due process of law."

Four Supreme Court justices, including Oliver Wendell Holmes, Jr., dissented from this judgment, maintaining that the health and welfare needs of citizens are properly matters for the judgment of the democratically elected New York legislature, not the judiciary. In the words of Justice John Harlan, "the state is not amenable to the judiciary, in respect of its legislative enactments, unless such enactments are plainly, palpably, beyond all question, inconsistent with the Constitution of the United States."[2] The dissent here suggests that judicial restraint should be exercised regarding legislation. Statutes should be presumed constitutional unless their conflict with the Constitution is unmistakable, such as when they conflict with a clear, specific prohibition of the sort contained in the Bill of Rights, for example, when they abridge "the free-dom of speech, or of the press" (First Amendment) or involve "unrea-sonable searches and seizures" (Fourth Amendment). This is similar to what I call the Moderate view of constitutional interpretation (see the Introduction).

The majority view of Justice Peckham is much closer to what I call the extreme Liberal view because it relies on the very general concept of liberty in the Due Process Clause to invalidate legislation that regulates economic relationships. This liberal interpretation of liberty held sway for more than thirty years. Many statutes designed to ameliorate the conditions of poor working people were held unconstitutional because they limited people's freedom of contract, thereby violating substantive due process. Legislatures were severely hampered in their efforts to reg-ulate the wages, hours, and working conditions of people who were so poor as to be powerless to improve their lot through contract negotia-tions. Some early New Deal legislation was thus held unconstitutional, though, as we see in the next section, the Court began to change its view in 1934.[3]

Due Process and the Family

The doctrine of substantive due process was abandoned in the 1930s for three basic reasons, all related to the Great Depression. First, with the problems of poverty and unemployment major national concerns, a method of interpreting the Constitution that hampered legislative ef-forts to ameliorate these problems seemed morally indefensible. Also, the depression created doubt about the underlying assumption of sub-stantive due process—that individuals are masters of their own eco-nomic fates whenever they are free of governmental interference. Dur-ing the depression many skilled, hard-working people were thrown out of work through no fault of their own. Finally, the depression made it apparent that a successful industrial society required governmental oversight and regulation of its economy if maximum productivity and widespread prosperity are to be attained. The hands-off approach of economic substantive due process relied on the increasingly discredited view that adequate economic coordination would be supplied by Adam Smith's invisible hand. Thus the doctrine of substantive due process has long been held in disrepute. Yet it influences *Roe v. Wade* in two ways. Stewart's opinion in *Roe* appeals directly to a noneconomic version of substantive due process. Blackmun's privacy rationale rests in part on a line of cases whose earliest members embody the doctrine of economic substantive due process. Consider that line of cases.

In *Meyer v. Nebraska* (1923) the Court held unconstitutional a 1919 Nebraska statute that made it unlawful to teach the German language in school to anyone "who had not attained and successfully passed the eighth grade."[4] Justice James McReynolds maintained that "mere knowledge of the German language cannot reasonably be regarded as harmful." The liberty guaranteed by the Fourteenth Amendment's Due Process Clause (i.e., substantive due process) includes the right to make one's living by teaching the German language to children who have not yet completed the eighth grade.

Two years later, in *Pierce v. Society of Sisters*, the Court invalidated an Oregon statute that prohibited gainfully providing private (including parochial) education for schoolchildren. Justice McReynolds, again speaking for the Court, held that because "these parties are engaged in a kind of undertaking not inherently harmful, but long regarded as useful and meritorious,"[5] the prohibiting statute deprives them of liberty and property without due process of law. So far, this case is like the first two cases we considered (*Lochner* and *Meyer*). Substantive due process is used to guarantee laissez-faire economic arrangements against state regulation.

But then the Court reinforced its conclusion with a second consideration. The statute also "unreasonably interferes with the liberty of parents and guardians to direct the upbringing and education of children under their control." "The child is not the mere creature of the state; those who nurture him and direct his destiny have the right, coupled with the high duty, to recognize and prepare him for additional obligations."[6] Here we have the first use of the concept of due process to defend people's liberty with regard to special family relationships.

Strictly speaking, the second reason should not have been taken, as it was by later courts, to form part of the precedent established in *Pierce*. Judicial opinions are considered under two headings, *ratio* and *dicta*. The ratio is the reasoning in the opinion that is put forward as justifying the result reached. A dictum is anything else in the opinion that is not presented as a necessary part of its rationale. Only the ratio is supposed to be considered by later courts when, following *stare decisis*, they cite the case as a precedent. In *Pierce* the consideration that Oregon's statute deprived private and parochial schools of their property without due process of law was argued to be sufficient to justify the conclusion that the law is unconstitutional. This is a fairly straightforward application of the doctrine of substantive due process as enunciated in *Lochner* and employed in *Meyer*. Because no reference to parental rights was argued to be essential to reach the result in *Pierce*, this whole line of thinking is, strictly speaking, dictum. It should not have formed a precedent for future cases.

Why, then, is the case taken to provide a precedent concerning parents' rights? A major reason is the doctrine of *stare decisis*. As we saw in the Introduction, it is important for people's knowledge of and reliance on the law that precedents be followed. This applies to the decision reached in *Pierce* no less than to other precedents. But a Supreme Court decision needs a justification. After the repudiation of appeals to substantive due process, the only remaining aspect of the Court's opinion that could plausibly be taken to justify the decision was the reference to "the liberty of parents and guardians to direct the upbringing and education of children under their control." So the consideration of parental rights has been transformed into the ratio of the decision to replace the original ratio, which is no longer considered constitutionally respectable. In this way, the doctrine of *stare decisis* has come to make the principle that parents have special prerogatives in childrearing no less a part of constitutional law than the result reached in *Pierce*, that states may not legislate private and parochial schools out of existence. Generalizing the principle that parents have special liberties regarding the upbringing and education of their children yields the principle that a state needs stronger justifications for regulations governing relationships among family members than for regulations governing most other relationships.

This kind of shift in rationale can account for some of the changes that occur in accepted constitutional law. On the extreme Conservative view, all such changes are unwarranted, whereas on the Liberal view the fact of change is not, by itself, considered to be a problem. On the Moderate view that I employ, the only acceptable changes are those in the meaning, extent and implications of relatively specific rights that are actually mentioned in the Constitution. According to the Moderate view, the rights announced in both *Meyer* and *Pierce* are not well grounded in the Constitution because they are tied to the Constitution only through a very general right to liberty.

Another case to influence *Roe v. Wade* was not officially decided on grounds of substantive due process. It is cited here because Justice William Douglas employed as a prominent aspect of his rationale the belief that the ability to procreate is a fundamental right. This right, announced for the first time in *Skinner v. Oklahoma* (1942), was later generalized to accord fundamental status to the right to control one's procreative powers. When combined with the *Pierce* holding, which was taken to require of states special deference to relationships within the family unit, the right to control one's procreative powers led to the next major decision in the line of cases culminating in *Roe v. Wade.*

The context of *Skinner*, in which the ability to procreate was first declared a fundamental right, was an Oklahoma statute that authorized the sterilization of people convicted and imprisoned for a third time of a felony "involving moral turpitude." Included among such felonies were robbery and larceny, but not embezzlement, political offenses and revenue act violations. Justice Douglas, writing for the Court, believed that the legislation "involves one of the basic civil rights of man. Marriage and procreation are fundamental to the very existence of the human race."[7] Combine this sentiment with the view that the act cannot plausibly serve a public purpose—it is predicated on the belief, already rejected by science, that criminality of the sort here in question is transmitted through biological heredity—and there is a strong due process argument against the act's constitutionality. The act deprives people of liberty without due process of law.

But the case was not officially decided on these grounds. Probably because the doctrine of substantive due process was already in disrepute, Douglas seized on the fact that according to the act, those convicted three times of larceny could be legally sterilized, whereas those similarly convicted of embezzlement could not. Since "the nature of the two crimes is intrinsically the same," the "legislation runs afoul of the equal protection clause."[8] As explained in the introductory chapter, besides due process, the Fourteenth Amendment requires states to provide people with "equal protection of the laws." States must, in other words, have good reasons for treating some people differently than others. The more significant are the individual rights affected by legislation, the better the state's rationale must be for different treatment. In this case, because the right to procreate is so fundamental, and the distinction between larceny and embezzlement so devoid of justification, Douglas was on firm ground in declaring that the statute violated people's rights to equal protection of the laws.

The case could just have easily been decided on grounds of substantive due process. Douglas maintains in *Skinner* that the ability to procreate is a fundamental right. As already noted, this belief is sufficient to trigger the strict judicial scrutiny that would justify the Court's rejection of Oklahoma's statute on grounds of substantive due process. It is not surprising, then, that at least two of Douglas's colleagues on the Court have since referred to *Skinner* as a decision resting on the Due

Process Clause.[9] *Skinner* is important for our purposes also because the fundamental right to procreate that is there taken for granted is nowhere mentioned explicitly in the Constitution. Douglas employs an extreme Liberal view of constitutional interpretation, as he makes no attempt to tie this right to any word, phrase, or clause in the Constitution. If the Supreme Court is allowed, as in this case, to declare rights not found in the Constitution to be nevertheless constitutionally fundamental, the opportunities for strict judicial scrutiny and invalidation of legislation are significantly increased.[10] Finally, *Skinner* is important for our purposes because, as already noted, through the process of generalization *Skinner* has come to be viewed as granting fundamental status to the right to control one's procreative powers. *Pierce* has come to be viewed as requiring of states special deference to relationships within the family unit. These are combined in the next case that leads to *Roe v. Wade*.

Contraception and Privacy in Griswold v. Connecticut

Respect for the rights of people to control their procreative powers and their intrafamilial relationships were combined in *Griswold v. Connecticut*.[11] Connecticut had a law that forbade the *use* of contraceptives by everyone, including married couples. This is simultaneously a state regulation of the most intimate intrafamilial relationship and state interference with people's use of their procreative powers. In view of the decisions made in *Pierce* and *Skinner*, it is not surprising that Justice Harlan, writing about the statute in a previous case,[12] considered it to violate rights that are fundamental and belong to the "citizens of all free governments." In his view, due process represents "the balance which our nation, built upon postulates of respect for the liberty of the individual, has struck between that liberty and the demands of organized society."[13] For this reason, "the full scope of the liberty guaranteed by the Due Process Clause cannot be found in or limited by the precise terms of the specific guarantees elsewhere provided in the Constitution," such as "freedom of speech, press, and religion." Instead, due process "includes a freedom from all substantial arbitrary impositions and purposeless restraints" on the exercise of fundamental rights.[14] Harlan refers explicitly to the *Skinner* decision to indicate that he considers control of one's procreative powers to be such a right. So, in Harlan's view, the "Connecticut Statute infringes the Due Process Clause of the Fourteenth Amendment because the enactment violates basic values 'implicit in the concept of ordered liberty.'"[15]

Harlan refers here to basic values because views about legitimate government reflect such values. We saw in the Introduction that our constitutional form of government reflects the values associated with majority rule and individual rights. Majority rule is important when people depend on others whom they do not know personally and with whom they have no realistic opportunity to negotiate privately the conditions of their interaction. Allowing people to act under these conditions in any way they choose would subject each person to the effects of the behavior of others whom they cannot influence in a peaceful way. The results could be violent, contrary to the value of peace. They could also involve the undue subordination of some people's interests, contrary to the values of justice and equality. Peace requires that order be established, and the belief in the equal dignity and importance of each human being requires that the order in question show equal respect for everyone's interests. Assuming that people can generally define their own interests and act on their own behalf, majority rule preserves order and peace while providing, as well as possible, for the just and equal consideration of everyone's interests. The value of democracy rests, then, on the values of peace and of equal respect for people and for their powers of self-determination. In principle, democracy gives each an equal chance to determine for herself the rules that will govern everyone's behavior.

But respect for the value of individual self-determination cannot be maintained by submitting all matters to a democratic vote. Democracy is required only in situations where people depend on others with whom they cannot realistically negotiate a private accord. Where people are independent of one another, or can protect their interests through private negotiations without jeopardizing the interests of others, the value of self-determination is best served by allowing adults to act as they choose as long as consent is obtained from all those who are significantly affected.

Harlan believes the use of contraceptives to fall into this latter category, where individual rights, rather than majority rule, should prevail. Stressing liberty in "the concept of ordered liberty," he believes that the Due Process Clause should be interpreted to protect the "basic values" of individual dignity and self-determination against the unwarranted intrusions of majority rule. To protect these values, the Due Process Clause guarantees to people fundamental rights to life, liberty, and property. This is the substantive due process interpretation of the clause. Harlan believes that this interpretation justifies the result in *Skinner* because he believes that procreation is not an aspect of human life where people must have recourse to majority rule. He believes that in procreation people are independent of most other people, and they can protect their interests through private interactions that do not significantly affect the general welfare. So, derivative from the fundamental right to liberty that Harlan finds in the Due Process Clause is a fundamental right to control one's procreative powers. The Connecticut statute that Harlan was writing about violated this fundamental right by proscribing the use of contraceptives.

Harlan's argument here is structurally identical to Stewart's substantive due process rationale in *Roe v. Wade*. Since we are mainly interested in *Roe*, I postpone criticism of this kind of rationale until I consider it in the context of Stewart's opinion in *Roe*. Suffice it to say that the problems are formidable and account for the fact that Douglas avoided appealing to substantive due process in his *Griswold* opinion, as he had earlier tried to avoid it in his *Skinner* opinion.

Writing for the Court, which agreed with Harlan that Connecticut's statute was unconstitutional, Douglas based his decision in *Griswold* on the statute's authorization of undue interference with intrafamilial relationships. He considered the statute "repulsive to the notions of privacy surrounding the marriage relationship," as it suggests that "we allow the police to search the sacred precincts of marital bedrooms for telltale signs of the use of contraceptives."[16]

But no such right of privacy is mentioned in the Constitution, so how can a statute be unconstitutional because it limits people's privacy? Douglas deftly produces an *implicit* right of privacy from no fewer than four of the ten amendments that constitute the Bill of Rights.[17] Douglas finds an implicit endorsement of a right of privacy in the First Amendment's "right of the people peacefully to assemble," as this suggests that people have a right to private association with one another. "The Third Amendment in its prohibition against the quartering of soldiers 'in any house' in time of peace without the consent of the owner is another facet of that privacy." The Fourth Amendment's prohibition of "unreasonable searches and seizures" suggests a right of privacy in one's home, as the Fifth Amendment's guarantee against enforced self-incrimination suggests a right of privacy in one's dealings. Finally, the Ninth Amendment states: "The enumeration in the Constitution of certain rights, shall not be construed to deny or disparage others retained by the people." Douglas infers from this that the absence of explicit mention in the Constitution of a right of privacy does not mean that there is no such fundamental right, especially in the marriage relationship where "we deal with a right of privacy older than the Bill of Rights."[18] This appeal to the Ninth Amendment amounts to a constitutional argument favoring what I have called a Liberal view of constitutional interpretation. According to this view, judges may "discover" implicit in the Constitution rights that are not mentioned explicitly. The Liberal view is discussed at length later in this chapter (see "Stewart's Due Process Rationale in *Roe v. Wade*" and "Tribe on Substantive Due Process").

In sum, according to Douglas, a right of privacy is implicit in the First, Third, Fourth, and Fifth amendments, and is provided for in the Ninth Amendment. Connecticut's law is unconstitutional because it violates this right. So the *Griswold* decision reinforces the view generalized from the *Pierce* decision that people have special rights regarding intrafamilial relationships. Harlan, in contrast, rejected the view that the Bill of Rights protects more than the rights explicitly mentioned therein. He maintained, instead, that the Due Process Clause of the Fourteenth Amendment protects certain fundamental rights, regardless of the fact that those rights are not mentioned in the Constitution. Following a generalization from the *Skinner* decision, he includes among these the right to control one's own procreative powers. Harlan, no less than Douglas, employs a relatively Liberal view of constitutional interpretation.

Justices Black and Stewart dissented from the Court's view that Connecticut's law was unconstitutional. They agreed with Douglas that Harlan's appeal to the Fourteenth Amendment was out of place, and with Harlan, against Douglas, that the Bill of Rights guarantees only those rights explicitly mentioned and so does not include a right of privacy. Reserving until later a discussion of substantive due process, I here include the main arguments of Black and Stewart against Douglas's finding in the Constitution an implicit right of privacy.

Black writes: "There are, of course, guarantees in certain specific provisions which are designed in part to protect privacy at certain times and places with respect to certain activities."[19] But "'Privacy' is a broad, abstract and ambiguous concept which can . . . easily be interpreted as a constitutional ban against many other things."[20] Agreeing with Black, Stewart points out that this is just what Douglas does in the majority opinion. Douglas declares that the Connecticut statute violates a constitutional right of privacy. Stewart counters: "No soldier has been quartered in any house. There has been no search and no seizure. Nobody has been compelled to be a witness against himself."[21] Thus, according to Stewart, the Connecticut statute is not unconstitutional, because it does not run afoul of any specific constitutional guarantee.

These objections are important because they concern the extent to which the Supreme Court should depart from or expand on the specific,

limited guarantees contained in the Constitution. This is the underlying
issue also in disputes about the Court's use of substantive due process,
as that use is inherently expansive. It is the issue of the merits of the
relatively Liberal view versus the relatively Conservative view of constitutional interpretation. For the moment, it is sufficient to note that a
general constitutional right of privacy is insecure as long as a more
restrictive (Moderate or Conservative) view of the Court's role is cogent
and legally recognized. The more general issue is discussed below in
connection with Stewart's use of substantive due process in his *Roe*
opinion.[22]

Contraception and Privacy in Eisenstadt v. Baird

In *Eisenstadt v. Baird*[23] the Supreme Court considered a Massachusetts
law concerning the distribution, rather than the use, of contraceptives.
The law made it legal for contraceptives to be distributed for birth control only to married people and only by registered physicians and pharmacists. All distribution of contraceptives to unmarried people for birth
control was against the law. The Court found this statute unconstitutional. Writing for the Court, Justice Brennan argued that the statute's
distinction between married and unmarried people was an unconstitutional denial of equal protection of the laws.

But why should a state be constitutionally debarred from making a
distinction between married and unmarried people regarding the distribution of contraceptives? The reason, said Brennan, is this: "The marital couple is not an independent entity with a mind and heart of its
own, but an association of two individuals, each with a separate intel-
lectual and emotional makeup. If the right of privacy means anything, it
is the right of the *individual*, married or single, to be free from unwarranted governmental intrusion into matters so fundamentally affecting a
person as the decision whether to bear or beget a child."[24]

Brennan here takes the notion of privacy away from the intrafamilial context in which it was developed by Douglas in *Griswold* and
applies it to the notion developed in *Skinner* that people have a fundamental right to control their procreation. The influence of *Skinner* is in
the fact that Brennan centers the right to control procreation in the
individual, rather than in the family. In Brennan's view, the issue in
Eisenstadt, like that in *Skinner*, concerns the rights of individuals as
individuals, not their rights as family members. But this right to control
one's procreation does not appear explicitly in the Constitution. It must

be somehow attached to the Constitution to make it a *constitutional* right that the Court can enforce. For this purpose, Brennan enlists the constitutional right of privacy, claiming that the individual's right to control his or her procreation is a species of the right of privacy found and invoked in *Griswold*. In sum, in *Eisenstadt*, Brennan attaches the idea of a fundamental right to control one's procreation to the right of privacy that Douglas, writing for the Court in *Griswold*, had found implicit in the Bill of Rights. This constitutionally unmentioned but implicit right of privacy is the only significant thread that ties the *Eisenstadt* decision to the Constitution.

Unfortunately, the thread is considerably frayed. The Connecticut statute invalidated in *Griswold* concerned the *use* of contraceptives. Its enforcement, therefore, could plausibly involve police intrusions into "the sacred precincts of marital bedrooms." The Massachusetts statute invalidated in *Eisenstadt* concerned the *distribution* of contraceptives. In this case, interdiction would not ordinarily involve encroachments on privacy greater than those accompanying the enforcement of any ban on a controlled substance—heroin, for example. Even if there is a fundamental, general right of privacy in the Bill of Rights, it cannot reasonably be thought to disallow the interdiction of commerce in controlled substances and paraphernalia that may be used in the home.

This appears to have been the view of Justice Douglas, whose majority opinion in *Griswold* originated the privacy rationale. He did not apply that rationale in *Eisentadt*. Instead, he wrote an opinion concurring in the Court's result, but on grounds of free speech. Seizing on the fact that the distribution of contraceptives at issue in *Eisenstadt* followed a speech about contraception, Douglas interpreted the contraceptive as a visual aid and its transfer "to a member of the audience" as "merely a projection of the visual aid."[25] Thus, Douglas neither presented nor accepted in *Eisenstadt* the argument that the right of privacy, or any other constitutional right, prevents states from outlawing the sale of contraceptives.

Another weakness in the thread tying *Eisenstadt* to the Constitution through *Griswold* concerns the marriage relationship. Connecticut's statute controlled the actions of married people. Since our society depends for the primary nurturing and enculturation of the young on marital and family relationships, special deference is often given to intrafamilial association. It is far from clear, despite the unsupported dictum in *Pierce*, that there is a *constitutional* guarantee of such deference. But be that as it may, the Massachusetts law considered in *Eisenstadt* was invalidated by the Court insofar as it controls the distribution of contraceptives to unmarried people.[26] So any force that the notion of privacy may gain from connotations of marital intimacy is unavailable in *Eisenstadt*, where unmarried people are concerned.

Thus, the Court's rationale in the *Eisenstadt* decision is weak as a statement of constitutional law. This is not to say that the Massachusetts law was wise or justified as a matter of public policy. Personally, I think is was unwise and obnoxious. I think the same of the Connecticut law invalidated in *Griswold*, the Oklahoma law invalidated in *Skinner*, and the Nebraska law invalidated in *Meyer*. But in our system, as noted earlier, it is generally the right of legislatures and the duty of voters to remedy the situation through the ballot box. The exceptions to this general rule concern statutes that contravene the Constitution. It is essential in such cases to explain clearly the manner of inconsistency between the statute and the Constitution, lest judges sit as a super-legislature that substitutes its public policies for those of democratically elected legislatures.

Blackmun's Privacy Rationale in Roe v. Wade

The preceding sections focus on the Supreme Court's development and use of the notions of privacy and substantive due process because these are the only two notions used by the Court in *Roe v. Wade* to connect its decision to the Constitution. Writing for the Court, Justice Blackmun based his view (the official Court view) on the notion of privacy. The present section critically examines this part of Blackmun's opinion. After noting Blackmun's use of precedents, the section articulates four senses of privacy. It shows that a constitutional right to terminate one's pregnancy cannot be supported cogently by appeals to a right of privacy in any of these senses. The first two senses—the right of privacy as the right to avoid intrusive government snooping, and the right of privacy as the right to control the dissemination of information about oneself— are only tenuously related to antiabortion statutes of the sort invalidated in *Roe* and subsequent cases. The second two senses—the right of privacy as the right to create and follow one's own self-definition and life plan, and the right of privacy as the right to be free of undue government pressure toward standardization—are not plausibly protected by the Constitution. There are too many unproblematically constitutional statutes that contravene the right of privacy in either or both of these senses. The section concludes with speculation about the thought process that led Blackmun to maintain that his decision was based on the right of privacy.

Blackmun introduced his privacy rationale in *Roe v. Wade* by briefly reviewing the history of the Court's derivation of and appeal to the right of privacy. Referring to this history, Blackmun declared the right of privacy "broad enough to encompass a woman's decision whether or not to terminate her pregnancy."[27] One is amazed to find *Meyer v. Nebraska* mentioned twice in this quick review of history, since that case was decided squarely on grounds of substantive due process. Nebraska's law illegitimately limited the opportunities for gainful employment of people who teach the German language.

Blackmun also mentions *Pierce v. Society of Sisters*, which calls for the constitutional protection of some intrafamilial relationships. But even assuming that the protection of such relationships can be considered the protection of privacy, that case was actually decided on grounds of substantive due process relating to the ownership of property by the Society of Sisters. References to special relationships within the family are pure dicta and should not be taken to create a new rule of law. And even if they did create a new rule of law, that rule would have little to do with "a woman's decision whether or not to terminate her pregnancy." A woman is an individual, not a family. Subsequent Supreme Court decisions have maintained, moreover, that the right to terminate her pregnancy is hers alone. Her decision cannot be vetoed by a spouse or, if she is a minor, by either or both parents.[28] The dictum in *Pierce* endorses special rights of parents to direct their children's lives (i.e., the right of parents to send their children to parochial schools). It cannot be more than a bad joke to derive from *Pierce* the right of a woman to terminate her pregnancy when this right is clarified to mean that a minor need not gain parental permission.

Of course, Supreme Court justices cannot be faulted for failing to foresee future developments. The reference to *Pierce* may have seemed more reasonable to a justice who anticipated the abortion right of a minor to be controlled by her parents. Now that the abortion right in *Roe* has been clarified to exclude parental control, however, those who would defend *Roe* against future challenges can hardly use *Pierce* in its defense.

Griswold v. Connecticut, also referred to by Blackmun, concerns privacy in a common-sense way because it declares unconstitutional governmental snooping in bed chambers. This is the old "one's home is one's castle" sense of privacy, and it is the first of the four senses of privacy examined in the present section. Abortions are not private in this sense, however, because they generally take place outside the home and are performed by paid professionals licensed by the state. This seems to be what Justice Rehnquist meant when he remarked in dissent,

"A transaction resulting in an operation such as this is not 'private' in the ordinary usage of that word."[29]

Blackmun mentions *Eisenstadt v. Baird* as well. As we have seen, however, this case concerns activities that are no more private "in the ordinary usage of that word" than is an abortion. Whatever connects *Eisenstadt* and *Roe*, it is not privacy in the sense that calls for government to curtail its intrusive snooping.

Ironically, two cases that do concern privacy in this sense were decided by the Court during the 1972–73 session against the asserted interest in privacy. Thirteen days before the *Roe* decision, the Court found in *Couch v. United States*[30] no privacy interest in records a taxpayer had given to her accountant. The Court decided on the same day as *Roe* that a grand jury could force someone to provide a voice exemplar (a recording of the voice used, like a fingerprint, to identify people).[31] Subsequently, the Court has gone so far as to allow governmental snooping in bedrooms. In *Bowers v. Hardwick* Justice White declared for the Court's (new) majority that an antisodomy statute in Georgia is constitutional despite the possibility of its enforcement involving invasions of private bedrooms.[32] If this is not an invasion of privacy, then nothing is, certainly not the interdiction of the distribution of contraceptives (which the Court invalidated in *Eisenstadt*) or the criminalization of licensed physicians performing abortions in facilities that serve the public (which the Court invalidated in *Roe*).

Defenders of Blackmun's privacy rationale point out that other senses of privacy, not yet articulated in the present work, may vindicate Blackmun's reasoning. One of these is the informational sense of privacy. This is "an interest in keeping certain matters out of public view."[33] In this sense, medical matters are ordinarily considered private.[34] Contraception and abortion are medical matters, so privacy in the informational sense would reasonably apply to them. But the privacy rights asserted in *Eisenstadt* and *Roe* do not concern the right to keep out of public view one's contraceptives or abortion. They concern the right to *have* contraceptives and abortions. The issue is not publicity, but access. The controversial right is to have and do certain things, not to prevent others from knowing about them.

Another (third, if you are counting) sense of privacy concerns the importance of an activity to an individual. Activities are private in this sense when they are central to a person's plan of life and self-definition. Decisions about contraception and abortion are private in this sense because they affect parenthood, and parenthood can have profound effects on one's life plan and self-definition. But many other matters, equally central to people's life plans and self-definitions, are regulated by the state with few, if any, complaints that a *constitutional* right of privacy is thereby infringed. Someone given to self-exposure (of the anatomical kind) is legally restrained out of deference to the sensibilities of those who are offended and disturbed by the sight of a stranger's genitals. There is no constitutional right of privacy to expose oneself, no matter how important the practice may be to someone's life plan and self-definition.

Even when unconsenting others are not involved, decisions central to one's life plan are not all considered constitutionally protected from state control. Polygamy among consenting adults is illegal in every state. Statutes prohibiting polygamy are not usually mentioned among those that infringe the constitutional right of privacy. Yet marriage and family, like procreation, are widely viewed as central to people's life plan and self-definition. Again, few matters can be more central to a cancer patient than the therapy options available to her. In spite of this fact, the government limits those options, making illegal, for example, the use of laetrile. Whether or not this government decision is wise, it is not viewed as infringing on anyone's constitutional right of privacy. In sum, there is no general constitutional right of privacy to have or do those things that are central to one's life plan or self-definition. If laws prohibiting abortion and the sale of contraceptives are unconstitutional, as I believe they (mostly) are (for reasons explained in Chapter 6), it is not because they infringe upon anyone's privacy in this sense.

Another related sense of privacy concerns the laws' "profound capacity to direct and to occupy individuals' lives through their affirmative consequences."[35] This is why, according to Jed Rubenfeld, the Court struck down laws prohibiting the following activities: teaching foreign languages (*Meyer*), maintaining parochial schools (*Pierce*), using and selling contraceptives (*Griswold* and *Eisenstadt*), and having an abortion (*Roe*). In each case the prohibition, if obeyed, forces the individual's life into relatively narrow channels of development. "Antiabortion laws" for example, "produce motherhood: they take diverse women with every variety of career, life-plan, and so on, and make mothers of them all."[36] According to Rubenfeld, such laws violate the constitutional right of privacy because they "radically and affirmatively redirect women's lives."[37] Other laws, such as those against murder, theft, self-exposure, and incest, remove narrow channels of action and self-expression, but leave the individual otherwise free to develop as she sees fit. Such laws do not infringe the constitutional right of privacy. But laws that tend, like those in a totalitarian regime, to cause people's lives to be standardized and taken over by state objectives do infringe upon the right of privacy.

As Rubenfeld recognizes, "we are all so powerfully influenced by the institutions within which we are raised that it is probably impossible . . . to speak of defining one's own identity."[38] But it is still important, he maintains, "to prevent the state from taking over, or taking undue advantage of, those processes by which individuals are defined in order to produce overly standardized, functional citizens."[39] This is why there is a constitutional right of privacy.

But, contrary to Rubenfeld, privacy in this sense is not, for the most part, respected in our society or in our law. Many valid laws have as their goal the production of "standardized, functional citizens." The most obvious are laws concerning compulsory education. Even though, since the *Pierce* decision, the state may not outlaw private and parochial schools, it may still standardize education to a great degree. It may require all schools to be state certified, and may require for certification that teachers have certain credentials, that curricula include certain subjects, and that average students attain certain levels of proficiency in those subjects.

The promotion of common, standard values is the goal of many educational, and other, public policies. Children in private and parochial schools, no less than in public schools, are taught to view democracy as a blessing, hard work as a virtue, and our country as a (mostly or wholly) benevolent influence in the world. We all learn that slavery and racism are bad and that toleration of religious differences is (usually) good.

Other public policies carry many of the same messages, and additional messages, designed to effect greater uniformity of outlook in our country. Public service advertisements encourage us to value forests, the nuclear family, and endangered species. Affirmative action programs and equal employment opportunity legislation are designed to encourage actions and outlooks that are hostile to sexism and racism in employment.

Most of these attempts to impart standard language, information, outlooks, and values are reasonable. Countries lacking such standardization sometimes suffer greatly as a result of ethnic strife, for example, the Soviet Union, Lebanon, and Sri Lanka. So if the right of privacy is the right to avoid powerful influences of standardization, then many laws and public policies in our country violate that right. Since the vast majority of these laws and public policies are unproblematically constitutional, our Constitution contains no such right of privacy. Finally, since a great deal of standardization or uniformity is necessary for society to function well, the addition to our Constitution of a right to avoid powerful influences of standardization would not improve our basic charter.

Of course, attempts at standardization can go too far. One might argue that the Constitution does not protect us from *all* influences of standardization, but it does protect us from influences that are *too strong*. The constitutional right of privacy, according to this view, renders unconstitutional laws that impose on people prohibitions or requirements or both that have the effect of *overly* standardizing citizens. Thus, anti-contraception and antiabortion laws are unconstitutional because they tend too strongly to standardize women in the role of mothers.

But the influences of compulsory education and other government efforts at standardization are much more pervasive and basic than is the influence of parenthood. In fact, our prevailing social outlook is responsible for the fact that parenthood structures people's lives in the manner and to the extent that it does. Promotion of the nuclear family and of the woman's special role in that family powerfully influence women, more than men, to organize their lives around child care. If we lived in a society where childrearing were communal, for example, on an Israeli kibbutz, the impact (after pregnancy) of motherhood might be no greater than that of fatherhood. With different cultural attitudes, putting children up for adoption would be much less emotionally difficult than it is at present in our society. Thus, the standardizing effect of motherhood is largely influenced by cultural attitudes that the government helps to promote through its commonly accepted, and mostly effective, efforts at standardization. Objecting on constitutional grounds to anti-contraception and antiabortion laws because they overly standardize women in the role of mothers, while not objecting to more fundamental, pervasive, and effective government efforts at such standardization, is inconsistent. The former cannot violate the alleged constitutional right of privacy if the latter do not, and there is general consensus that in the main, the government's efforts at standardization are perfectly constitutional.

In response to these considerations, proponents of the privacy rationale shift emphasis from motherhood to pregnancy. Anti-contraception and antiabortion laws affect women initially not by making them mothers but by influencing them to become, and then by requiring them to remain, pregnant. During pregnancy, according to Rubenfeld, "the woman's body will be subjected to a continuous regimen of diet, exercise, medical examination, and possibly surgical procedures. . . . In these ways, anti-abortion laws exert power productively over a woman's body and, through the uses to which her body is put, forcefully reshape and redirect her life."[40] Rubenfeld maintains that this violates the woman's right of privacy.

But this reasoning overlooks the constitutionality of the peacetime military draft. Pregnancy is shorter in duration and (usually) less all-consuming in effect than is the military duty of draftees. During peacetime, the draft is used primarily to save money for the government. The government generally pays less for services that are required by law. Draftees typically spend two years, not just nine months, in government service. Their lives are almost entirely occupied by this service. In Laurence Tribe's words, "the state's power of military conscription . . . completely denies a young person's physical liberty."[41] Yet even Tribe and other supporters of a constitutional right of privacy acknowledge the constitutionality of a peacetime draft. If the alleged constitutional right of privacy permits a peacetime draft (applied, by the way, to males only), it must also permit antiabortion laws that have a lesser impact (on females only).

In sum, four senses of privacy have been explored: privacy as freedom from physically intrusive government snooping, privacy as the ability to control the dissemination of information about oneself, privacy as the ability to establish and follow one's own self-definition and life plan, and privacy as the ability to avoid government efforts at occupying and standardizing people's lives. The first two are irrelevant to antiabortion legislation of the sort invalidated in *Roe*. Such legislation called merely for the same kind of government snooping as other criminal statutes and primarily affected people's activities, not the dissemination of information about those activities. The second two senses of privacy are relevant to abortion, but privacy in neither sense is generally protected by the Constitution.

Thus, the general right of privacy declared in *Griswold* and invoked in *Eisenstadt* and *Roe* fails adequately to justify the decision reached in *Roe*. It fails to meet the first criterion for interpretations of the Constitution. It does not reflect explicit and specific language in the Constitution, nor does it reflect many Supreme Court interpretations of the Constitution where privacy is clearly at issue. Further, in light of its tenuous relationship to the text of the Constitution, rationales relying on a general right of privacy represent a relatively Liberal view of constitutional interpretation and contain the defects inherent in applications of that view. These defects include undue derogation of a central political ideal: majority rule (see the Introduction). So how are we to understand Blackmun's references to privacy?

The crux of the matter seems to be contained in Blackmun's contention that "only personal rights that can be deemed 'fundamental' or 'implicit in the concept of ordered liberty,' are included in this guarantee of personal privacy."[42] Citing a string of cases, some of which we have just reviewed, Blackmun contends that the right of privacy "has some extension to activities relating to marriage; procreation; contraception; family relationships; and child rearing and education."[43] But not all the cases cited concern matters of privacy. The Court ties them together with *Roe* merely by asserting in each case that a state law contravened a "fundamental" right.

These rights are not fundamental because they are rights of privacy. Instead, they are called rights of privacy by Blackmun because he already considers them all to be fundamental personal rights. "Right of privacy" is just a new, misleading term used here to designate fundamental personal rights that are not enumerated in the Constitution.

The reason for the misnomer, one must suppose, is that Douglas did a reasonably good job in *Griswold* of finding an implicit right of privacy in the Bill of Rights. Blackmun calls any and all unenumerated fundamental personal rights "rights of privacy" to ensure that they are connected to the Constitution through Douglas's rationale.

But the implicit, general right of privacy "discovered" by Douglas in *Griswold* is privacy in the sense that disallows intrusive government snooping. As already noted, Douglas indicated this to be his meaning not only in his *Griswold* opinion but also in his unwillingness to employ the *Griswold* analysis in *Eisenstadt*, where there was no issue of snooping. In Douglas's sense of the right of privacy, the right to terminate one's pregnancy is not a right of privacy at all. So Blackmun's assertion of the right cannot reasonably rest on the privacy analysis as Douglas understood it. Nor can that assertion be otherwise connected to the Constitution. And this is as good as Blackmun's opinion gets, insofar as connection to the Constitution is concerned.

As John Hart Ely put it, "though the identification of a constitutional connection is only the beginning of analysis, it is a necessary beginning."[44] *Roe v. Wade* is "a very bad decision," he writes, "because it is bad constitutional law, or rather because it is not constitutional law and gives almost no sense of an obligation to try to be."[45] Professor

Ely's judgment is certainly a fair assessment of Blackmun's opinion. The concept of privacy on which Blackmun relies does not connect the Court's decision to the Constitution.

Stewart's Due Process Rationale in Roe v. Wade

Justice Stewart's concurring opinion does better. He argues for the woman's right to terminate her pregnancy on the basis of the Fourteenth Amendment's Due Process Clause. He writes that "the Constitution nowhere mentions a specific right of personal choice in matters of marriage and family life, but the 'liberty' protected by the Due Process Clause of the Fourteenth Amendment covers more than those freedoms explicitly named in the Bill of Rights."[46] Stewart quotes with approval Harlan's view that the liberty referred to in the Fourteenth Amendment "includes a freedom from all substantial arbitrary impositions and purposeless restraints, . . . and . . . recognizes . . . that certain interests require particularly careful scrutiny of the state needs asserted to justify their abridgment."[47]

This reasoning is better than Blackmun's because liberty in general is mentioned in the Constitution, whereas privacy is not, and restrictions on abortions do affect liberty, in a constitutionally relevant sense. So why was this not the Court's rationale in the first place? The answer lies in the unfortunate history and inherent dangers of substantive due process. I now turn to that topic.

We saw earlier that substantive due process was appealed to early in our century to protect property rights and economic liberties against state economic regulations. Almost everyone now applauds the definitive rejection in 1937 of appeals to substantive due process in the economic sphere, as that rejection allows for the kind of governmental regulation of the marketplace that almost everyone now considers necessary in an advanced industrial society.[48] For example, the government must be able constitutionally to promote public health, among other goals, through regulation of hours and working conditions.

But this rejection of substantive due process in the economic realm means that property rights and individual liberty in a competitive marketplace are not among the fundamental, substantive rights protected by the Due Process Clause. Property rights and economic liberty can be limited by the state whenever the limitations are plausibly related to a legitimate public purpose. The limitations do not have to be necessary to meet a compelling public need.[49] This is very strange. If *any* substan-

tive rights are secured by the prohibition of governmental deprivations
of "life, *liberty*, or *property*, without due process of law," surely economic liberty in general, and property rights in particular, would be
among those protected. Property is explicitly mentioned in the Due
Process Clause. Besides, our society prides itself on upholding rights to
private property and to economic liberty in a competitive marketplace.
These rights embody values that we consistently oppose to the collecti-
vist vision pursued in other societies. So if substantive due process protects any rights, one would expect economic rights to be among those
protected.[50] Since they are not so protected, the most consistent view
would seem to require the rejection of substantive due process altogether, including Harlan's use of that doctrine in his *Griswold* opinion
(see "Contraception and Privacy in *Griswold v. Connecticut*) and Stewart's use of it in his concurrence in *Roe*.[51]

It has been suggested that substantive due process may be justifiably
appealed to in noneconomic contexts, even while such appeals are rejected in economic contexts. Economic relationships tend to affect unconsenting third parties or involve parties of unequal power. Legislation
is often needed to protect third parties and weaker parties. For example,
environmental legislation is needed to protect third parties from the effects of environmental deterioration, and labor legislation is needed to
protect workers from exploitation by the relatively wealthy people who
employ them. But, the argument continues, where many personal rights
are concerned, rights of procreation and sexual preference, for example,
the situation is different. Except in extraordinary cases, problems regarding exploitation and harm to unconsenting third parties cannot justify legislative intervention. So statutes regulating behavior in these
areas should be subject to strict scrutiny to protect people's fundamental right to liberty.

The fatal defect in this line of reasoning is the assumption that the
distinction between economic and noneconomic activities corresponds
neatly to the distinction between those activities that do, and those that
do not, significantly affect third parties or risk exploitation of the weak.
Many people would maintain, for example, that polygamy risks the exploitation of women and can therefore appropriately be made illegal,
even when all parties to a desired polygamous union are consenting
adults. Thus, noneconomic exploitation can be a legitimate legislative
concern.

Effects on third parties, too, can be significant in noneconomic contexts. Consider private dueling with pistols as a mutually agreed-upon
method of settling disputes among consenting adults. Such duels are not

regulated to protect third parties from being accidentally fired upon. They are banned outright, in part, because the effects on third parties extend well beyond the dangers of accidental gunshot wounds. A society in which private dueling with pistols was an accepted method of settling disputes among consenting adults would value differently than we the importance of domestic tranquility and peaceful coexistence. It would be a society in which many people are raised to be ashamed of compromising or apologizing instead of fighting a duel. The difference would affect almost everyone in profound ways. So even though dueling is a noneconomic activity, its practice among consenting adults can legitimately be proscribed in view of its *indirect* effects on others.

Since the dangers of exploiting the weak and harming third parties exist in noneconomic as well as in economic contexts, one cannot legitimately extend to all noneconomic personal liberties the protection afforded by substantive due process. If such protection is uniformly denied in the economic realm in order to allow legislatures to protect third parties from harm and weaker parties from exploitation, then it must be denied for the same reasons where certain noneconomic, personal liberties are concerned, as the exercise of these liberties may have similar adverse effects.

Consider, for example, sodomy between consenting adults. I do not think that the Georgia prohibition, upheld in *Bowers v. Hardwick*, is at all wise or justified. But the mere fact that sexual preference is a personal, rather than an economic, liberty provides no assurance that the weak are not being exploited and third parties are not being harmed. The case must be judged on its specific merits, not on the general merits of personal, as opposed to economic, liberties.[52] This is the job of legislatures, not the courts, because where people's actions may plausibly affect unconsenting others, majority rule serves best the values of peace, and of equal respect for people and for their powers of self-determination (see above). So if the possibilities of harm and exploitation in the economic realm justify legislative determinations by majority rule, as against judicial recourse to substantive due process, consistency requires the same where noneconomic personal liberties may also plausibly involve harm and exploitation.

Related to the problem of justifying the use of substantive due process in the noneconomic area while it is not used in the economic area is the problem of identifying within the noneconomic area just which substantive liberties the Due Process Clause protects. Unless the scope of "liberty" is narrowed, Justice Black points out in his *Griswold* dissent, "every state criminal statute—since it must inevitably curtail 'liberty' to some extent—would be suspect."[53] But like most other statutes, most criminal statutes are presumed by the Court to be valid. So the substantive liberties protected by due process as fundamental constitutional rights must be a limited, select group of liberties. Since they are to range beyond those liberties expressly guaranteed in the Constitution, the text of that document cannot be our chief guide. What, then, is supposed to guide judges in the identification of fundamental liberties?

Concurring in *Griswold*, Justice Arthur Goldberg wrote, "The Court stated many years ago that the Due Process Clause protects those liberties that are 'so rooted in the traditions and conscience of our people as to be ranked as fundamental.'"[54] Justice Black dissented from this use of substantive due process on the grounds that "the scientific miracles of our age have not yet produced a gadget which the Court can use to determine what traditions are rooted in the '[collective] conscience of our people.'"[55] I would add to this that democratically elected legislatures would seem better representatives of the "conscience of our people" than are unelected judges. To the extent that the constitutionality of legislation depends on its restrictions of liberty reflecting the collective conscience, the legislature's work should be presumed valid, and strict scrutiny should not be employed by the Court to protect fundamental liberties guaranteed by the Due Process Clause.

If neither the text of the Constitution nor the "conscience of our people" can guide judges' selections of those liberties they deem fundamental, Black suggests that the judges employing substantive due process must have recourse to their own notions of what is fair and just. They must assume that there is an unwritten natural law of right and wrong that they are consulting through examination of their own conscience. With this possibility in mind, Black quoted part of an opinion of Justice James Iredell from 1798. "The ideas of natural justice are regulated by no fixed standard: the ablest and purest men have differed on the subject."[56] Overturning legislation on this basis amounts to the substitution, without any fixed standards for guidance, of the dictates of the judges' conscience for that of the legislature. Because there are no standards, Black pointed out, "any limitation upon [judges] using the natural law due process philosophy to strike down any state law, dealing with any activity whatsoever, will obviously be only self-imposed."[57] History teaches us the dangers of relying within this framework on judicial self-restraint. According to Black,

> the Due Process Clause with an "arbitrary and capricious" or "shocking to the conscience" formula was liberally used by this Court to strike

down economic legislation in the early decades of this century, threatening, many people thought, the tranquility and stability of the Nation. . . .
That formula, based on subjective considerations of "natural justice," is
no less dangerous when used to enforce this Court's views about personal rights than those about economic rights.[58]

These dangers can be illustrated with a few cases. In *Loving v. Virginia*[59] the Court invalidated Virginia's anti-miscegenation statute. In his
opinion in *Roe*, Stewart properly lists this case as involving substantive
due process. But if one has a substantive due process right to marry
someone of a different race, why does one not have such a right to
marry more than one consenting adult of the opposite sex?[60] People
have moral and religious objections to polygamy, but so did the people
of Virginia have moral and religious objections to miscegenation. How
is one to decide which such scruples the law should impose on the general public?

Here is a more controversial example. In *Bowers v. Hardwick*
(1986) the Court let stand a Georgia statute that makes sodomy a criminal act. Justice Stevens noted in dissent, "The fact that the governing
majority in a state has traditionally viewed a particular practice as immoral is not a sufficient reason for upholding a law prohibiting the
practice."[61] Justice Blackmun, also dissenting, wrote: "This case involves no real interference with the rights of others, for the mere knowledge that other individuals do not adhere to one's value system cannot
be a legally cognizable interest, . . . let alone an interest that can justify
invading the houses, hearts, and minds of citizens who choose to live
their lives differently."[62]

Do these statements imply that Blackmun objects to typical anticruelty statutes that make illegal the private torture of animals for personal amusement at home? Does Stevens object to such statutes because
"the fact that the governing majority" views "a particular practice as
immoral is not a sufficient reason for upholding a law prohibiting the
practice."[63] I strongly suspect that neither Stevens nor Blackmun considers such statutes to be unconstitutional. Why? *They share* the majority's moral objections to cruelty to animals, so they have no problem
with the state imposing that moral judgment on the population at large.
It seems that they do not similarly object to sodomy, so on that issue
they would bar the state from imposing the majority's moral views on
everyone else. It is hard to see in this application of substantive due
process anything more or less than the justices substituting their moral
judgments for those of elected legislative majorities. Where they agree
with the majority's moral judgment, they find no problem of substan-

tive due process in the state's enforcement of it. Where they strongly disagree with the majority's moral judgment, they find the state's law unduly to constrain the liberty guaranteed to all individuals by the Fourteenth Amendment.

The same analysis applies to the different judicial treatment accorded statutes that forbid marriage to someone of a different race and those that forbid marriage to more than one person at a time. The judiciary finds the former, but not the latter, morally obnoxious. So anti-miscegenation statutes are invalidated on constitutional grounds that Stevens identifies with substantive due process, while there are no serious constitutional challenges to anti-polygamy statutes.

I find troublesome the close correspondence between judges' moral codes and their judgments that substantive due process is or is not violated by a given statute. The law inevitably incorporates many aspects of morality. Substantive due process is a doctrine that seems to allow judges to substitute their moral judgments for those of the people's elected representatives. This is extremely antidemocratic. Representative democracy requires that the majority rule. Representative democracy in a country with a constitution requires that the majority's rule be limited only by that constitution. If the Constitution is so interpreted by the judiciary as to allow judges to override the moral judgments of the majority whenever enough appropriately placed judges have strong feelings about an issue, then the Constitution has been misused to erode the republican form of government that it is supposed to assist. In sum, reliance on substantive due process suffers from the defects inherent in the Liberal view of constitutional interpretation.

The antidote is the Moderate view. Justice White, for example, would disallow any constitutional grounds for overturning statutes except those that are supported by clear language in the Constitution. So, writing for the Court in *Bowers*, he refuses to take "a more expansive view of our authority to discover new fundamental rights imbedded in the Due Process Clause. The Court is most vulnerable and comes nearest to illegitimacy when it deals with judge-made constitutional law having little or no cognizable roots in the language or design of the Constitution."[64]

The Court "comes nearest to illegitimacy" in these cases because its legitimacy is a function of its place in a governmental system that includes the separation of powers between the legislative, executive, and judicial branches. If judges can invalidate any legislation they find morally offensive, they sit as a kind of superlegislature. It is with this thought in mind that Black wrote in his *Griswold* dissent: "Subjecting federal and state laws to . . . an unrestrained and unrestrainable judicial control as to the wisdom of legislative enactments would, I fear, jeopardize the separation of governmental powers that the Framers set up."[65]

Black then quoted Holmes's suggested cure for these ills. "I think the proper course is to recognize that a state legislature can do whatever it sees fit to do unless it is restrained by some express prohibition in the Constitution of the United States or of the State."[66] In short, like Justices Black and White, Holmes recommended the rejection of the Liberal view of constitutional interpretation and, therewith, any reliance on considerations of substantive due process.

These are important problems. The use by the Court of substantive due process seems to be in principle antidemocratic, antiseparation of powers, and not susceptible of reliable limitation. It makes judges loose cannons on the decks of the ship of state. Yet the decision in *Roe v. Wade* is often regarded as resting on these controversial due process grounds. Justice Brennan maintained in *Carey v. Population Services International* (1977) that the abortion rights declared in *Roe* rest on "one aspect of the 'liberty' protected by the Due Process Clause of the Fourteenth Amendment."[67] Laurence Tribe writes, in a similar vein: "What is truly implicated in the decision whether to abort or to give birth is not privacy, but autonomy."[68] The literal meaning of "autonomy" is self-rule. In political contexts this means liberty, freedom from legal constraints, and brings us back to the constitutional guarantee of liberty in the Due Process Clause. Other commentators, too, explicitly attribute the *Roe* decision to considerations of liberty under the Fourteenth Amendment.[69] So Stewart's due process rationale is widely accepted as the best foundation for the decision in *Roe*. Unless and until powerful objections to the use of substantive due process can be adequately answered, this justification of the result in *Roe v. Wade* remains problematic.

Tribe on Substantive Due Process

In *Abortion: The Clash of Absolutes*, Laurence Tribe defends the general use of substantive due process and its specific application to antiabortion legislation. The present section explains and then refutes Tribe's argument for substantive due process.

At the heart of Tribe's argument is the claim that the only "principled" alternative to accepting substantive due process is what I have called the *extreme* Conservative view of constitutional interpretation. Apart from the Due Process Clause, Tribe points out, the text of the Constitution contains no words to suggest application to the states of the guarantees contained in the Bill of Rights. Only through the Court's gradual incorporation of the Bill of Rights into the Fourteenth Amendment's Due Process Clause has our Constitution come to prohibit states from denying freedom of speech, employing cruel and unusual punishments, and establishing a religion. But since the Fourteenth Amendment does not specify that the Bill of Rights should be applied to the states, the incorporation of the Bill of Rights into the Fourteenth Amendment is justified merely by judicial interpretations of the general guarantee of liberty. So the application of the Bill of Rights to the states is justified solely by an application of substantive due process. Only an extreme Conservative would reject this application. Thus, the only alternative to accepting substantive due process is an extremely Conservative view of constitutional interpretation. Tribe writes:

> The application of the Bill of Rights to the states, although not specifically intended by the framers of the Fourteenth Amendment and although once highly controversial, is now common ground. No sitting justice questions it. . . . Indeed, without incorporation of the Bill of Rights, we would have a world in which, although the federal government could not censor an anti-government newspaper, the state of Illinois could. . . . Or in which, though there could be no official church of the United States, the state of New York could declare Presbyterianism the official state religion.[70]

In light of the incorporation of the Bill of Rights, Tribe maintains, "the claim that the liberty clause is 'entirely' procedural is unsustainable."[71] The existence of substantive due process, in other words, is uncontroversial. The only real issue is "whether or not there is any basis for limiting the meaning of 'liberty' *only* to rights specifically mentioned in the Bill of Rights."[72]

Tribe points next to the Ninth Amendment, which states: "The enumeration in the Constitution, of certain rights, shall not be construed to deny or disparage others retained by the people." Tribe interprets this to mean that individuals in the United States retain substantive rights in addition to those enumerated in the Constitution. These rights are referred to in their general form (life, liberty, and property) in the Fourteenth Amendment's Due Process Clause. So, according to Tribe, it is the Court's job to apply, and thereby give more specific substantive content to, these provisions of the Due Process Clause. Thus, any principled, consistent, contemporary understanding of the Constitution accepts substantive due process.

In sum, Tribe's argument is this. There is only one principled alternative to accepting substantive due process, by which he means what I have called the extreme Liberal view of constitutional interpretation, that is the judicial "discovery" of additional, unenumerated constitutional guarantees of individual liberty. The only alternative is the extremely Conservative View that rejects applying to the states the explicit guarantees contained in the Bill of Rights. Since no one accepts that alternative, adherence to principle requires accepting substantive due process and the extreme Liberal view.

This reasoning is flawed. The alternatives mentioned by Tribe are not exhaustive. One can reject the extreme Conservative View of constitutional interpretation, as I do, without adopting substantive due process and the extreme Liberal view. There is a *principled* compromise between these extremes. I begin by illustrating in a different legal context the nature of principled compromise.

Two important values in our society are security in one's home and the effective control of crime. If the first value were given absolute priority, searches of people's homes would be absolutely prohibited, and crime control would suffer greatly. Criminals would often be able to use their homes effectively to hide their activities from the authorities. In contrast, if the value of crime control were given absolute priority, police would be given unlimited power to search people's homes, and security in one's home would suffer greatly. One would never know when the police might barge in. Recognizing the importance of both values, and the potential for conflict between them, Congress included the Fourth Amendment in the Bill of Rights. That amendment provides for searches of people's homes, but only reasonable searches. Such searches must be justified by "probable cause" and follow issuance of a warrant "particularly describing the place to be searched, and the persons or things to be seized." This is a compromise, but it is principled. The principle is the Principle of Compromise. The principle is simply that, because both values are important, neither should be ignored completely. So each must be slighted *somewhat* in order to accommodate the other.

This principle is employed often in the law. Freedom of speech is important, but so is freedom from bodily injury. So free speech is generally allowed, but not when there is a clear and present danger of that speech leading to bodily injury. For example, one may not shout "Fire!"

in a crowded theater (where one does not believe there is a fire). "Fighting words" may also be prohibited.

Again, the value of majority rule supports a system of representative democracy. But particular matters of legal justice should seldom be greatly influenced by majority will. So the Constitution provides that federal judges be appointed for life, thereby insulating them from most pressures of majority rule. But a judiciary entirely out of touch with the values and perspectives of the majority may, through its power to invalidate legislation, unduly obstruct the will of the majority. The Constitution addresses this problem by requiring federal judges to be appointed and confirmed by elected officials: the president and Senate. Congress may also increase the number of federal judges, including the number of justices of the Supreme Court, so as to influence judicial opinion.

Thus, individual amendments, interpretations of constitutional guarantees, and the constitutional system of checks and balances are all justified in large part by the principle that where two important values come into conflict, each should be compromised somewhat. Such compromises are not unprincipled simply because they are compromises. If they give reasonable weight to each of the principles involved, they are justified by the Principle of Compromise itself. While the particular compromise reached in any given case may be controversial, the Principle of Compromise is not itself controversial.

Let us return now to the extreme Liberal view and the extreme Conservative view of constitutional interpretation. Tribe maintains that no principled compromise between these extremes is possible. As we have seen, the extreme Conservative view would deny application of the Bill of Rights to the states. States would be permitted to establish religions, conduct unlimited searches and seizures, and so forth. Respect for individual rights would be greatly impaired.

In contrast, the extreme Liberal view would permit judicial "discoveries" of unenumerated constitutional rights. These "discoveries" would be limited only by the self-restraint of life-tenured, unelected judges. History shows that majority rule may thereby suffer more than most people consider acceptable in a republican form of government. Even Tribe maintains that "judges certainly should not feel free simply to import into the Constitution their own personal moral views."[73] But the suggestions he makes to avoid this result are unavailing. Recourse to natural law may be no more than different terminology for recourse to the judge's "own personal moral views." Appeals to unenumerated rights "deeply rooted in this nation's history and tradition"[74] provide judges with little guidance and suggest that legislators, who are equally aware of the "nation's history and tradition," be unhindered by judicial "discoveries." These considerations suggest, in keeping with the lessons of history, that the extreme Liberal view of constitutional interpretation menaces proper respect for majority rule.

We have here another example of conflict between two values that we deem worthy of respect: individual rights and majority rule. The extreme Liberal view of constitutional interpretation serves well the value of individual rights, but unduly menaces majority rule. The extreme Conservative view has the opposite effect. A compromise between them can rest on the principle, embodied in our Constitution and employed in constitutional interpretations, that where two important values come into conflict, each should be compromised somewhat.

The Moderate view of constitutional interpretation represents such a compromise. It rejects appeals to substantive due process, which is to say, judicial "discoveries" of unenumerated rights implicit in the "liberty" guaranteed by the Due Process Clause. But the rights specifically enumerated in the Constitution are applied, according to the Moderate view, to all levels of government: federal, state, and local. Further, the meaning of these rights evolves with changes in our society's secular values (see Chapters 3 and 4). So courts are able to protect many individual rights against majority rule. But, out of deference to majority rule, this protection extends only to rights specifically mentioned in the Constitution.

The worth of this particular compromise is, of course, open to challenge. But it can hardly be denied that the Moderate view represents a compromise, and applies the uncontroversial Principle of Compromise. In short, Tribe's thesis that no such compromise can be principled ignores the Principle of Compromise.

Tribe's other argument for the extreme Liberal view is that horrible consequences would follow from its rejection. "A world with only enumerated rights would be a vastly different one from the world we know today."[75] There would be no constitutional right to have an abortion or even to use contraceptives. Worse yet, "not only could abortion be *prohibited*, but abortion as well as sterilization could be *mandated* by the state . . . for reasons of population control or eugenics. . . . The courts would be unable to interfere in the name of the Constitution."[76]

Chapter 6 argues that the Establishment Clause of the First Amendment is sufficient to provide constitutional guarantees of access to contraceptives and abortions. If these arguments are sound, they undercut some of Tribe's dire predictions. Other decisions thought to rest on substantive due process may be justified by appeal to the Equal Protection Clause of the Fourteenth Amendment. *Loving v. Virginia*, for example, which upheld the right of people to marry those of a different race, is in this category.

In general, Tribe's global predictions of dire consequences are unsubstantiated. Each matter will have to be investigated specifically to see whether, and to what extent, the Moderate view yields judicial decisions different from those that Tribe favors. That general task is beyond the scope of the present work. It is sufficient for our purposes that rights to contraception and abortion are constitutionally protected as well, or better, through the present work's use of the Moderate view than they are through Tribe's use of the extreme Liberal view.

Conclusion

The Supreme Court declared in *Roe v. Wade* that a woman has a fundamental right to terminate her pregnancy. This chapter examined the way the Court found that right in, or attached that right to, the Constitution so as to declare it a constitutional right. Two lines of argument have been explored. The first concerns privacy. But the existence in the Constitution of a general right of privacy is uncertain, and abortion is not a private act in any sense in which privacy may be protected by the Constitution. The choice of abortion is an exercise of liberty, which is guaranteed in general terms in the Fourteenth Amendment. But this general liberty can be brought to bear on specific state limitations of liberty only by the Court's using the controversial doctrine of substantive due process, whose legitimacy is uncertain.

In sum, the *Roe* opinions do an inadequate job of anchoring in the Constitution a woman's right to terminate her pregnancy. If the arguments used there are the sole protections of that right, it is in grave jeopardy. For this reason, an alternate justification for the right is provided in the present work.

Before moving on to alternate grounds for abortion rights, however, we should look at some of the specifications of those rights in *Roe* and subsequent abortion-related decisions. Here, controversy surrounds the Court's use of the concept of viability.

CHAPTER 2

Potentiality and Viability

T HIS CHAPTER EXAMINES three basic approaches to the issue of legalizing abortion. One approach maintains that abortions should be restricted severely, or prohibited completely, because the unborn is, from the moment of fertilization, a (human) person with the same right to life as every other person. A second approach justifies severe restrictions, but views the unborn as a *potential* (human) person. Disentangling this approach (potential personhood) from the first approach (actual personhood) is a major goal of the chapter. Viability is discussed because viability is sometimes taken to mark the distinction between potential and actual personhood, and because the Supreme Court employs the concept of viability in some of its major decisions regarding abortion.

The third basic approach separates the issue of abortion's legality from that of the unborn's humanity. There are two general varieties. According to one, abortion should be restricted significantly even if the unborn are not regarded as (human) persons. Restrictions are justified on this view because abortion's availability has adverse consequences for society in general or for identifiable individuals who are unproblematically persons. The other variety separates the status of abortion from that of the unborn by arguing to the opposite effect. Even if the unborn are regarded as persons, it is argued, abortions should not be restricted because restrictions constitute unfair burdens on women. Again, the consequences for others, rather than the rights of the unborn, are featured. In rejecting all varieties of this approach, I maintain in this chapter that the personhood of the unborn, not the consequences for others, is central to the major issue: Should state legislatures be permitted to restrict severely, or even prohibit completely, women's access to abortion?

Considerations regarding the personhood of the unborn have influenced Supreme Court decisions beginning with *Roe v. Wade*. This chapter first discusses that case and then subsequent Supreme Court decisions that concern the personhood of the unborn. Chapters 7 and 8 relate abortion rights to the permissibility of state regulations concerning such matters as health care, spousal consent (for married women), parental consent (for minors), and public funding (for the poor).

Before beginning, a word about terminology is needed. Following some medical usage, I use three terms for the unborn. I call it a *zygote* from the time of fertilization to that of implantation on the uterine wall, about a week later. I call it an *embryo* during the following six or seven weeks, and then a *fetus* (until it is born).

The Roe v. Wade *Decision*

Justice Blackmun, writing for the Court in *Roe v. Wade*, declared that a woman has a fundamental right to decide "whether or not to terminate her pregnancy."[1] Although fundamental rights are not absolute and may be limited by the state (see introductory chapter), Blackmun qualified this limitation: "Where certain 'fundamental rights' are involved, the Court has held that regulation limiting these rights may be justified *only* by a 'compelling state interest,' and that legislative enactments must be narrowly drawn to express only the legitimate state interests at stake."[2]

Blackmun went on to specify the nature of the compelling state interests relevant to abortion and the limits that these interests place on a woman's right to terminate her pregnancy. He divided pregnancy into three roughly equal time segments, or trimesters, and declared it unconstitutional for a state to regulate abortion during the first of those trimesters. "The attending physician, in consultation with his patient, is free to determine, without regulation by the State, that, in his medical judgment, the patient's pregnancy should be terminated."[3] During the first trimester, then, the Court recognized no compelling state interests sufficient to override or limit the right to have an abortion.

Starting with the second trimester, however, "a State may regulate the abortion procedure to the extent that the regulation reasonably relates to the preservation and protection of maternal health."[4] The protection of people's health is a legitimate public purpose. The greater the jeopardy to people's health in any situation, the greater the need for protective state regulations. The Court maintained in *Roe* that during the first trimester of pregnancy an abortion does not jeopardize a woman's health sufficiently to justify limiting abortion rights. But in the second trimester the abortion procedure involves greater risks to maternal health. The Court maintained that the jeopardy is so great as to create the kind of compelling state interest (in protecting maternal health) that justifies the limitation of even a fundamental right (to terminate one's pregnancy). I discuss this in Chapter 7.

Finally, during the third trimester, which is "the stage subsequent to viability, the State in promoting its interest in the potentiality of human life may, if it chooses, regulate, and even proscribe, abortion except where it is necessary, in appropriate medical judgment, for the preservation of the life or health of the mother."[5] The compelling state interest in the third trimester is in the preservation of the life of the fetus. This interest is compelling in the third trimester because the fetus is viable.

The Court professes agnosticism on the issue of fetal humanity, whether at viability or at any other stage of gestation. Blackmun writes: "We need not resolve the difficult question of when life begins. When those trained in the respective disciplines of medicine, philosophy and theology are unable to arrive at any consensus, the judiciary, at this point in the development of man's knowledge, is not in a position to speculate as to the answer."[6] The key to the Court's attitude, however, is its requirement that legislatures act similarly as agnostics until the fetus is viable. After the point of viability, the Court remains agnostic, but does not require the same of legislatures.

Before viability, then, the state may not "by adopting one theory of life, . . . override the rights of the pregnant woman."[7] It may not regulate or proscribe abortion in the interest of protecting fetal life. This amounts to saying that it may not treat the fetus as a human being, nor may it judge that the fetus' at least *potential* humanity carries such weight as to override a woman's fundamental right to terminate her pregnancy.

This all changes with viability. After viability the state is permitted by the Court to value the fetus's humanity, or its potential for humanity, to such an extent as "to proscribe abortion during that period, except when it is necessary to preserve the life or health of the mother."[8] After viability, the state is permitted to act on the theory that the fetus is a human being with human rights that the state is obligated to protect against all abortions except those relatively few that are needed to preserve a woman's life or health.

We see here that viability plays an important role in the Court's specification of a woman's right to terminate her pregnancy. But what is viability, and why is it important? I begin by discussing the concept of viability employed by the Court's majority. I then consider dissenting judicial opinions and scholarly articles that challenge the view that viability marks the point in pregnancy when a state may legitimately protect the fetus (almost) as if it were a newborn or older human being. Justices White, Rehnquist, and O'Connor maintain that viability is not important. They maintain that a state should be able to provide to all fetuses whatever protections it is allowed to provide for viable fetuses. O'Connor's defense of this view may depend on her confusing two different senses of potentiality; White's arguments for the same view are considered and rejected next. I then present and defend my own view. I agree that viability is not crucial. I maintain that the proper criterion is not viability but the similarity of the unborn to newborns. I conclude that if women have a fundamental right to terminate their pregnancies, this right is limited by the unborn's right to life. No such right exists early in pregnancy, but eight-month fetuses typically do have such a right. I defer to Chapter 6 a consideration of in-between cases.

The Concept of Viability in Abortion Cases

There are three major aspects to the concept of viability that the Court used in *Roe v. Wade*. Viability refers to a condition that could exist immediately, so *immediacy* is one aspect of viability. But what could exist immediately does not exist at present. Because the condition does not exist at present, it is currently contrary to fact. Philosophers call such conditions counterfactuals. For example, because I am at present at home, my being at the office is contrary to fact and, therefore, counterfactual. Viability refers to a *counterfactual* condition, that of the fetus's existence outside its mother. The third aspect of viability is the *reasonable likelihood* of fetal survival outside its mother. This section is devoted primarily to explaining these three aspects of the concept of viability—counterfactuality, reasonable likelihood, and immediacy— with special attention to the relationship between viability and potentiality. I conclude the section by showing that Justice O'Connor's argument against the importance of viability may turn on a failure to distinguish two different senses of potentiality that are implicit in the Court's concept of viability.

According to the Court, viability exists by definition when "the fetus

. . . has the capability of meaningful life outside the mother's womb,"[9] that is, when the fetus is "potentially able to live outside the mother's womb, albeit with artificial aid."[10] A third formulation approved by the Court is contained in Missouri's definition of viability as "that stage of fetal development when the life of the unborn child may be continued indefinitely outside the womb by natural or artificial life support systems."[11]

All three of these formulations refer to a *counterfactual*, but possible, condition. As already stated, this is a condition that is not a fact, but that could be, or could have been, a fact.

The first formulation refers to "capability," the second to what the fetus can do "potentially," and the third to what "may be" done. These are the key terms in the formulations that show viability to be concerned with a counterfactual possibility. And in all three cases the possibility is that of the survival of the fetus "outside the mother's womb." The fetus can be separated from the mother and survive ("albeit with artificial aid"). Just as I am not currently at my office, but could be there, a viable fetus is not currently in the hospital's incubator, but could be there. In sum, a fetus is viable when it can survive separation from the woman in whose body it is growing. The "potentiality" and "capability" at viability is for survival on separation.

The result of the separation that could take place at viability is "meaningful life," which is to say, a life whose development "may be continued indefinitely." The Court notes that the "mere possibility of momentary survival is not the medical standard of viability."[12] The "potentiality," the "capability," what "may be" at viability, then, is the development of the fetus into an adult human being without any further help from, or contact with, the woman who is carrying it.

Because a fetus at any stage of gestation is a delicate being, one cannot require for viability the certainty of the fetus's survival outside its mother. What is more, "the probability of any particular fetus' obtaining meaningful life outside the womb can be determined only with difficulty," and "even if agreement may be reached on the probability of survival, different physicians equate viability with different probabilities of survival."[13] Some physicians require a 10 percent chance of survival, others 5 percent, and still others only 2 or 3 percent to consider a fetus viable.[14] Amid such disagreement, the Court laid down the standard of "*reasonable likelihood.*" "Viability exists when . . . there is a reasonable likelihood of the fetus' sustained survival outside the womb, with or without artificial support."[15] (Contrary to common usage, the Court considers "reasonably likely" outcomes with only a 10, 5, or even 2 percent probability.)

Besides referring to a counterfactual condition of which there is a reasonable likelihood, the Court's use of viability involves the notion of *immediacy*. If a fetus is viable, it has *right now* "the capability of meaningful life outside the mother's womb." It is *at present* "potentially able to live outside the mother's womb, albeit with artificial aid." Such immediacy must be part of the Court's concept of viability because without the notion of immediacy in the concept, there would be no point during pregnancy when a fetus is not viable. If "the capability for meaningful life outside the mother's womb" (which defines viability) were one that would exist someday, in the near or distant future, with no time limit, then a fetus would be viable virtually throughout pregnancy. Most embryos become, in time, fetuses that develop through time the capability of living outside the mother's womb. But, the Court clearly means by viability a condition that comes into being at a certain point during pregnancy (generally at the end of the second trimester), not a condition that exists throughout pregnancy. It is only after the fetus is viable, and not before, that the Court permits "State regulation protective of fetal life."[16] So "the capability for meaningful life outside the mother's womb," which defines viability, must be one that exists at present. To be viable a fetus must be capable right now of existing outside the mother's womb. The counterfactual condition is current, not merely future.

The same point can be made with reference to the concept of potentiality. Aristotle, who explained and employed the concept extensively, distinguished between what he called first and second potentiality. A person who is not currently trained to build houses is potentially a builder in the first of Aristotle's two senses of potentiality. In order to build a house she would have to learn the trade and then employ her newly acquired skills. A person who is not currently building a house, but who currently has all the requisite skills, is potentially a builder in the second of Aristotle's two senses. Because she is not currently engaged in the act of building, her building activity is counterfactual and potential, rather than actual. But because she is now fully capable of building a house, her building activity is in a state of second potentiality. This distinction, though not this terminology, is important in everyday life. If I am contracting with an unemployed person to build a house, it is crucial that she be a potential builder in the second, not merely in the first, sense of potentiality.

When Blackmun defines a viable fetus as one "potentially able to live outside the mother's womb, albeit with artificial aid," he is using potentiality in the second of Aristotle's two senses. In the first sense of potentiality, a fetus is "potentially able to live outside the mother's womb" virtually throughout pregnancy. First potentiality exists when an ability can be developed, and fetuses are capable throughout pregnancy of developing the ability to live separately from their mothers. Since we know that the concept of viability is used by the Court to denote a condition that appears during pregnancy, we know that it is second potentiality that the Court employs in its definition of viability. A viable fetus is able immediately to live outside the womb.

This point requires emphasis because some current Supreme Court justices reject the viability criterion as a result of failure to appreciate the distinction between first and second potentiality. Dissenting in *Akron v. Akron Center for Reproductive Health*, Justice O'Connor wrote that "*potential* life is no less potential in the first weeks of pregnancy than it is at viability or afterward. At any stage in pregnancy, there is potential for human life."[17] Three years later Justice White, dissenting in *Thornburgh v. American College of Obstetricians and Gynecologists*, referred approvingly to O'Connor's line of reasoning in *Akron* and concluded that "the Court's choice of viability as the point at which the State's interest becomes compelling is entirely arbitrary."[18] Justice Rehnquist joined in White's opinion on this matter. So three justices are on record as believing on the following grounds that the viability standard is arbitrary. The viability standard is designed to protect potential human life. Since potential human life exists throughout pregnancy, it is arbitrary to provide protection only during the later stages of pregnancy.

The flaw in this argument is its failure to recognize the distinction between first and second potentiality that is implicit in the Court's viability criterion. During the early stages of pregnancy there exists only the first potentiality for life outside the mother's womb. The fetus can develop the ability to live separately from its mother. At viability, in contrast, there is second potentiality of separate existence. It has the *current* ability to live separately, but is not actually doing so. Thus, the viability criterion does not involve irrationally protecting a potentiality and at the same time denying protection to that same kind of potentiality.

Dividing the Gestational Continuum

In addition to seconding O'Connor's objections to the viability criterion, White objects to the criterion on other grounds. Writing for both himself and Rehnquist, he argues:

The Governmental interest at issue is in protecting those who will be citizens if their lives are not ended in the womb. The substantiality of this
interest is in no way dependent on the probability that the fetus may be
capable of surviving outside the womb at any given point in its development. . . . The State's interest is in the fetus as an entity in itself, and the
character of this entity does not change at the point of viability under
conventional medical wisdom. Accordingly, the State's interest, if compelling after viability, is equally compelling before viability.[19]

According to White, the state has an interest at all stages of pregnancy
"in the fetus as an entity in itself." So states may prohibit abortions just
as they prohibit "assaults committed upon children by parents."[20] In
short, states are entitled to protect the unborn at all stages of gestation,
just as they protect infants, children, and all other human beings.

This is White's position. His argument for this position is the following:

However one answers the metaphysical or theological question whether
the fetus is a "human being" or the legal question whether it is a "person" as that term is used in the Constitution, one must at least recognize, first, that the fetus is an entity that bears in its cells all the genetic
information that characterizes a member of the species *homo sapiens*
and distinguishes an individual member of that species from all others,
and second, that there is no nonarbitrary line separating a fetus from a
child or, indeed, an adult human being.[21]

Writing for both himself and Rehnquist, White here notes two considerations supporting the view that fetuses are enough like "persons"
to be entitled to legal protection. They have the genetic code of persons,
and they develop gradually into those who are undoubtedly persons
(children and adult human beings) through a process containing no
nonarbitrary lines of division. In this section I explain and reject the
second of these reasons for granting a right to life to previable fetuses. I
deal with the first consideration in the section that follows.

The fact that change takes place gradually with no nonarbitrary
lines of division does not imply that what existed at the beginning of the
change belongs to the same category as what existed at the end. For
example, some people start adulthood with a full head of hair and lose
it gradually. There is no nonarbitrary line in terms of numbers of hairs
on one's head that distinguishes the state of being bald from the state of
not being bald. Yet, even when the process of change from one state to
the other is gradual, a term can properly be applied late in the process
that could not be applied early. Thus, looking at an old photograph of

the person, it can be correctly, if not politely, declared, "He wasn't bald yet when this picture was taken."

The law recognizes this phenomenon. Writing about the concept of negligence in *Daniels v. Williams*, Justice Rehnquist acknowledged that the subject was complex, abounding in "nice distinctions that may be troublesome." But this does not prevent the law from distinguishing negligence from intent, because "the difference between one end of the spectrum—negligence—and the other—intent—is abundantly clear."[22] In legal distinctions as in everyday life, the fact that there are many in-between cases that cannot be readily identified with either extreme does not call into question the significance of distinctions between extremes.

This is also true where the law deals with gradual processes affecting people's fundamental rights. White notes that a child develops into an adult through a continuation of the process begun at conception.[23] One might, therefore, parody his thought by arguing as follows: We recognize that mentally competent citizens of the United States who have attained the age of forty years have a fundamental right to vote in democratic elections. These people have developed during their lives through a continuous process. "There is no nonarbitrary line separating . . . a child [from] an adult human being."[24] So whatever fundamental rights are enjoyed by adults should be accorded children, even newborns, as well. Newborns should have the right to vote in democratic elections.

The fallacy in this form of reasoning is, first, the supposition already discussed and rejected that one cannot distinguish extreme cases from one another if there are in-between cases that are difficult to classify. The fact that it is sometimes difficult to decide whether a seventeen-year-old is a child or an adult does not impair one's ability to say that a newborn is a child and a thirty-year-old is an adult.

The second fallacy is the related supposition that if there is no nonarbitrary line separating two cases, then the cases should not be treated differently, especially where fundamental rights are concerned. The fallacy is exposed by the voting example, which illustrates that the law *must* sometimes make somewhat arbitrary distinctions, even where fundamental rights are concerned. An agreed-upon line is needed to separate two kinds of cases because at the extremes there is enough difference to require different treatment, there are problematic in-between cases, and legal certainty is best served by a sharp line of division. In such cases, it is not arbitrary that there be a sharp line of division, and it is not arbitrary that the line of division be among the in-between cases, but the exact location among those cases is arbitrary. Thus, there is enough difference between an infant and a forty-year-old to require that they be treated differently with regard to voting rights. There are in-between cases (e.g., people from fifteen to twenty-five) about whom there can be legitimate disagreement concerning the propriety of voting rights. Nevertheless, a sharp and general division is needed so that people can know their rights. Also, individual (administrative or judicial) determinations of people's voting rights would risk the abuse of power that impairs the democratic process. So it is not arbitrary that a sharp line be drawn; it is not arbitrary that the line be drawn somewhere between ages fifteen and twenty-five, but the choice of eighteen, as opposed to seventeen or twenty-one, is somewhat arbitrary.

Analogously, one can maintain that a zygote and a newborn are as different from one another as are a newborn and an adult. It may, therefore, be inappropriate for them to have the same right to life. Since people need to know what rights exist at various gestational stages, it is necessary to create some lines of division. Because the transition is continuous between the zygote and the newborn, all lines of division will contain an element of arbitrariness, even though it is not arbitrary that such lines be drawn, nor is it arbitrary that they be drawn among the problematic cases. I believe that these are the sorts of considerations that Justice Stevens had in mind when he wrote:

> The State's interest in the protection of an embryo—even if that interest is defined as "protecting those who will be citizens"—increases progressively and dramatically as the organism's capacity to feel pain, to experience pleasure, to survive and to react to its surroundings increases day by day. The development of a fetus—and pregnancy itself—are not static conditions, and the assertion that the government's interest is static simply ignores this reality.[25]

The government's interest changes with the development of the fetus because that development involves changes to which the law should be responsive, just as it is responsive to the changes that take place as people grow from infancy to adulthood. Later in this chapter I present some considerations bearing on the point in the gestational process where it is reasonable to draw a line of division. Chapter 6 returns to this topic and is more specific.

White has a ready reply to the argument in this section. He maintains that because the genetic code does not change during gestation, there is warrant to treat pregnancy the same way in all its stages. This view is discussed in the section that follows.

The Genetic Approach to Personhood

As noted in the last section, White thinks it important "that the fetus is an entity that bears in its cells all the genetic information that characterizes a member of the species *homo sapiens* and distinguishes an individual member of that species from all others."[26] Let us suppose, at least for the sake of argument, that White means by this that it is reasonable, if not required, for a state to treat a developing life as being both morally and legally a complete human being from the moment it has a human genetic code. This may not be exactly what White intended. Nevertheless, it is a view worth exploring because it is only on this view that we can avoid drawing one or more distinctions among the unborn at different gestational stages, and White objects that all such distinctions are drawn arbitrarily.

The view is worth exploring also because the Missouri law upheld in *Webster v. Reproductive Health Services* contains a preamble with "findings" that "the life of each human being begins at conception" and that "unborn children have protectable interests in life, health, and well-being."[27] The Human Life bill debated, but not passed, by Congress contains the same view: "Congress hereby declares that for the purpose of enforcing the obligation of the States under the fourteenth amendment not to deprive persons of life without due process of law, human life shall be deemed to exist from conception, without regard to race, sex, age, health, defect, or condition of dependency; and for this purpose 'person' shall include all human life as defined herein."[28]

Because of these attempts to alter the law so as to incorporate the view that human life, and full, legal personhood begin at conception, it is worth exploring the implications of this view when it is taken seriously, that is, literally. So the present section considers the implications without any dilutions that common sense may suggest, as all compromises involve the use of distinctions that White considers arbitrary. I find the rule that a being is a person within the meaning of the Fourteenth Amendment from the moment it has a human genetic code to entail radical departures from our legal traditions and to yield what can only be called absurdities. These absurdities are conceptual, practical, and legal. I begin by pointing out conceptual absurdities.

First, there is the puzzle about *whose* human life is deemed to exist from the moment of fertilization, when a zygote comes into existence with its own, human genetic code. The zygote may split within several days to become two (or more) identical zygotes, thus creating monozygotic twins or triplets. Which of these is the "person" who came into existence at fertilization? Who are the others? Do they, too, have full human rights? If so, does their personhood come into existence not at fertilization (when there was only one) but at some time (possibly days) later when the zygote splits? How do we know which one became a person at fertilization and which one(s) attained personhood later? These are all ridiculous questions. They cannot be answered because they cannot be understood. They make no sense within the conceptual scheme available to us. Our normal assumption that full personhood does not begin at fertilization protects us from such absurdities. Reverse this assumption and we are led to absurd questions. It is a postulate of logic that one should avoid commitments to views that lead to absurdities.

Other absurdities relate to conflicts with common practice and common sense. As Joel Feinberg notes, "Embryologists have estimated that only 58 percent of fertilized ova survive until implantation (seven days after conception) and that the spontaneous abortion rate after that stage is from 10 to 15 percent."[29] Combined with these facts, the belief that personhood begins at fertilizations yields the conclusion that more than half of all human deaths occur before birth. If these prenatal human lives are to be respected equally with all others, the greatest expenditure of resources in medicine and in medical research should be devoted to saving these lives "without regard to race, sex, age, *health, defect,* or condition of dependency." After all, for every child that suffers from spina bifida, cerebral palsy, or muscular dystrophy, there are thousands who die from a failure to implant on the uterine wall, so medical efforts should be geared primarily to address this problem. If we are successful, we could move from a population where about 2 percent suffer from relatively minor congenital defects to one where as many as 10 to 20 percent suffer from major defects. When this implication is recognized, how many people really want to attribute personhood from the moment of fertilization regardless of health or defect?

Another implication at odds with common practice and common sense is that we should mourn the death of all these "people," and have death certificates and burial requirements. Never mind that in most cases the only clue that such a death has occurred is a late or particularly heavy menstrual flow. A person is a person. All should be treated with respect. Surely none should be flushed down the toilet or thrown into the garbage.

Population statistics would have to be revised to reflect the (often brief) existence of these people. A state may gain additional members in the House of Representatives if it has more pregnant women than do other states. Actuarial tables would have to be revised as well. Since more than half of the human population dies before birth through failure of implantation or spontaneous abortion, a country where the life expectancy is currently thought to be about seventy years would actually be one with a life expectancy under thirty-five.

Of course, individuals who survive to childhood would be older than is currently thought, about nine months older in most cases, because we currently date the beginning of life at birth, which is nine months after the person has actually come into existence. Appropriate adjustments would have to be made in the ages at which a person is permitted to drive, vote, drink, and so forth.

Many thousands of frozen human embryos exist at present. If personhood begins at conception, then these are all (chilly) people. When decisions are made about their future, they would all need guardians *ad litem* (legal counsel) to protect their rights. If their parents are getting divorced, any dispute over them would be a matter of child custody. If their parents, whether divorcing or not, do not want them to develop further, the court would have to protect their rights by removing them from their parents' custody. As soon as immunosuppressive drugs are available that enable a genetically unrelated woman to carry an embryo to term, these "children" should be put up for adoption just as other children are.

Adopting any new idea is likely to have some consequences that are unexpected and unwelcome. It is important to realize in this case, first, that the implications noted above are surprising because the idea of treating zygotes as people is new. It is not, and has not been, the norm in our society. Abortion is not the only area in which our practice deviates from the implications of placing the advent of personhood at fertilization. We need to realize also that while some of the implications are merely odd, funny, or ridiculous, others are truly disturbing. Especially disturbing are the implications concerning the allocation of medical resources. It would be tragic to diminish efforts in areas of postnatal care and treatment because many more "people's" lives could be saved through attention to problems of uterine implantation, when success in this latter pursuit results in millions of additional postnatal people being subject to lives afflicted with debilitating genetic defects. It is also absurd at a practical level. When health care already consumes nearly 11 percent of the gross national product, and millions of (postnatal) people are nevertheless poorly served, it is absurd to add a burden that is incalculable and incomparable.

By contrast, the legal implications of this view are less absurd than frightening. Abortion would, of course, be illegal. That is the main reason for maintaining, in the first place, that beings become persons on receipt of a human genetic code. But it is one thing to maintain that abortion is illegal, and quite another to treat it seriously as murder. Murder is among the most serious crimes, and carries some of the heaviest penalties. Life in prison and even the death penalty are considered by the Supreme Court to be permissible penalties for murder. If fetuses are considered persons under the Fourteenth Amendment, then performing an abortion can be nothing less than premeditated murder, planning an abortion would be conspiracy to commit murder, and having an abortion would be a felony that results in the unlawful death of another. Wherever there is a felony murder rule, a law that declares people guilty of murder whenever a felony they commit results in an unlawful death, all women who have abortions would be guilty of murder.

Any lesser treatment of abortion would show unwarranted disrespect for fetal people. One purpose of punishing murderers is to express the community's condemnation of murder. If fetuses are people with equal status, their murder should be condemned as emphatically as anyone else's. Another purpose of punishing murderers is to deter potential murderers, thereby saving the lives of potential victims. The only way to give fetuses equal protection of the laws is to punish abortion with the same severity as other murders. To do less would be like punishing those who murder blacks less severely than those who murder whites. This would obviously be unconstitutional. Thus, if personhood begins at fertilization, the implication is not that abortion could be treated as murder, but that it would have to be treated as murder.

This treatment of abortion contrasts sharply with any treatment previously known in our system. The typical statute, such as the one invalidated in *Roe v. Wade*, was directed solely at the person who performed the abortion. The woman who requested, planned, and voluntarily submitted to the abortion was not considered an accessory, as she would have to be if abortion were murder. Nor was the doctor subject to penalties anything like those that Texas associated with murder. This was true everywhere and at all times in our legal tradition.[30] As Justice Tom C. Clark wrote after his retirement from the Supreme Court, "no prosecutor has ever returned a murder indictment charging the taking of the life of a fetus. This would not be the case if the fetus constituted a human life."[31]

The implications of treating fertilized eggs as human beings are more ominous where contraception is concerned, because some contraceptives are actually abortifacients. The IUD is the most prominent among these. It prevents fertilized eggs from implanting on the uterine wall, thereby depriving the zygote of the nutrition it requires for further development. The zygote is then expelled in the menstrual flow. If fertilized eggs are human beings, this is murder by starvation and exposure, and would have to be dealt with accordingly if all people are to be given equal protection of the laws.

A major distinction would have to be made among hormonal contraceptives. Those, like "the pill," which prevent fertilization, would be blameless. But any intervention, such as a "morning after" pill, which killed eggs after fertilization, would have to be made strictly illegal. Since, unlike abortions, morning after pills are self-administered, the woman taking them would herself be guilty of murder (if a zygote was actually killed) or attempted murder or reckless endangerment (if there was no fertilized egg). Finding a woman in possession of such a pill would constitute probable cause for an investigation that would have to include collection and inspection of her next menstrual flow to determine whether or not a fertilized egg was present. Surely the difference between murder and either attempted murder or reckless endangerment is serious enough to warrant such inspections. The impositions on privacy and the expenditures of police time involved in these inspections are justified by the seriousness of the criminal activity in question. The equal protection of zygotes *requires* as much.

In sum, absurdities abound when fertilized ova are considered persons with the same right to life as the rest of us. These absurdities are conceptual, practical, and legal. That is the message of this section. The preceding section showed, contrary to the suggestion of Justice White, that both law and common sense sometimes require that (partly) arbitrary divisions be made in matters that, like the gestational process, involve continua. Since newborns, at the end of the gestational process, are uncontroversially accorded the status of persons in our law, whereas absurdities follow from the same attribution to zygotes, at the beginning of the process, we conclude that gestational development is one of those continua where one or more lines of division *must* be drawn. In other words, practical reason requires that we decide to accord significance to differences between one gestational stage and another because this is the only way to avoid absurdities. Further, to avoid absurdities, these differences must be considered relevant to the acquisition of personhood and its attendant rights. So Justice Douglas was perfectly justified in his concurring opinion in *Doe v. Bolton* (1973) when he declared a Georgia statute to be "overbroad because it equates the value of embryonic life immediately after conception with the worth of life immediately before birth."[32]

Having established that one or more lines must be drawn, I consider and reject in the next section the proposal that the most important line be drawn at viability. I find that the viability criterion should be replaced by a consideration of the similarity of the unborn to the newborn.

Viability versus Similarity to Newborns

As White correctly notes, the issue of where in the gestational process to mark the acquisition of personhood affects "the State's interest . . . in the fetus as an entity in itself."[33] The issue is whether and when this entity has *in itself* rights that the state has a duty to protect.

Viability as defined by the Court in *Roe* and subsequent cases concerns the possibility of fetal survival on separation from its mother. This possibility varies with medical technology. Fertilization can already be accomplished *in vitro* (outside a woman). The development of an artificial placenta would enable such zygotes to gestate fully outside any human body. Such a technological breakthrough is not imminent, but could occur in the next generation, so it is not too early to adjust our thinking to include its occurrence. At that point zygotes would be viable, making the viability criterion equivalent to the view that a right to life differs by gestational stage no more than it currently differs by race or religion. But the preceding section has shown the absurdity of according zygotes a full right to life. White is thus correct to reject the Court's viability criterion for assigning a right to life to the fetus. He is justified in maintaining that "the possibility of fetal survival is contingent on the state of medical practice and technology, factors that are in essence morally and constitutionally irrelevant."[34]

The relevant factor is the current nature of the fetus, just as the relevant factor in according many other rights is the current state of the right holder. Five year olds are not accorded the right to drive a car. They are potentially seventeen year olds with appropriate driving skills, but their current rights are geared to their current state of being. The high school biology student has no current right to practice medicine, even though she is potentially a physician. The absurdities discussed in the preceding section can be avoided if the fetus's right to life is similarly geared to its current state (current at the time the right is ascribed), and if possession of a human genetic code is not sufficient for this ascription.

If the genetic code is not sufficient, what is? Surely being just like newborns except in location is sufficient to be accorded the same right to life as newborns (and other human beings). It is a well-established principle that, other things being equal, the right to life does not differ with mere location. Morally and legally, my right to life is the same at home, at work, and in a foreign country. An eight-month fetus can be removed and simply survive, given ordinary care.[35] This shows it to differ from a newborn primarily in location. A secondary difference is the eight-month fetus's attachment to its mother, from whom it receives oxygen and nutrition. A healthy newborn breathes to extract oxygen from the air. An eight-month fetus receives its oxygen from its mother, whose breathing extracts oxygen from the air. The newborn and fetus differ analogously in their acquisition of nutrition. So, in addition to location, the newborn and the eight month fetus differ in the manner of their acquisition of oxygen and nutrition. This difference resembles that between a healthy person and a person who is in a hospital receiving oxygen by respirator and nutrition by intravenous feeding. Other things being equal, the unusual dependency for oxygen and nutrition of hospitalized people does not diminish their right to life, especially when they are capable immediately of breathing and eating normally. Similarly, the eight month fetus's dependency, which can be ended immediately by its removal from its mother, provides no grounds for denying to it the same right to life ascribed to a newborn.

In sum, the eight-month fetus differs from a newborn only in location and dependency. But it is capable *immediately* of being removed from its mother and surviving like a newborn. So, like a newborn, it should have a human being's right to life. It is not an in-between case.

Zygotes and embryos are entirely different in this regard. They do not have the organs or the sensitivities of newborns. The fact that embryos can be frozen for later implantation shows that they are more like simpler organisms than like infants (except in their genetic code, and absurdities follow from relying on the genetic code alone). Zygotes and embryos lack the right to life because they are so unlike newborns and other human beings. Their current state of being is biologically much more primitive than that of birds and mammals, which lack the right to life in our law, but do have a right to be free of wanton cruelty. Unlike birds and mammals, however, embryos cannot feel pain, as they have no central nervous system, making cruelty to them no more possible than cruelty to plants. These facts would not be altered by the development of an artificial placenta that enables embryos to develop into infants outside a human mother. As long as an embryo is still an embryo (has not yet developed further), its rights are the same as those of other comparably simple organisms. In short, it has no rights at all because its degree of biological complexity is similar to that of insects, to whom we ascribe no rights at all. In one respect, however, an embryo is like an eight-month fetus. Like an eight-month fetus, an embryo is not an in-between case. But whereas an eight-month fetus clearly has all the rights of a newborn (other things being equal), an embryo clearly has none of these rights.

As Nancy Rhoden points out, this line of reasoning is not entirely foreign to Blackmun's in *Roe v. Wade*. At the time of the *Roe* decision, fetuses that were viable in the sense of having the current ability "to live outside the mother's womb, albeit with artificial aid,"[36] were in their general nature "substantially similar to a baby."[37] At that level of technology the Court's viability standard approximates an application of the principle endorsed here that a fetus gains a right to life as its current state of being resembles that of a newborn. So the principle endorsed here may be seen as capturing the moral insight behind the Court's original viability standard.

In the intervening years technology has not (yet) altered matters significantly. But O'Connor is justified in her insistence that the Court's position be consistent with technological breakthroughs,[38] even if experts do not agree that such breakthroughs are imminent.[39] White is also correct when he insists that "medical practice and technology . . . are in essence morally and constitutionally irrelevant."[40] The viability standard in *Roe* should, therefore, be replaced by one that corresponds more reliably to the consideration of similarity to newborns. This consideration underlies the viability standard, is immune to technological change, and is morally and legally relevant. It yields the result that eight-month fetuses normally have the rights of newborns, whereas zygotes and embryos do not. A criterion for the treatment of in-between cases is proposed in Chapter 6.

Two Consequentialist Arguments

I have argued that fetuses late in the gestational process have the same right to life as infants. Like infants, children, and adult human beings, they should be treated as ends in themselves. They should be protected for their own sake. The two arguments considered and rejected in this section maintain, to the contrary, that fetuses should be protected not for their own sake but for the sake of others. Their protection does not stem from, or depend on, their own rights at the time they are being protected but on the impact of protecting them on real human beings (whose rights are the only ones at issue). In other words, (in terms familiar to philosophers) the arguments considered in this section treat the unborn as having merely instrumental value. Like hammers, automobiles, and tomatoes, fetuses are considered here only as means to the fulfillment of the ends of others. The treatment of fetuses is judged, and the protection of fetuses justified, by the resulting *consequences* for others. Because consequences for others are central to the arguments considered in this section, these arguments are labeled "consequentialist." The first of these two rationales applies only to viable fetuses. The second is more inclusive.

Ronald Dworkin argues that "even though a fetus is not a constitutional person," it can be legally protected on the following rationale: "A State might properly fear the impact of widespread abortion on its citizens' instinctive respect for the value of human life and their instinctive horror at human destruction and suffering, which are values essential for the maintenance of a just and decent civil society." These considerations are "particularly intense after viability when the fetus has assumed a postnatal baby's form. This is a matter of resemblance."[41]

This rationale for protecting viable fetuses parallels Immanuel Kant's reasons for protecting animals from the cruelty of human beings. Kant did not believe that the animals had any right to be protected from cruelty. But "he who is cruel to animals becomes hard also in his dealing with men."[42] Animals must be protected from cruelty in order indirectly to protect people from cruelty. Similarly, Dworkin argues that even though fetuses have no rights, those late in the gestational process should be protected. In view of their resemblance to people, failure to protect such fetuses could erode respect for human life.

I disagree with this rationale on two grounds. First, both Kant and Dworkin appeal to a highly speculative consideration that is deemed sufficient to settle an important matter in the absence of evidence. What evidence do we have that suppressing cruelty to animals will lessen, rather than aggravate, cruelty to human beings? Kant presents none. Dworkin's speculation that allowing abortions late in the gestational process will lead to disrespect for human life is equally unsupported.

My second reason for disagreeing with Dworkin concerns his denial that fetuses have rights. If, morally and constitutionally, the right to life is affected by a being's nature, but not by its physical location, and if an eight-month fetus has the same nature as a newborn, then it has the same moral and constitutional right to life. It should be protected for its own sake, for what it is in itself, not for what its destruction might mean to others.

The eight-month fetus is, to be sure, merely a potential infant, in one sense of potentiality. But, as we have seen this is second potentiality. People are similarly merely potential doctors when they are sleeping, even those who have medical degrees and practice medicine for a living. Potentiality in this sense does not deprive people of the rights associated with actuality. So, being in second potentiality for infancy, an eight-month fetus has an infant's right to life. Potentiality in the first sense is just the opposite. Someone who is potentially a doctor in the sense that she could someday learn the medical arts does not have any rights that belong specifically to doctors. Because embryos have only first potentiality, they lack the rights of infants and other human beings.

Failure to observe the subtleties of potentiality affects the other consequentialist argument for protecting fetuses. It is argued that the state has an interest in zygotes, embryos and fetuses (at all stages of gestation) because they "will be citizens if their lives are not ended in the womb."[43] White may mean by this that even if embryos, for example, have no rights, they should be treated as if they do because they are potential human beings in the first sense of potentiality. Left undisturbed, they will become the human beings of the future. They are the citizens of tomorrow. So even if they have no rights, their potential gives them *value*.

Blackmun, too, may have had this consideration in mind when he wrote in *Roe*, "as long as at least *potential* life is involved, the State may assert interests beyond the protection of the pregnant woman alone" apart from any "theory that a new human life is present from the moment of conception."[44]

If White and Blackmun are making a point about the instrumental value of prenatal life, rather than about the rights of the unborn, then clarity is required concerning the differences between claims of value and claims of rights. Claims of value can be of two different sorts: intrinsic and instrumental. Chapter 6 relates claims that fetuses have intrinsic value to claims that they have rights. This chapter considers claims that fetuses have instrumental value. So where I write "value" in this chapter, I mean "instrumental value," and when I contrast attributions of rights and values, I am contrasting attributions of rights and instrumental values.

As we have seen, a claim that the unborn have a right to life means that the unborn should be allowed to live for their own sakes, as ends in themselves, not for the good of others. Claims of (instrumental) value are just the opposite. Milk, for example, has value, but no rights. It is produced and preserved, not for its own sake at all, but for the sake of those who would drink it. The handling and treatment of milk is governed entirely by consequentialist considerations. The entire dairy industry is geared to produce good consequences for human beings, who are ends-in-themselves, and for whom the industry's practices and products are (supposed to be) of value.

Some beings, of course, have both value and rights. Newborns, for example, have rights. They are also valued by people who want to raise children and who look forward to being sustained in their old age by the next generation.

I have argued earlier in this chapter that embryos do not have any rights. But do they have value? In what ways, if any, do they serve the welfare of others? Every newborn must first be an embryo, and, as we have just seen, newborns have value as well as rights. It might be argued that embryos must have the same value to others that newborns have, as they are a necessary step in the process that results in the newborn satisfying other people's needs and desires.

These considerations do not, however, sustain any governmental regulations designed to protect embryos from destruction. Restricting the destruction of something that is valuable, but that has no rights of its own, makes sense only when there is a limited supply relative to people's wants or needs. It is on this ground that we restrict the killing of bald eagles, for example, but not of most fungi. Fungi are valuable as essential elements in the biosphere that sustains human life. We could not live without them. But no restriction on killing them is rational where they are in abundant supply, that is, where no endangered species of fungus is in question.

There is no reason to believe that embryos are in short supply in a world of more than five billion people. And whenever they are in relatively short supply, people can be encouraged through government incentives to increase the rate of their production. France, for example, augments significantly government aid to families that have three or more children. Thus, even though embryos are valuable, the consideration of this value cannot rationally sustain restrictions on their destruction.

A contrary judgment may result from the following, confused argument. A given embryo is valuable because, if allowed to survive, it will become a certain newborn, which has a right to life. Since the life of that newborn depends on the survival of that particular embryo, destruction of the embryo results in denial to the newborn of its right to life. The fallacy here is in supposing that one can, during the early gestational stages predicate a moral or legal decision on the right to life of a potential newborn whose actual existence is affected by that decision. Rights are predicated on what a being is, not on what it will become. On the assumption that embryos do not themselves have rights, appeals to a right to life cannot be made in this context until the newborn, or a fetus similar to a newborn, is actually in being. An embryo cannot have value in relation to the rights of the newborn that it could become because while it is yet an embryo, neither the newborn, nor its rights, exist.

Of course, one can speak intelligibly in some other contexts of the rights of those not yet in being. We speak of the rights of those not yet conceived to inherit an environment that is relatively free of toxic chemicals. It would seem reasonable, too, that a person be able to recover in tort law for damages that he or she sustained *in utero*, regardless of the gestational stage at which the harm was originally done.[45] But in such cases as these, the rights of those not yet in being are predicated on the supposition that they will exist in the future as human beings. It is the future human beings who really have these rights. The same is true when "unborn children have been recognized as acquiring rights or interests by way of inheritance." The rights are those of the human beings they are expected to become, not of the unborn as such. So rights of inheritance "have generally been contingent on live birth."[46] But the supposition that birth will occur cannot be made when the destruction of an embryo is at issue. If it is destroyed, the person who it would have become will never exist, and so will never have any rights. The value of the embryo cannot be predicated on the rights of a being that will not exist, and so will not have those rights. To have value one must have value for a being that already exists or will exist, and that has rights.[47]

Confusion on this point may result from failure to distinguish first from second potentiality. People may suppose that an eight-month fetus should be protected because it is potentially a newborn, which has rights. An embryo is also potentially a newborn, which has rights, so it should enjoy the same protection as an eight-month fetus. As noted earlier, however, the eight-month fetus should be protected because it has second potentiality for infancy and, therefore, its very own rights. An embryo, in contrast, has only first potentiality for being a newborn and therefore has no rights of its own. Its protection must be predicated on its value, and that must be value to some being with rights whose existence is not problematic.

We have seen in this section that considerations of value do not justify protecting embryos. Embryos are not generally in short supply, and where they are locally in short supply, government incentives are sufficient to increase people's production of them. Value considerations are beside the point also where healthy eight-month fetuses are concerned because such fetuses have rights of their own that are sufficient to justify their protection.

It is difficult to know if any of the Supreme Court justices are guilty of the confusions discussed in this section. When Blackmun refers in *Roe* to the state's interest "in protecting potential life,"[48] it is not clear whether he is endorsing the consequentialist, value-based argument rejected here or whether he is making a rights-based argument that he properly applies only to fetuses late in the gestational process. Similarly, when White refers in *Thornburgh* to "the governmental interest . . . in protecting those who will be citizens if their lives are not ended in the womb,"[49] he may be arguing fallaciously that the rights of a being (a newborn) who does not exist, and will not exist if an abortion is performed, are violated by the destruction of a being that has no such rights. Alternatively, he may just be repeating the error discussed earlier of supposing that zygotes and embryos must have all the rights of infants because the developmental process is a continuum in which all cutoff points are somewhat arbitrary. In any case, Stevens seems to be on the right track when he emphasizes the difference between "an embryo" and a fetus with the "capacity to feel pain, to experience pleasure, to survive, and to react to its surroundings."[50] These are the kinds of characteristics that make an eight-month fetus an infant inside its mother and, therefore, a human being with human rights.

Feminism and Viability

In the last section I examined and rejected the view that the unborn should be protected as if they were persons even if and when they are not. In this section I examine and reject the view that the unborn should not be protected as persons even if and when they are persons. My conclusion from these two sections is that the personhood of the unborn is necessary (last section) and sufficient (this section) to justify protecting the right to life of the unborn as we protect the rights of other people.

As just noted, some people argue that even if fetuses are persons with human rights, women should still have a right to terminate their pregnancies before the fetus is viable. I consider three feminist arguments of this sort for a constitutional right to previability abortions. These arguments turn on considerations of self-defense, good samaritanism, and the equal protection of the laws.

When the state asserts before viability its compelling interest in "the fetus as an entity in itself," it imposes on pregnant women the burden of continued pregnancy. Even if the fetus is a person, this burden is unjust, according to some writers, because the laws in our society do not generally require of anyone a sacrifice to preserve the life of another comparable to the sacrifice required of women when they are denied access to abortions. One author compares the growing fetus of an unwanted pregnancy to an imaginary invader against whom abortion is an act of self-defense.[51] Women should be as entitled as others to defend themselves. Before viability, they can only do this through abortions that take the life of the fetus. Even if fetuses have a right to life, taking their lives is justified in this context. After viability, in contrast, the fetus can, in principle, be separated from its mother without being killed, so abortions that kill the fetus lose their legitimacy.

A problem with this defense of the viability criterion is that knowingly taking the life of another in self-defense is seldom morally or legally justified except to avoid one's own death or severe injury. Self-defense would, then, justify only those previability abortions that are necessary to preserve "the life or health of the mother." Such abortions constitute a small fraction of those legalized in *Roe v. Wade*, where the viability criterion is employed.

A related line of reasoning compares continuing an unwanted pregnancy to a heroic act of self-sacrifice, like that of remaining bedridden and attached through catheters for nine months to save the life of a stranger.[52] Though the stranger is a human being with a right to life, she does not have any legal right to require this kind of sacrifice by others. Good samaritan behavior is seldom a legal requirement. Before viability the fetus is similarly dependent on its mother. Even if it has a right to life, it has no right that its mother be compelled to act as a good samaritan. Forbidding previability abortions amounts to unjustly imposing on pregnant women a level of samaritanism not required of others.

There is a cogent reply to this. Remember, we are assuming for the sake of argument in this section that fetuses have a protectable right to life throughout their gestation. On this assumption, the relation between a woman and a fetus is like that between two people. They are related more like parent and child than like strangers, however, and it is not uncommon in the law to require of parents the sacrifices needed for their children's survival. For example, parents owe child support for eighteen years. The similarity of the mother-fetus to the parent-child relationship is weakest in the case of rape, where the fetus is the product of a criminal, degrading, frightening assault. Even if such fetuses may be regarded as strangers whom the pregnant woman has no obligation to save, only a small percentage of the abortions legalized in *Roe* would thereby be justified. So this argument does not justify the more general appeal to viability in the *Roe v. Wade* decision.

A third defense of previable abortions has more general applicability. Even if the previable fetus is a human being, it is dependent on a particular woman who is alone capable of sustaining it. The denial of abortion rights, according to Sylvia Law, "dramatically impairs the woman's capacity for individual self-determination,"[53] "denies the capacity of women as independent decision makers," and "imposes a crushing restraint on the heterosexual women's capacity for sexual expression."[54] Thus, "state restrictions on access to abortion plainly oppress women." Such restrictions deny to women equal protection of the laws because the direct, negative impact is exclusively on women. So it is only "*women* who are oppressed when abortion is denied."[55] Previability abortions should be available because "control of reproduction is the *sine qua non* of women's capacity to live as equal people" and equality has a "high place . . . in our constellation of democratic and constitutional values."[56] Laurence Tribe agrees: "One may discern a constitutionally problematic subjugation of women in the law's *indifference* to the biological reality that sometimes requires women, but never men, to resort to abortion if they are to avoid pregnancy and retain control of their own bodies."[57] But once the fetus "has the capability of meaningful life outside the mother's womb—that is, once the responsibility for the nurture that is essential to life can be assumed by others with the aid of medical technology—the state may limit abortions."[58] "Justice White is thus surely mistaken when he argues that fetal viability and the state of medical technology are morally and constitutionally irrelevant."[59]

This feminist rationale applies generally to previability abortions. One corollary recognized by Tribe is that if and when medical science develops artificial aids that enable fetuses to survive at earlier stages of pregnancy, women's rights to abortions should be altered to reflect the new, shorter previability period. "As technology enhances the ability to relieve the pregnant woman of the burden of her pregnancy and transfer nurture of the fetus to other hands, the state's power to protect fetal life expands—*as it should*."[60] Tribe takes this to mean that "the state may limit abortions so long as it poses no danger to the woman's life or health,"[61] which was the Court's view in *Roe v. Wade* regarding post-viability abortions.

Tribe seems not to recognize that the logic of the feminist argument does not yield the Court's view regarding postviability abortions. The feminist argument is that women are afforded unequal constitutional protection when they are prevented from terminating unwanted pregnancies. Viability is important merely as the point at which "the woman's right to terminate her pregnancy and the fetus' right to life may be vindicated simultaneously."[62] It follows that women should retain throughout pregnancy the right to be separated from the fetus. All that changes at viability, at whatever point technology places viability, is the possibility that the fetus's removal be accomplished without its death. So fetal removal ("abortion" is a misleading term if it suggests the death of the fetus) should be allowed throughout pregnancy, subject to regulations designed to enhance the chances for survival of viable fetuses. In this way women's rights to equality would be vindicated, while the fetus's right to life would be respected to the greatest extent that technology makes this compatible with equality for women.

In sum, what changes at viability is not the permissibility of abortions, but the rationality of legal requirements designed to save the life of the fetus. In view of the definition of viability earlier in this chapter, such requirements would make sense when the chances of fetal survival exceed 2 or 5 or 10 percent. Alternatively, one might reasonably maintain that since human life is precious, regarding the fetus as a human being justifies legal requirements to save the lives of fetuses whose chances of survival are meaningful but less than 2 percent. One might support, in this context, regulations such as those upheld in *Webster v. Reproductive Health Services*[63] (which require a presumption of viability) or those invalidated in *Thornburgh v. American College of Obstetricians and Gynecologists* (which required a second physician to attend to a "possibly viable" fetus).[64] Pro-choice feminists have generally opposed such regulations, considering them to limit unduly a woman's right to terminate her pregnancy. Thus, like the lines of reasoning examined earlier in this section, this feminist rationale may not yield the extensive abortion rights that many people seek to justify.

More important, all feminist rationales for constitutional rights rest on the problematic view that gender is a constitutionally suspect classification, like race and religion. Suspect classifications, like fundamental rights, are occasions for strict judicial scrutiny of legislation to ensure that democratically elected majorities do not unfairly impose their will on minorities. Such unfairness is considered a danger worth taking precautions against where "discrete and insular minorities" are concerned because the voice of such minorities can go unheard indefinitely in a political process geared to the creation of majority coalitions.[65] For this reason, racial and religious minorities are afforded special constitutional protection through strict judicial scrutiny of legislative classifications according to race or religion.

Women are not a minority, much less an insular minority, in our society. Though they have a long history of suffering oppression, and certainly do not (yet) share power equally with men, there is reason to believe that most of their current legal liabilities can be remedied at the ballot box. Exceptions to this general rule might plausibly include demands for economic equality which an entrenched male economic establishment might be able to deny indefinitely. Abortion, however, does not seem to be that kind of issue. Male and female attitudes do not differ markedly enough for the results of majority politics to be seen as the imposition of men's attitudes on women. What is more, if fetuses are to be accepted as having rights, which is one of the assumptions underlying the feminist thought in this section, then they are more plausible candidates than women for special protection. They cannot speak for themselves at all in the political process. As John Hart Ely put it, "I'm not sure I'd know a discrete and insular minority if I saw one, but confronted with a multiple choice question requiring me to designate (a) women or (b) fetuses as one, I'd expect no credit for the former answer."[66] A feminist equal protection rationale is not persuasive when conjoined with the assumption that fetuses are people with rights of their own. When this assumption is withdrawn, a feminist equal protection rationale is not needed.

Conclusion

If women have a fundamental right to terminate their pregnancies, that right is properly limited by considerations related to preserving the life of the unborn if and only if the unborn in question is a person. I reject arguments that the unborn should be protected even if they are not people and that they should not be protected even if they are people. I also reject arguments for attributing personhood to everyone with a human genetic code because these arguments contain fallacies and their conclusion entails absurdities and evils. I reject the viability criterion of personhood because technological developments could make it equivalent to the rejected identification of personhood with the presence of a human genetic code. Instead, I maintain that the unborn become persons (with a right to life) when they become substantially similar to newborns. Zygotes and embryos are not people, whereas eight-month fetuses (usually) are people. Chapter 6 discusses considerations bearing on the specific point in the gestational process where the line should be drawn between those who are not yet, and those who already are, people.

In the meantime, it is necessary to address again the issue of whether or not women have a fundamental constitutional right to terminate their pregnancies. I argued in Chapter 1 against the privacy rationale employed by Blackmun in *Roe v. Wade*. I maintained also that the liberty rationale offered by Stewart was weak and uncertain. So I turn in the next four chapters to a rationale related to constitutional rights regarding religion. I argue that the religion guarantees of the First Amendment prohibit states from legislation designed to save the lives of fetuses that are not yet twenty-one weeks old.

CHAPTER 3

The Evolution of "Religion"

WE SAW IN CHAPTER 1 that the Supreme Court failed in its *Roe v. Wade* decision to justify adequately its claim that women have a fundamental (constitutional) right to terminate their pregnancies. Two rationales were given in that case, one based on privacy and the other on substantive due process. Neither one convincingly connects the alleged right to the text of the Constitution.

Chapter 2 maintained that in both law and morality, the principal objections to abortion rest on beliefs about the humanity of the fetus. I argued that the legal ascription of full personhood to newly fertilized human ova leads to absurdities, but that ascriptions of personhood should ordinarily take place before birth. I argued also that the Court's viability standard is poorly understood by some members of the Court, and that it cannot be relied upon in the future to yield an acceptable legal standard. In none of this discussion, however, was the Constitution shown to protect abortion rights. That issue was not even addressed.

The argument begun in this chapter and concluded in Chapter 6 shows that abortion rights are constitutionally protected. In outline, the argument is the following: The First Amendment says that "Congress shall make no law respecting an establishment of religion, or prohibiting the free exercise thereof." These are termed the Establishment Clause and the Free Exercise Clause, and together they are called the Religion Clauses. I analyze the meaning of religion as it appears in these clauses and find that beliefs concerning the personhood of fetuses twenty weeks or younger are religious beliefs. Legislation having no justification except the protection of such fetuses for their own sakes

78

amounts to the unconstitutional establishment of religion. Thus the constitutional point is not that women have a right to terminate their pregnancies. Rather, the only plausible legislative goal for much anti-abortion legislation is constitutionally forbidden by the First Amendment.

I begin the present chapter by reviewing others' attempts to tie abortion rights to the Religion Clauses of the First Amendment. I find especially that Justice Stevens has the right idea, but the idea needs elaboration and defense. I begin that defense by describing the purposes and original understanding of the Religion Clauses; I then recount the changes in understanding that have occurred in the last one hundred years. I next defend the legitimacy of this kind of evolution of understanding by comparing Robert Bork's Original Understanding view of constitutional interpretation with my own Moderate view.

Having secured the legitimacy in general of evolutionary changes in the meaning of constitutional guarantees, I question the adequacy of the particular changes wrought by the Court in its understanding of the Religion Clauses. I note that the Court has brought the Free Exercise Clause into apparent conflict with the Establishment Clause. Some writers and courts have maintained that "religion" must be defined differently in the one clause than in the other. Yet the word "religion" appears only once in the First Amendment, suggesting that the amendment's authors intended "religion" to have a single meaning. Worse than this, I next point out, there appears to be no definition of religion capable of encompassing the meaning of religion implied in some judicial decisions under the Free Exercise Clause. These problems raise doubts about the Court's expanded meaning of "religion" in the First Amendment.

Since I rely in the rest of my argument on the expanded meaning of religion, I develop in the next chapter a definition of religion that eliminates these problems. I then use this definition in Chapter 6 to show that legislation whose sole purpose is protecting fetuses twenty weeks or younger for their own sakes violates the rights that women have under the Religion Clauses.

Religion in the Abortion Debate

Professor Laurence Tribe of Harvard University attempted shortly after the *Roe v. Wade* decision to justify a woman's right to terminate her pregnancy as an aspect of religious liberty. He began by noting that the most promising case for governmental prohibitions of abortion rests on the claim that the fetus is a human being.[1] But "some regard the fetus as merely another part of the woman's body until quite late in pregnancy or even until birth; others believe the fetus must be regarded as a helpless human child from the time of its conception."[2] Because no secular concepts can settle this issue, it is no accident, according to Tribe, that "the only bodies of thought that have purported in this century to locate the crucial line between potential and actual life have been those of organized religious doctrine."[3] But "whenever the views of organized religious groups . . . play a pervasive role in an entire subject's legislative consideration," there is a danger that governmental regulation amounts to the unconstitutional establishment of religion. This danger is realized when the reason for the pervasive role of religious groups is "intrinsic to the subject matter as then understood," that is, when the subject matter cannot be addressed in purely secular terms.[4] Because there is no secular way to determine the humanity of the fetus, religious groups *necessarily* play a pervasive role in the entire area of legislation designed to restrict access to abortions. Under these circumstances, "the involvement of religious groups in the political process"[5] makes any legislation in the area a violation of the Establishment Clause. Any governmental regulation of abortion, then, because it involves "excessive entanglement" with religion, is unconstitutional. Women must be allowed to make abortion decisions for themselves.

Professor Tribe has subsequently repudiated this reasoning for over a decade. He writes:

> Suggestions have been advanced that the . . . inescapable involvement of religious groups in the debate over abortion render the subject inappropriate for political resolution and hence proper only for decision by the woman herself. But, on reflection, that view appears to give too little weight to the value of allowing religious groups freely to express their convictions in the political process, underestimates the power of moral convictions unattached to religious beliefs on this issue, and makes the unrealistic assumption that a constitutional ruling could somehow disentangle religion from future public debate on the question.[6]

Tribe is surely correct here, when he writes that the involvement of religious groups in discussion of an issue cannot make that issue constitutionally off-limits to legislation. Church groups have taken the lead, at times, in providing food for the hungry, housing for the homeless, and medical care for the poor. Food, housing, and medical care remain appropriate areas of governmental concern. Tribe's earlier reasoning was certainly flawed when suggesting that the extensive, even predominant, involvement of religious groups in a subject matter rendered unconstitutional all legislative initiatives in that area. There is another aspect to Tribe's reasoning, however, apparently underappreciated by Tribe himself, which is used in Chapters 6, 7,and 8 of this work to show that most legislation aimed at restricting access to abortions does indeed unconstitutionally impair people's religious freedom.

The first Supreme Court discussion of abortion rights as an aspect of religious freedom appeared in *Harris v. McRae*[7] (1980). Because the context was the public funding of abortions, discussion of that case is postponed until Chapter 8. More recently, Justice Stevens has maintained that "unless the religious view that a fetus is a 'person' is adopted . . . there is a fundamental and well-recognized difference between a fetus and a human being."[8] So legislation designed to restrict access to abortions in order to protect the fetus is unconstitutional. The fetus merits such protection only if it has human rights. But the fetus has such rights only on a religious view of the matter. Thus, legislation designed to protect the fetus is unconstitutional because it amounts to the establishment of religion.

Stevens explained this further while dissenting in *Webster v. Reproductive Health Services*. A Missouri statute regulating abortion procedures contains a preamble with "'findings' by the state legislature that 'the life of each human being begins at conception' and that 'unborn children have protectable interests in life, health and well-being.'"[9] Stevens argued that these legislative "findings" amount to the unconstitutional establishment of religion:

> If the views of St. Thomas were held as widely today as they were in the Middle Ages, and if a state legislature were to enact a statute prefaced with a "finding" that female life begins 80 days after conception and male life begins 40 days after conception [which was St. Thomas's view], I have no doubt that this Court would promptly conclude that such an endorsement of a particular religious tenet is violative of the Establishment Clause.
>
> In my opinion the difference between that hypothetical statute and Missouri's preamble reflects nothing more than a difference in theological doctrine.[10]

An unsympathetic reader might suppose that Stevens objects to a legislative determination that human life begins at conception—as he would to a similar "finding" that male life begins at forty days and female life at eighty days—because this view coincides with the theological teachings of certain religious groups. Today, the Roman Catholic church and several Protestant sects adopt the view that life begins at the moment of conception. On this unsympathetic reading, Stevens considers all legislation that reflects a religious belief to violate the First Amendment's guarantee against laws regarding the establishment of religion. I call this reading unsympathetic because, so understood, such a position would be clearly untenable. Laws against murder and fraud coincide with religious beliefs, as do those designed to feed the hungry and house the poor. So mere coincidence of a statute with a religious view does not make that statute an establishment of religion.

Stevens's cogent objection to the statute rests on his claim that, unlike other laws that coincide with religious views, Missouri's preamble has *no secular justification*. Laws against murder and fraud, and those designed to feed the hungry and house the poor, serve secular as well as religious goals. According to Stevens, however, there is no secular justification for a "finding" that "the life of each human being begins at conception." "In fact, if one prescinds from the theological concept of ensoulment . . . a State has no greater secular interest in protecting the potential life of an embryo that is still 'seed' than in protecting the potential life of a sperm or an unfertilized ovum."[11]

This reasoning, which I believe to be essentially correct, was not so much rejected as avoided by the majority in *Webster*. Chief Justice Rehnquist, writing for the majority, noted that Missouri predicated none of its regulations of abortion on the "findings" in the statute's preamble. So the preamble cannot amount to an unconstitutional restriction of abortion rights.[12] Thus it remains to be seen whether, and to what extent, the Court will allow antiabortion measures to be predicated on a state "finding" that human life begins at conception. Stevens's argument is that any restriction would be invalid as an establishment of religion. For this argument to carry the day, however, an appropriate understanding of religion, and of the Religion Clauses must be developed. I do this in the present chapter and in the two to follow. The present chapter recounts the historical purposes of the Religion Clauses, and the historical evolution of the meaning attached by the Supreme Court to the word "religion" as it appears in those Clauses. The two following chapters complete my account of the constitutional understanding of religion. Chapter 6 relates this understanding to the general issue of abortion's permissibility. Chapters 7 and 8 discuss specific limitations on abortion.

The Original Understanding of the Religion Clauses

On several occasions during the past fifty years the Supreme Court has explained the original reasons for, and meaning of, the Religion Clauses of the First Amendment. There is general agreement that fear of the civil strife that religious dissention can bring was a principal motivation for including the Religion Clauses in the Bill of Rights. In 1785 James Madison addressed his "Memorial and Remonstrance Against Religious Assessments" to those in Virginia who were contemplating state support of an established church: "Torrents of blood have been spilt in the old world, by vain attempts of the secular arm to extinguish Religious discord, by proscribing all difference in Religious opinions. Time has at length revealed the true remedy. Every relaxation of narrow and rigorous policy, wherever it has been tried, has been found to assuage the disease."[13] Madison later played a leading role in the Constitutional Convention and in the Congress that adopted the First Amendment. His "Remonstrance" is quoted in full by Justice Wiley Rutledge in *Everson v. Board of Education* (1947).[14]

Justice Black, writing for the Court in *Everson*, echoed Madison's opinion, and maintained that the Establishment Clause in particular was needed to reduce the threat of religiously motivated civil disturbance:

> The centuries immediately before and contemporaneous with the colonization of America had been filled with turmoil, civil strife, and persecutions generated in large part by established sects determined to maintain their absolute political and religious supremacy.
>
> These practices of the old world were transplanted to and began to thrive in the soil of the new America. . . . Catholics found themselves hounded and proscribed because of their faith; Quakers who followed their conscience went to jail.
>
> These practices became so commonplace as to shock the freedom-loving colonials into a feeling of abhorrence.[15]

Convinced that "cruel persecutions were the inevitable result of government-established religions,"[16] Black continued, James Madison and Thomas Jefferson led the successful fight for the disestablishment of the state-supported church in their native state of Virginia. The same fear led to the inclusion of the Establishment Clause in the First Amendment.

But this was not the only concern. Several states had established religions and feared imposition by the new federal Congress of a different established religion. By denying to Congress power to make a "law respecting an establishment of religion," the First Amendment secured to the states the power to establish churches of their own.[17] This state practice waned and ended during the first half of the nineteenth century,[18] but not in response to the federal Constitution, which, as originally understood, was silent on this point.

According to our best information about the Framers' understanding, the Religion Clauses were limited not only jurisdictionally (to the federal level) but also doctrinally (to beliefs of some major Christian sects). Rehnquist quotes Joseph Story, a member of the Court from 1811 to 1845, whose *Commentaries on the Constitution of the United States* are widely regarded as reflecting the Framers' understanding of the newly created document. Story writes: "The real object of the [First] [A]mendment was not to countenance, much less to advance, Mahometanism, or Judaism, or infidelity, by prostrating Christianity; but to exclude all rivalry among Christian sects, and to prevent any national ecclesiastical establishment which should give to a hierarchy the exclusive patronage of the national government. It thus cut off the means of religious persecution."[19] This is not to say that the means of persecuting Moslems, Jews, atheists, and others were curtailed by the First Amendment as originally understood. Only Christians were granted freedom from persecution, according to Justice Story's understanding of the Framers' original intent.

This doctrinal limitation prevailed in the Supreme Court for over a hundred years. In 1890, for example, the Court upheld a statute of the territory of Utah[20] that disenfranchised anyone "who teaches, advises, counsels, or encourages any person or persons to become bigamists or polygamists, . . . or who is a member of any order, organization or association which teaches, advises, counsels, or encourages its members . . . to commit the crime of bigamy or polygamy." The Court found that this legislation "is not open to any constitutional or legal objection."[21] According to the Court in 1890, then, the constitutionally guaranteed freedoms of speech, association, and religion did not protect people from losing their rights to vote and hold public office merely for the fault of belonging to the Mormon church. On this understanding, the guarantee of free exercise of religion did not cover all who considered themselves Christians and permitted the imposition of substantial penalties on those who belonged to or proselytized for a disfavored sect. If anything, the breadth of protection under the First Amendment extended to a narrower range of beliefs than it had originally (according to Justice Story's understanding of the Framers' original intent).

This was not an isolated decision. Two years later, in *Church of the Holy Trinity v. United States*, the Supreme Court noted with approval a provision in Maryland's Constitution (1867) that excluded from jury duty anyone who disbelieved in the existence of God and a system of divine rewards and punishments.[22] The Court similarly endorsed a Massachusetts constitutional provision that allowed the legislature to require municipalities to pay "for the institution of public worship of God and for the support and maintenance of public Protestant teachers of piety, religion and morality."[23] Also endorsed is an opinion of the chief justice of the New York Supreme Court that "the free, equal and undisturbed enjoyment of religious opinion" does not permit "blasphemous contempt" of Christianity, but is no bar to "the like attacks upon the religion of Mahomet or of the Grand Lama; and for the plain reason, that . . . we are a Christian people, and the morality of the country is deeply ingrafted upon Christianity, and not upon the doctrines or worship of those impostors."[24] Finally, after noting "that the Christian religion is a part of the common law of Pennsylvania," the Supreme Court of the United States concluded in 1892 that "this is a Christian nation."[25] So for more than a hundred years, more than half of the time that separates us from the adoption of the Bill of Rights in 1791, the First Amendment guarantees of religious freedom were limited doctrinally to Christianity.

The Evolution of Religion Clause Doctrine

The evolution of the Supreme Court's understanding of the First Amendment's Religion Clauses has four aspects: (1) the gradual incorporation of the Bill of Rights, including the First Amendment, into the Fourteenth Amendment's guarantee of due process; (2) the change from the protection merely of religious beliefs to that of many practices associated with those beliefs; (3) the extension of constitutional protection from prohibition of direct burdens on the free exercise of religion to prohibition of many indirect burdens as well; and (4) the expansion of the meaning that the Court attaches to the word "religion."

INCORPORATION OF THE RELIGION CLAUSES

As noted in the introductory chapter, the Constitution and the Bill of Rights applied originally only to actions of the federal government. The Bill of Rights was considered inapplicable to state legislation even after the Fourteenth Amendment, adopted in 1868, provided that no *state* "shall . . . deprive any person of life, liberty or property, without due process of law; nor deny to any person within its jurisdiction the equal protection of the laws." The use of this amendment to apply the Bill of Rights to the states is called the incorporation of the Bill of Rights into the Fourteenth Amendment. Justice Douglas described the history of the process of this incorporation:[26]

> The process of the "selective incorporation" of various provisions of the Bill of Rights into the Fourteenth Amendment . . . has been a steady one. It started in 1897 with *Chicago, B. and Q.R.R. Co. v. Chicago*,[27] in which the Court held that the Fourteenth Amendment precluded a state from taking private property for public use without payment of just compensation, as provided in the Fifth Amendment. The first direct holding as to the incorporation of the First Amendment into the Four-teenth occurred in 1931 in *Stromberg v. California*,[28] a case involving the right of free speech, although that holding in *Stromberg* had been foreshadowed in 1925 by the Court's opinion in *Gitlow v. New York*.[29]

Our concern is primarily with the First Amendment guarantees of reli-gious freedom. Justice Brennan tells us:[30]

> The process of absorption of the religious guarantees of the First Amendment as protection against the States under the Fourteenth Amendment began with the Free Exercise Clause. In 1923 the Court held that the protections of the Fourteenth included at least a person's freedom "to worship God according to the dictates of his own con-science."[31] The Court's opinion in *Hamilton v. Regents* (1934) includes indications to the same effect.[32]

Finally, "*Cantwell v. Connecticut*[33] completed in 1940 the process of absorption of the Free Exercise Clause,"[34] and the Establishment Clause was incorporated seven years later in *Everson v. Board of Education*.[35] In sum, the process of expanding the jurisdiction of the Bill of Rights so as to apply to states the religion guarantees of the First Amendment spanned fifty years. It was gradual, deliberate, and moderately paced.

FROM BELIEF TO PRACTICE

The Court's understanding of the meaning of the religion guarantees evolved at the same time as their jurisdiction was expanded. During the 1878–1879 term the Supreme Court held in *Reynolds v. United States*[36] that a statute prohibiting bigamy and polygamy in the territory of Utah was constitutional, notwithstanding the fact that the accused was a

Mormon who believed multiple marriage to be a religious duty. The Court distinguished religious belief from religious conduct, and maintained that the First Amendment protected only the former." Congress was deprived of all legislative power over mere opinion, but was left free to reach actions which were in violation of social duties or subversive of good order.[37] Suppose one believed that human sacrifices were a necessary part of religious worship . . . or . . . a wife religiously believed it was her duty to burn herself upon the funeral pile of her dead husband."[38] To permit such things "would make the professed doctrines of religious belief superior to the law of the land, and in effect to permit every citizen to become a law unto himself."[39] So while laws "cannot interfere with mere religious belief and opinions, they may with practices."[40]

By 1940, however, the Court was ready to make subtler distinctions. Justice Owen Roberts declared for the Court in *Cantwell v. Connecticut* that "the Amendment embraces two concepts,—freedom to believe and freedom to act. The first is absolute but, in the nature of things, the second cannot be."[41] The freedom to act cannot be absolute, for reasons well stated in *Reynolds*. But the impossibility of a right being absolute is no justification for denying the right altogether. If it were, we would have few rights indeed, because almost no right is absolute. Like most other (constitutionally) fundamental rights, then, the right to act on our religious convictions can be limited by the state when this is truly necessary to meet a compelling public need. In this way the free exercise of religion, which includes action as well as belief (as the word "exercise" suggests), is reconciled with the need of public order.

ALLEVIATING INDIRECT BURDENS ON RELIGIOUS PRACTICE

The Court's understanding of the Free Exercise Clause has expanded to include another aspect as well. As understood earlier, the Clause protected people only against direct governmental interference with the exercise of their religion. The Court's current understanding includes protection also against some forms of indirect governmental interference. The transition took place between 1961 and 1963. In 1961 the Court considered in *Braunfeld v. Brown*[42] the constitutionality of a Pennsylvania law that forbade most retail sales on Sundays. This law did not directly require of Orthodox Jewish merchants any acts or omissions inconsistent with their religion. There is no rule in Judaism requiring work on Sunday. But the law did place additional burdens on the exercise of Orthodox Jewish merchants' religiously mandated practice of

observing the sabbath on Saturday. In order both to observe their sabbath and to comply with the law, these merchants were required to
close two days per week, rather than the one day (Sunday) required of
their competitors. Thus the law caused the exercise of their religion to
involve commercial jeopardy.

The Court rejected the claim that such an imposition constituted a
violation of the Free Exercise Clause. Writing for the Court, Chief Justice Earl Warren maintained: "To strike down, without the most critical
scrutiny, legislation which imposes only an indirect burden on the exercise of religion, i.e., legislation which does not make unlawful the religious practice itself, would radically restrict the operating latitude of the
legislature."[43] So the Pennsylvania law was declared constitutional.

Two years later, however, in *Sherbert v. Verner*, the Court began to
consider some indirect burdens on the exercise of religion to constitute
violations of the Free Exercise Clause. "Appellant, a member of the
Seventh-day Adventist Church, was discharged by her South Carolina
employer because she would not work on Saturday, the Sabbath Day of
her faith."[44] She was then denied unemployment benefits by the state,
and the issue was whether this denial by the state infringed on her right
to the free exercise of religion. Like the Pennsylvania law upheld in
Braunfeld v. Brown, South Carolina's denial of unemployment benefits
made it more expensive for the Sabbatarian to exercise her religious
beliefs. Writing for the Court, Justice Brennan maintained: "Here not
only is it apparent that appellant's declared ineligibility for benefits derives solely from the practice of her religion, but the pressure upon her
to forego that practice is unmistakable." The government's denial of
benefits "puts the same kind of burden on the free exercise of religion
as would a fine imposed against appellant for her Saturday worship."[45]
Such an indirect burden is therefore unconstitutional. This perspective is
now a well-entrenched Court doctrine, as it was reaffirmed in 1981[46]
and 1987.[47]

EXPANDING THE MEANING OF "RELIGION"

The Court has expanded the meaning it attaches to the word "religion."
As we saw in the last section, for over a hundred years the Court interpreted "religion" in the First Amendment to refer exclusively to Christianity. The meaning of "religion" was expanded gradually to include
deviant Christian sects, non-Christian religions, nontheistic belief systems, essentially moral views, and arguably nonsectarian metaphysical
beliefs about spirits. This part recounts the history of that expansion.

As far as we can tell, the Framers originally identified religion with Christianity. But, they intended the Religion Clauses to defuse the kind of sectarian strife that had drastically impaired domestic tranquility in the Old World. In an increasingly pluralistic nation such as ours, domestic tranquility would not be preserved if the guarantees of religious freedom excluded Jews, Moslems, and others. Out of respect, then, for the original purpose of the Religion Clauses, the Court has gradually expanded the meaning of "religion" beyond its original reference.

The first expansion occurred in 1944. It did not constitute a break with Christianity, but only with orthodox Christianity. Guy Ballard organized and promoted through the mail what he called the "I Am" movement. He claimed that he and two relatives could "cure persons of those diseases . . . which are ordinarily classified by the medical profession as being incurable diseases."[48] He was convicted of fraudulent use of the mail. Because his claims of cure were considered religious claims, the Court maintained that the only relevant issue was Ballard's sincerity in making them. The truth of the claims was properly withheld from consideration by the jury. Legal judgments concerning the truth of religious claims resemble heresy trials. Writing for the Court, Justice Douglas maintained:

> Heresy trials are foreign to our Constitution. Men may believe what they cannot prove. They may not be put to the proof of their religious doctrines or beliefs. Religious experiences which are as real as life to some may be incomprehensible to others.[49] The Fathers of the Constitution were not unaware of the varied and extreme views of religious sects, of the violence of disagreement among them, and of the lack of any one religious creed on which all men would agree.[50]

So unorthodox sects are given the full protection of the Constitution's religion guarantees, notwithstanding the fact that their views "might seem incredible, if not preposterous, to most people."[51]

Three years later, the Court moved unmistakably beyond Christianity in its understanding of "religion." It maintained in *Everson v. Board of Education* (1947) that in view of the Establishment Clause, the state "cannot exclude individual Catholics, Lutherans, Mohammedans, Baptists, Jews, Methodists, Non-believers, Presbyterians, or members of any other faith, *because of their faith, or lack of it,* from receiving the benefits of public welfare legislation."[52] Religious freedom is here guaranteed to those of all religious faiths. But once Christianity is no longer the common standard, how does one know what counts as a religious faith?

We learn in *Torcaso v. Watkins* that, by 1961, the Court considered belief in God to be a sufficient condition for a body of thought to be considered religious. Maryland required that holders of public office make a "declaration of belief in the existence of God."[53] The Court found this requirement to be unconstitutional. "It sets up a religious test," and Article VI of the Constitution says that "no religious Test shall ever be required as a Qualification to any Office or public trust under the United States." If, according to the Court, a required declaration of belief in the existence of God is a religious test, then the Court considers belief in the existence of God to be an inherently religious belief. To this extent, the constitutional concept of religion is not only broader than Christianity, it is broader also than Judaism, Islam, and all other organized religious sects, as belief in the existence of God can be maintained apart from any and all organized religions.

Justice Black, writing for the Court, added the dictum that there are several "religions in this country which do not teach what would generally be considered a belief in the existence of God." They include "Buddhism, Taoism, Ethical Culture, Secular Humanism and others."[54] So while belief in the existence of God is sufficient to justify classifying something as religious, it is not necessary, as there can be religions that do not include this belief.

The Court explained its views further in *United States v. Seeger* (1965)[55] when it was called on to interpret the phrase "religious training and belief" as it is used to indicate those eligible for conscientious objector status in the Universal Military Training and Service Act. Though the case concerns the interpretation of a statute, not of the Constitution, the Court has applied its understanding of "religion" in this statute to its understanding of the Religion Clauses of the First Amendment. The statute defines the phrase "religious training and belief" to mean "an individual's belief in a relation to a Supreme Being involving duties superior to those arising from any human relation, but [not to include] essentially political, sociological, or philosophical views or a merely personal moral code."[56] But the Court had already concluded in *Torcaso* that religions need not include a belief in the existence of a personal God. Can the congressional definition be understood in a way that makes it consistent with the Court's understanding of the meaning of religion? Of course it can. Seizing on the fact that Congress had chosen the term Supreme Being, rather than God, Justice Douglas, concurring in the result, argued that Hinduism, Buddhism, and other Oriental religions that do not include belief in a personal God do nevertheless center on a transcendental Reality that could be designated a Supreme Being.[57]

Writing for the majority, Justice Clark went further. He ensured that "religious training and belief" were kept distinct from any organized group or sect. He wrote:

> The test of belief "in a relation to a Supreme Being" is whether a given belief that is sincere and meaningful occupies a place in the life of its possessor parallel to that filled by the orthodox belief in God of one who clearly qualifies for the exemption. Where such beliefs have parallel positions in the lives of their respective holders we cannot say that one is "in a relation to a Supreme Being" and the other is not.[58]

Clark maintained that this understanding of religion accords with that of prominent contemporary Protestant theologians Paul Tillich and A. T. Robinson, and is consistent with the Catholic understanding as articulated in documents related to Vatican II.[59] Tillich's views were emphasized. Tillich identified God with "the depth of your life, . . . the source of your being, . . . your ultimate concern, . . . *what you take seriously without any reservation.*"[60] Because one's religion on this view is one's "ultimate concern," nontheistic and nonsectarian views can be unproblematically classified as religious.

The Court developed this perspective further in *Welsh v. United States* (1970), another case concerning conscientious objection to military service. The main difference is that Welsh, unlike Seeger, rejected the characterization of his beliefs as religious. "But very few registrants," reasoned Justice Black, "are fully aware of the broad scope of the word 'religious' as used" in this legislation.[61] So Welsh's own characterization of his beliefs may be in error. Following *Seeger*, the issue "is whether these beliefs play the role of a religion and function as a religion in the registrant's life."[62] Despite the fact that "Welsh . . . characterized his beliefs as having been formed 'by reading in the fields of history and sociology,'"[63] denied that they concern a duty "superior to those arising from any human relation,"[64] and said that he "believe[d] the taking of life—anyone's life—to be morally wrong,"[65] the Court concluded that "Welsh was clearly entitled to a conscientious objector exemption."[66] The act "exempts from military service all those whose consciences, spurred by deeply held moral, ethical, or religious beliefs, would give them no rest or peace if they allowed themselves to become a part of an instrument of war."[67]

Among the implications of the cases considered so far is the following: The fear of civil strife based on differences of religious belief has abated. The Court does not include, among its reasons for honoring the beliefs of Seeger or Welsh, that failure to do so is likely to result in disruptive lawlessness, nor did they include the fear of civil disruption among their reasons for objecting to Maryland's required "declaration of belief in the existence of God."[68]

More recently, Justice O'Connor has maintained that "political divisiveness along religious lines should not be an independent test of constitutionality."[69] Even though, according to O'Connor, "Political divisiveness is admittedly an evil addressed by the Establishment Clause," it is not "an independent ground for holding a government practice unconstitutional." One reason is this. "Guessing the potential for political divisiveness inherent in a government practice is simply too speculative an enterprise."[70] In sum, even though the Establishment Clause was adopted originally with an eye toward avoiding religiously motivated civil strife, the Court's current interpretation of the clause is largely free of preoccupation with that concern. Even where statutory interpretation is involved, as in the conscientious objector cases (*Seeger* and *Welsh*), the Court's classification of beliefs as religious is largely unaffected by considerations of political divisiveness.

So far, all the beliefs considered religious have been associated with well-articulated belief systems that form the doctrine of a sect. In *Thomas v. Review Board* (1981) the Court further expanded its concept of religious belief. Thomas, a Jehovah's Witness, quit work "when he was transferred from the roll foundry to a department that produced turrets for military tanks. He claimed his religious beliefs prevented him from participating in the production of war materials. The respondent Review Board denied him unemployment compensation benefits."[71] To this point, the case resembles *Sherbert v. Verner*, where it was held that a woman had a free exercise right to unemployment compensation benefits. She had lost her job because of her religiously motivated refusal to work on Saturdays. But the religious belief, in her case, was well articulated and held in common by members of her religious group. It was the official position of the Church. Thomas's views, however, were somewhat idiosyncratic. A friend, colleague, and fellow Jehovah's Witness "advised him that working on weapons parts . . . was not 'unscriptural.'"[72] But Chief Justice Burger maintained that "the guarantee of free exercise is not limited to beliefs which are shared by all of the members of a religious sect."[73]

Thomas's views were also suspected of inconsistency. He maintained that conscience forbade "actually producing the tank itself, hammering it out."[74] But he would not object to "produc[ing] the new product necessary for the production of any kind of tank . . . [because I] would not be a direct party to whoever they shipped it to [and] would not be . . .

chargeable in . . . conscience."[75] The lower court "found this position inconsistent with Thomas's stated opposition to participation in the production of armaments."[76] But, Burger maintained, "it is not for us to say that the line he drew was an unreasonable one. Courts should not undertake to dissect religious beliefs because the believer admits that he is 'struggling' with his position or because his beliefs are not articulated with the clarity and precision that a more sophisticated person might employ."[77] Thus, sincerely held beliefs that are idiosyncratic and of uncertain consistency can nevertheless qualify as religious beliefs deserving constitutional protection.

Bowen v. Roy (1987) illustrates and extends this view. "Stephen Roy and Karen Miller . . . contended that obtaining a Social Security number for their 2-year-old daughter, Little Bird of the Snow, would violate their Native American religious beliefs."[78] After it was determined that the Social Security Administration had already assigned a number to his daughter, Roy "testified that her spirit would be robbed only by the 'use' of the number."[79] He explained: "We try to keep her spirit unique, and we're scared that if we were to use this number, she would lose control of that and she would have no ability to protect herself from any evil that that number might be used against her." This is an unusual belief. It seems not to represent the view of any organized religious sect of which Roy was a member. "Roy testified that he had recently developed" this belief.[80] Nevertheless, every member of the Supreme Court accepted Roy's belief as religious. Furthermore, following *Sherbert* and *Thomas*, a majority believed that the government should accommodate Roy's belief and continue to provide benefits for Little Bird of the Snow even if Roy refused to place her social security number on the appropriate forms. Thus the concept of religion has been expanded from referring merely to Christianity to include non-Christian and nontheistic religions, to encompass some strongly held moral views (*Welsh*), and to denote some metaphysical, spiritual beliefs that are arguably unrelated to any organized religion (*Bowen*).

The Original Understanding View

The last two sections explained first the original meaning of the Religion Clauses and then the evolution of the Court's understanding of their meaning. Because I endorse and rely on such evolutionary changes of meaning, I defend their legitimacy against conservative challenges. In outline, my argument is this: The Conservative view of constitutional interpretation, if taken to the extreme, rejects all changes in the meaning of constitutional guarantees. But that view is for several reasons clearly unacceptable. Robert Bork's Original Understanding view of constitutional interpretation,[81] in contrast, is a *relatively* Conservative view. The qualifications Bork introduces to render his view reasonable make it compatible with evolutionary changes of meaning. The next section illustrates this through a consideration of Bork's treatment of the Fourteenth Amendment. In practice, Bork's interpretive method is nearly the same as my Moderate view. So Bork's Original Understanding view allows the kind of evolution of judicial interpretation on which I rely.

The Introduction distinguished three approaches to constitutional interpretation—the Liberal view, the Moderate view, and the Conservative view—and preliminarily explained defects of Liberal and Conservative views. Chapter 1 illustrated and criticized some versions of the Liberal view. Now the Conservative view is examined and criticized.

The extreme Conservative view maintains that the meaning of the Constitution was fixed forever by those who wrote and ratified it and its amendments. Hence, if "religion" in the First Amendment was understood originally to refer exclusively to Christianity, it must be so understood today. The history of its expanded meaning is a history of judicial error. We should reject this expansion altogether and return to the realization that the religion guarantees protect only Christian sects and their members. Jews, Moslems, Hindus, and Buddhists have no constitutional right to free exercise of their religion.

Of course, virtually no one today endorses this extreme Conservative view. The implications concerning religion alone make it intolerable. In addition, as noted in the Introduction, the Fourteenth Amendment was not originally intended to apply the Bill of Rights to state legislation. So by adhering to the original understanding of the Fourteenth Amendment, the extreme Conservative view sees no constitutional difficulty in state legislation that abrogates freedom of speech (First Amendment violation), mandates random searches of people's homes (Fourth Amendment violation), or prescribes public castration of adulterers (Eighth Amendment violation). These consequences, too, would be unacceptable.

A more general problem with the extreme Conservative view is that it reduces the current relevance of the Constitution. For example, the Framers had no opinions or intentions about wiretapping telephones, because they had no telephones. So if constitutional interpretation is restricted to the Framers' particular thought and meaning, the Fourth

Amendment's prohibition of unreasonable searches and seizures would not apply one way or the other to telephone taps. As former Federal Judge Bork notes, this amounts to saying that "changes in circumstances must be permitted gradually to render constitutional guarantees meaningless."[82] It seems that no one favors this outcome, so it is unnecessary to discuss further the extreme Conservative view.

Relatively Conservative views differ by degrees from those resembling the extreme to those resembling the Moderate view that I endorse. I focus my analysis of the Conservative view on the exposition that Judge Bork, the view's chief contemporary exponent, provides in *The Tempting of America*.

Much of Bork's argument for what he calls "original understanding" consists in criticisms of extreme and relatively Liberal views of constitutional interpretation. I generally agree with his arguments on this matter and commend his treatment.

Bork's major argument for original understanding (his relatively Conservative view) is quite simple. The Constitution is our law. Like other laws, it consists of rules that everyone in appropriate jurisdictions is supposed to obey, judges included. A disfavored rule should be changed by prescribed procedures of amendment or repeal. In Bork's words:

> When we speak of "law," we ordinarily refer to a rule that we have no right to change except through prescribed procedures. That statement assumes that the rule has a meaning independent of our own desires. Otherwise there would be no need to agree on procedures for changing the rule. Statutes, we agree, may be changed by amendment or repeal. The Constitution may be changed pursuant to the procedures set out in article V. It is a necessary implication of the prescribed procedures that neither statute nor Constitution should be changed by judges.[83] What is the meaning of a rule that judges should not change? It is the meaning understood at the time of the law's enactment.[84]

In the case of the Constitution, it is "what the ratifiers understood themselves to be enacting," because their understanding "must be taken to be what the public of that time would have understood the words to mean." Because "law is a public act," its meaning is what the words employed "ordinarily mean," as this is the best indication of "what the public understood":[85] "The original understanding is thus manifested in the words used and in secondary materials, such as debates at the conventions, public discussion, newspaper articles, dictionaries in use at the time, and the like."[86]

In sum, "if the Constitution is law, then presumably, like all other law, the meaning the lawmakers intended is as binding upon judges as it is upon legislatures and executives."[87]

So far, Bork's "original understanding" approach seems indistinguishable from the extreme Conservative view, which, in Bork's own words, entails "that changes in circumstances must be permitted to render constitutional guarantees meaningless."[88] To avoid this result Bork softens the original understanding approach in three ways that transform it into a relatively Conservative view that is akin to the Moderate view that I endorse.

First, some precedents in derogation of original understanding should nevertheless be followed, rather than reversed, even by the Supreme Court.

> Previous decisions may be clearly incorrect but nevertheless have becomes so embedded in the life of the nation, so accepted by the society, so fundamental to the private and public expectations of individuals and institutions, that the result should not be changed now. Thus, it is too late to overrule not only the decision legalizing paper money, but also those decisions validating certain New Deal and Great Society programs pursuant to the congressional powers over commerce, taxation, and spending.[89]

Though he does not address the issue in this context, Bork seems to accept on this basis the application to the states of the first eight amendments through their gradual incorporation in the Fourteenth. But he writes that "it will probably never be too late to overrule the right of privacy cases, including *Roe v. Wade*, because they remain unaccepted and unacceptable to large segments of the body politic, and . . . could at once be replaced by restored legislative regulation of the subject.[90]

A second justification for departures from the legislators' original understanding rests on changes in circumstances. As noted, technological change can raise issues beyond the Framers' original understanding regarding the Fourth Amendment's prohibition of "unreasonable searches and seizures." Maintaining constitutional guarantees in such cases requires departing from the original understanding of the circumstances in which the prohibition could apply. Additionally, extensions of the original understanding can, according to Bork, be justified by nontechnological changes. Bork says that the evolution of the common-law doctrine of libel threatened First Amendment guarantees. Freedom of the press was jeopardized by public figures being able to sue for libel those periodicals whose coverage was unflattering. This situation justified the Supreme Court laying "down new rules making it more difficult for public figures to maintain actions for defamation."[91] I would guess, from these two examples, that Bork approves of the expansion of the First Amendment religion guarantees to protect the religious freedom of Jews, Moslems, Hindus, and other non-Christians. The increased religious diversity of the American population would be the change in circumstances that justifies departure in this case from original understanding.

Finally, Bork accepts departures from original understanding when the original understanding incorporated erroneous views of social situations. It is on this basis that Bork justifies the reversal of *Plessy v. Ferguson*[92] in *Brown v. Board of Education.*[93] *Plessy* (1896) had maintained that Fourteenth Amendment equal protection of the laws is accorded blacks even when the law mandates racial segregation, as long as the accommodations for blacks and whites are equal. This is the doctrine of "separate but equal," which Bork takes to be the original understanding of the Fourteenth Amendment. *Brown* (1954) maintained that separate facilities are inherently unequal, so legally mandated racial segregation inevitably denies to blacks the equal protection of the laws. This reversal was justified, according to Bork, because litigation earlier in this century had shown repeatedly that separate facilities tend invariably to be unequal. The change that justified reversal was not so much in social circumstances as in knowledge of social circumstances.

But if technological change, legal change, social change, and changes in the knowledge of social circumstances justify, according to Bork, departures from original understanding, is it not misleading of Bork to claim that he endorses adherence to original understanding? It all depends on what kind of original understanding you mean. Bork maintains that it is not the original author's understanding of particular matters that judges must seek to apply but, especially in the case of a constitution meant to last for centuries, their understanding of underlying principles or values. With regard to constitutional guarantees, it "is a principle or stated value that the ratifiers wanted to protect against hostile legislation or executive action."[94] The Fourth Amendment, for example, is clearly meant to protect the privacy of people in their homes, papers and effects from unwarranted governmental snooping and intrusion. This value preference can be protected in contemporary society against technological intrusions that the ratifiers never imagined without departing in the least from their original understanding of the underlying principle or value to be protected.

Uncertainty arises, however, because, according to Bork, much depends on the level of generality attributed to the underlying principle or value. Is the principle underlying the Fourteenth Amendment's guarantee of equal protection of the laws a guarantee of equality for blacks, for all people regardless of race, for all people regardless of genetic makeup, or what? A case can be made that the Fourteenth Amendment was understood originally by those who ratified it to apply only to blacks, as it was adopted after the Civil War to protect those who had formerly been slaves. On this understanding, as Bork notes, Alan Bakke would have had no Fourteenth Amendment grounds to challenge a preferential admissions policy that favored blacks over people like him, a white.[95] No matter how blatant or severe the discrimination, if the underlying value embodied in the Fourteenth Amendment is the protection of blacks, then adherence to the original understanding requires the rejection of claims made by whites, Hispanics, and Koreans, to name but a few. But if the fundamental value animating the amendment is the elimination of differential governmental treatment based on considerations of race, then whites, Hispanics, and Koreans are, like blacks, guaranteed equal protection of the laws. The level of generality attributed to the underlying value or principle is thus of great importance, as it alters considerably the nature and extent of the Constitution's guarantees.

If it were impossible to ascertain the originally understood level of generality of the principle underlying a constitutional provision, interpreters would have no recourse except either refusing to enforce that provision or supplying for themselves the level at which the provision should be understood. In the former case, people are denied the protections that the Constitution exists to provide. In the latter case, interpreters have wide latitude for insertion into the Constitution of their own value preferences. Those opposed on moral grounds to sexism, for example, could read into the Fourteenth Amendment a prohibition of discrimination (except, as always, when necessary to meet a compelling public need) on the basis of genetic makeup, including gender. This would afford Fourteenth Amendment protection to men and women of all races.

Because Bork maintains that original understanding should be the touchstone of constitutional interpretation, and the level of generality of principles underlying constitutional provisions affects the interpretation of those provisions, Bork maintains that current interpreters are able to capture the originally understood level of generality. He writes: "With many if not most textual provisions, the level of generality which is part of their meaning is readily apparent."[96] He acknowledges, however, that "the problem is most difficult when dealing with broadly stated provisions of the Bill of Rights."[97] In such cases, where the test itself does not supply an obviously appropriate level of generality, original understanding requires finding "the level of generality chosen by the ratifiers." This is "the level of generality that interpretation of the words, structure, and history of the Constitution fairly supports."[98] Bork's account would be improved by a clearer account of what is required for fairness in this regard.

Bork: Conservative or Moderate?

In practice, Bork's original understanding is nearly indistinguishable from the Moderate view that I support. Like the Conservative view, the Moderate view rejects the wide latitude that the Liberal view gives to judges to insert their own values into the Constitution. The Liberal view accepts, whereas the other two reject, judicial "discovery" of rights or guarantees not located in any particular provision of the Constitution but nevertheless implicit therein. Bork (conservative) and I (moderate) would confine constitutional interpretation to the Constitution's explicit provisions as they appear in particular articles, sections, sentences, and phrases of the document. This is, in John Hart Ely's phrase, "clause-bound interpretivism."[99] Bork and I accept clause-bound interpretation because we see the judicial expansion of constitutional guarantees to erode democracy. We oppose unelected judges increasingly substituting their judgments, and their moral principles, for those of democratically elected representatives.

Bork and I also agree that people under our scheme of government are supposed to have constitutional guarantees that remove certain matters from the hands of democratic majorities. In order for the Constitution's guarantees of individual rights to remain vital, the meaning attributed to the document's individual clauses must evolve. Bork mentions the necessity of evolution in response to well-entrenched Supreme Court precedents, changed circumstances (legal, technological, and social) and changed understanding of social reality. He recognizes also that such evolution is mandated by the nature of the Constitution because its clauses embody values or principles of some generality, and the particular meaning (for purposes of application) of a (somewhat) general principle changes with changes in knowledge and circumstances. I agree with all of this.

Bork acknowledges also, and I would stress, that "two judges equally devoted to the original purpose may disagree about the reach or application of the principle at stake and so arrive at different results."[100] "We must not expect too much of the search for original understanding in any legal context. The result of the search is never perfection, it is simply the best we can do; and the best we can do must be regarded as good enough—or we must abandon the enterprise of law and, most especially, that of judicial review."[101] One corollary is the following: "This version of original understanding certainly does not mean that judges will invariably decide cases the way the men of the ratifying conventions would if they could be resurrected to sit as courts."[102] Again, I believe that Bork is correct.

So what is the difference between Bork's view and what I call the Moderate view of constitutional interpretation? The most important difference is that the Moderate view acknowledges what Bork tends to ignore, but is no less committed to: Judges are inevitably and properly guided largely by their own moral and political values when choosing the level of generality that they attribute to a principle underlying a particular provision of the Constitution.

This inevitability can be seen by reviewing Bork's interpretation of the Fourteenth Amendment's Equal Protection Clause. Equal protection could be thought of very narrowly as applying only to the protection of blacks from violence and dispossession, more broadly as mandating full legal equality for blacks, or more broadly still as requiring legal equality regardless of race or ethnicity. It could even be construed to embody the principle of legal equality regardless of people's genetic makeup, which entails that gender is as irrelevant as race to a person's legal standing. Bork's choice among these possibilities reveals the inevitable injection of a judge's moral or political values, or both, in the process of interpreting some key constitutional clauses.

The Moderate view explicitly incorporates the two canons of interpretation explained in the Preface of this work. Interpretations should follow the text as closely as possible and, where there is doubt, should attribute to the text the most favorable meaning possible (within the margins of doubt). Attributing the most favorable meaning is an application of the principle of charity. To the extent that there is doubt, the doubt should be resolved in favor of the text by charitably attributing to it the best meaning possible. This is the meaning that agrees best with the interpreter's values. Thus, where there is uncertainty concerning the level of generality of principles embodied in constitutional clauses, judges should charitably attribute to the Constitution meanings that best reflects their own moral and political values.

This seems to trouble Bork because he is keenly aware of judges' tendencies to substitute their own values and policy judgments for those of the people's elected representatives. This certainly is a problem. But the solution to the illegitimate injection of judges' values into the law is not denial of their inevitable and legitimate injection. Injection is legitimate when it is needed to find an appropriate level of generality. Denying such injection of morality is self-deceiving. It fosters judges using their values unconsciously and therefore uncritically.

Bork's analysis of the Fourteenth Amendment's Equal Protection Clause illustrates the inevitability of judges injecting their moral and political values into their interpretations of constitutional guarantees that are framed in relatively general terms. Bork believes that "the original understanding of the equal protection clause" supports the decision in *Brown* that invalidated legislation mandating racial segregation. He argues as follows: "Suppose that *Plessy v. Ferguson* correctly represented the original understanding of the fourteenth amendment, that those who ratified it intended black equality. . . . But they also assumed that equality and state-compelled separation of the races were consistent."[103] So they allowed segregation laws to stand. By the middle of this century it was clear that separate facilities are inherently unequal. Combining this realization with the original understanding of equal protection, the Court properly overturned *Plessy v. Ferguson* and declared segregation laws to deny to blacks the equal protection of the laws.

This rationale is a flawed application of original understanding. There is little reason to believe as a matter of historical fact that the "separate but equal" doctrine in *Plessy* (1896) corresponds to the original understanding of those who ratified the Fourteenth Amendment *a generation earlier* (1868). The Thirteenth Amendment forbade slavery. But former slaves were liable to be denied their liberty, property, and even their lives by vindictive whites who were racist and bitter about their defeat in the Civil War. The Fourteenth Amendment was designed to prevent states from denying to blacks life, liberty, and property without due process of law. But blacks might still be deprived of basic needs through legislation that was procedurally correct. The same grim result could be fostered also through failure of legal officials to protect blacks against unofficial, private (but possibily organized) violence like that for which the Ku Klux Klan later became notorious. The Equal Protection Clause was therefore designed to require states to protect blacks against *violence* that would deprive them of life, liberty, and property. Equality in transportation and education were minor matters compared to the looming possibilities of mass murder and dispossession. The ratifiers' original understanding of the Fourteenth Amendment probably had nothing to do with the doctrine of separate but equal facilities in education and transportation.

This reading of the Fourteenth Amendment is reinforced by the fact that the Supreme Court's first interpretation of the amendment involved a matter of official violence against a black man.[104] West Virginia's law excluded blacks from juries, and for this reason the Court overturned a murder conviction that could have resulted in the death penalty being applied to a black man.

In addition, Bork acknowledged that in 1868 Congress, the states, and courts saw no inconsistency between segregation and the Fourteenth Amendment. Would Bork have us believe that in 1868 the segregated facilities of whites and blacks were actually equal and the inequalities began to appear only later? That requires us to believe in an unrealistically rapid recovery from slavery to equality. Or would Bork have us believe that inequalities existed but that people were unaware of them? Any claim about original understanding is suspect when it requires attributing to those who ratified the amendment massive ignorance of the obvious. In sum, the simultaneous acceptance of the Fourteenth Amendment and segregation reinforces the view derived from a social history of the period that the Equal Protection Clause was probably understood originally to protect from violence primarily the life, liberty, and property of blacks as of whites.

There is no way to be certain, of course. Because of this uncertainty, Bork, like every interpreter, must choose an underlying principle among the plausible candidates. He is legitimately influenced by his own moral abhorrence of segregation to choose a more general principle, the one later articulated in *Plessy*. Unlike the narrow principle that blacks should be protected from violence just as whites are protected, the more general principle that blacks and whites are to be equal in all respects before the law yields the conclusion that state-sponsored segregation is unconstitutional.

Additional evidence that Bork injects his own value preferences into his reading of the principle underlying the Equal Protection Clause comes from his view that the clause amounts to "a rule flatly prohibiting discrimination against blacks, whites, Americans of Polish descent, and so forth."[105] Such a broad prohibition follows only if the underlying principle is broader still than one requiring total, legal equality for blacks. The principle has to be even broader than one mandating equality not only for blacks but for people of any race. As Bork acknowledges explicitly, it must be the principle that the law should treat people equally regardless of "race or *ethnicity*."[106]

How can Bork justify the inclusion of ethnicity when that was clearly not at issue in 1868? The best rationale, I believe, consistent with Bork's understanding of "original understanding," is this: In the nineteenth century, and well into the twentieth, many people associated cultural differences with biological differences. Whereas we would say that Poles and Italians differ culturally, for example, they would call the differences racial and would attribute many differences of custom to differences of racial makeup. So in 1868 race as a category included what we now term *ethnicity*. We have subsequently narrowed the concept of race to exclude ethnicity. But if we go so far as to attribute to those who ratified the Fourteenth Amendment the understanding that everyone should be guaranteed equal protection of the laws regardless of race, then ethnicity should be included along with race in order to reflect their original understanding of race. In any case, whether on this basis or on some other, Bork does include ethnicity in his understanding of the principle underlying the Fourteenth Amendment.

Once Bork goes so far as to apply the Fourteenth Amendment to all racial and ethnic classifications, his original understanding approach to constitutional interpretation becomes virtually indistinguishable for purposes of the present work from what I call the Moderate view. According to the Moderate view, the fact that a value or right is believed by judges to be mandated by natural law, common decency, or our social traditions is insufficient to warrant believing it is mandated by the Constitution. Constitutional mandates are found in the individual clauses of the Constitution. (Thus, for example, there is no general constitutional right of privacy.) Other things being equal, interpretations are better grounded in the document when appeal is made to a relatively specific, rather than a more general, right or value actually found in the Constitution. Appeals to a guarantee of liberty, for example, provide less secure moorings in the Constitution than appeals to a guarantee of freedom specifically from double jeopardy in criminal trials. Being more specific, the latter reflects more clearly the morality of the Constitution. Being more general, the guarantee of liberty, though found in the Constitution, may be used to reflect the judge's morality more than the Constitution's. Appeals to substantive due process are egregious examples of this. Augmentation of constitutional guarantees by unelected judges erodes majority rule, which is one of our country's primary political values.

Yet, minority and individual rights are also important political values. The Constitution is supposed to guarantee these against intrusion by legislative majorities. In order to continue doing so, the meaning of specific clauses and guarantees must evolve to reflect changes in cir-

cumstances (legal, technological, and social) and changes in our knowledge. This evolution of constitutional doctrine is justified ultimately by
the claim that specific clauses or guarantees in the Constitution reflect
underlying principles or values. In order to be true to these values amid
changes in knowledge and circumstances, judges must sometimes alter
their understanding of specific clauses or guarantees. Because an underlying value can be viewed at more than one level of generality, judges
inevitably and legitimately employ their own values in the process of
constitutional interpretation. This is not an illegitimate derogation of
majority rule. It is necessary to preserve constitutional guarantees in a
form of government established by constitution.

As used in the present work, the Moderate view calls for no more
extensive liberty of interpretation than this. Chapter 6 shows that the
Moderate view yields an interpretation of the Religion Clauses that disallows all legislation, including antiabortion legislation, whose sole purpose is the protection of the lives of fetuses twenty weeks or younger.

Conflicts between the Religion Clauses

The preceding two sections showed that even Bork's Original Understanding view of constitutional interpretation permits the kind of
changes in the Court's understanding of the Religion Clauses recounted
earlier in this chapter. But it is one thing to show that change is acceptable in general, and quite another to defend certain changes in particular.
Someone might accept the principle that the Court's understanding of
the Religion Clauses should evolve, yet reject the particular course of
evolution that the Court has chosen. This section and the next explain
conceptual difficulties attendant on the particular course of evolution
charted by the Court. This section explains conflicts created by the
Court's current understanding of the clauses. Resolution of these conflicts may require that "religion" mean something different in the Establishment Clause than it means in the Free Exercise Clause. The next
section raises the specter that the Court's decisions have been so unprincipled as to render impossible any definition of religion at all in the Free
Exercise Clause. Inability to define religion would certainly hamper dis-
ciplined interpretations of that clause. Chapters 4 and 5 dispel the specter of confusion. I present a definition of religion that incorporates the
Court's current understanding and addresses adequately the conceptual
difficulties raised in this section and in the one that follows.

As we have seen, the Establishment Clause forbids laws respecting
an establishment of religion, while the Free Exercise Clause forbids laws

prohibiting the free exercise of religion. These clauses are, of course, supposed to be consistent with one another. But critics maintain that the Court's interpretation of the clauses has evolved so as to jeopardize their consistency.

Consider, for example, the case of *Thomas v. Review Board*[107] (1981) in which the Court required unemployment benefits be paid to Thomas. Thomas had quit his job because he opposed on religious grounds making implements of war. The Court concluded that by denying him unemployment compensation, the state was violating Thomas's right to free exercise of his religion. But since, in light of this decision, Thomas could quit his job (not be laid off, but *quit* his job) and nevertheless receive unemployment compensation, he is being treated more favorably by the state than are most other people. People usually receive unemployment compensation only if they are laid off (or are injured or ill), not if they quit. Why is Thomas given more favorable treatment? Because he quit for *religious* reasons. But then the government, it seems, is not being neutral regarding religion. It gives special treatment to people who quit their jobs for religious reasons, thereby favoring religion over nonreligion. This seems to violate the principle of governmental neutrality called for by the Establishment Clause. Thus, the Religion Clauses seem inconsistent with one another. Regarding unemployment compensation for people who quit work for religious reasons, it seems that the Free Exercise Clause requires special treatment that the Establishment Clause forbids. Chief Justice Burger, writing for the Court in *Thomas*, refers to this as "the tension between the two Religion Clauses."[108]

Justice Rehnquist's dissent is less kind. He suggests that this tension results from, and casts doubt on the wisdom of, the Court's expansion of the religion guarantees. He notes:

> The "tension" is of fairly recent vintage, unknown at the time of the framing and adoption of the First Amendment. The causes of the tension, it seems to me, are threefold. . . . The third, and perhaps most important, . . . is our overly expansive interpretation of *both* Clauses. By broadly construing both Clauses, the Court has constantly narrowed the channel between the Scylla and Charybdis through which any state or federal action must pass in order to survive constitutional scrutiny.[109]

If problems regarding relationships between the two Religion Clauses result from the Court's increasingly expansive interpretations of those clauses, Rehnquist suggests, there is reason to reject entirely (or for the most part) the evolution of judicial doctrine in this area.

A similar conflict seems to arise in a different kind of situation. The Constitution requires that the law be neutral in its treatment of different religious groups and in its treatment of religion versus nonreligion. This is why the state is forbidden, for example, from requiring prayers[110] or readings from the Bible[111] in public schools. All such state requirements constitute, according to the Court, the impermissible establishment of religion. But as we have seen, Justice Black considered Secular Humanism to be a religion. Since many works of literature may fairly be said to promote Secular Humanism, the introduction of these works into the school curriculum would seem also to constitute an impermissible establishment of religion. Such was the objection made by Carolyn Grove to the inclusion of Gordon Park's *The Learning Tree* in the public school curriculum. According to Grove, the book promotes Secular Humanism, which is a religion, and violates the Establishment Clause of the Constitution.[112]

Others object on similar grounds to including in public school curricula the theory of biological evolution.[113] This theory, they contend, directly contradicts their fundamentalist Christian religious beliefs and amounts to propaganda for a competing religion (i.e., Secular Humanism).

Surely something has gone wrong. It appears that the Supreme Court has so expanded the meaning of religion that the secular has become religious. This is a conceptual difficulty in itself. And it seems to have unacceptable legal implications. Since public education is supposed to be secular and nonreligious, the Court's definitions seem to make it impossible for public education to be constitutional. Any education that is secular is, for that reason, religious, and unconstitutional. But what can public education be if not secular? Thus the entire enterprise of public education would appear unconstituional. Surely this cannot be right. Again, the Court's expansive understanding of the Religion Clauses seems at fault, casting doubt on the wisdom of that expansion.

One response to these difficulties is to maintain that "religion" denotes different things in the two Religion Clauses. This is the dual definition approach to the Religion Clauses. Confronted with the claim that use of *The Learning Tree* in public schools amounts to the unconstitutional establishment of the religion of Secular Humanism, the Court distinguished the Establishment Clause from the Free Exercise Clause. Secular Humanism, according to the court of appeals that heard the case, is a religion for purposes of the Establishment Clause only when it is "characterized by tenets and organization,"[114] that is, only when it is embodied in a religious group. The Establishment Clause on this reading forbids certain kinds of government support only for sectarian activities—activities of an organized group with a creed and method of operation like that in most churches. Secular Humanist societies meet on Sundays, they have a Sunday school for children, collect dues, discuss the meaning and implications of their common beliefs, and have leaders who perform tasks similar to those performed by priests, ministers, and rabbis (pastoral care, marriage ceremonies, and the like). The Establishment Clause concerns Secular Humanism *as so organized*, because that clause denotes religion only as organized in sectarian groups. According to this view, "religion" means, in Establishment Clause contexts, "an organized sect, and its peculiarly sectarian ceremonies, activities, beliefs, artifacts, symbols, etc."[115] Because *The Learning Tree* is not an expression of the creed of any such organized group, it is not religious, so its inclusion in the public school curriculum does not amount to the unconstitutional establishment of religion.

But what of Thomas's belief in *Thomas v. Review Board* that making gun turrets violated his religious beliefs? This belief was not the official view of the Jehovah's Witnesses, the organized sect that he belonged to. If "religion" is limited to "sectarian religion," Thomas's belief would not count as religious. We have seen, however, that his belief was accepted by the Court as religious. This is why the Court ruled that denying him unemployment compensation violated his right to free exercise of religion. The dual definition approach to the Religion Clauses reconciles this ruling with that concerning *The Learning Tree* (the *Grove* decision). According to this approach, where free exercise is at issue, the meaning of "religion" is not limited to the creed of a sectarian organization. "Religion" is as expansive as individual conscience. So Thomas's idiosyncratic objections to making gun turrets are religious because "a generous . . . (and even idiosyncratic) definition best serves free exercise values,"[116] and Thomas's was a free exercise case. But "the same expansiveness in interpreting the establishment clause is simply intolerable."[117] As we have seen concerning *Grove*, it would make unconstitutional virtually all secular public education. The Court concludes, "there is much to be said for the view that the definition of religion should vary with the clause under review."[118]

Justice Rutledge articulated a problem with this dual definition approach a generation earlier in his *Everson* dissent. The clauses are contained in these words of the First Amendment: "Congress shall make no law respecting an establishment of religion, or prohibiting the free exercise thereof." Rutledge noted:

"Religion" appears only once in the Amendment. But the word governs
two prohibitions and governs them alike. It does not have two meanings, one narrow to forbid "an establishment" and another, much
broader, for securing "the free exercise thereof." "Thereof" brings down
"religion" with its entire and exact content, no more and no less, from
the first into the second guarantee, so that Congress and now the states
are as broadly restricted concerning the one as they are regarding the
other.[119]

This reasoning casts doubt on any dual definition analysis.[120] To the
extent that an expanded definition of religion creates the need for problematic dual definitions, the expanded definition of religion is itself
problematic.

The Elusive Meaning of "Religion"

More serious than the prospect of dual definitions is that one of those
two definitions (if two there must be) eludes formulation. There is at
present no widely accepted definition of "religion" for purpose of applying the Free Exercise Clause.

Religion can no longer be identified with Christianity, as it was in
the nineteenth century. *Thomas v Review Board* maintains that to be
protected by the Free Exercise Clause a religious belief need not be associated with the official position of any organized religion. The Jehovah's
Witnesses had no official position on the permissibility of manufactur-
ing gun turrets. *Bowen v. Roy* holds that to be protected by the Free
Exercise Clause a belief does not have to concern God or a Supreme
Being at all. Roy was concerned about the power over his daughter's
spirit involved in the use of her social security number. There was no
reference to God or to a Supreme Being, but the belief was accepted by
a majority of the Court as religious.

In sum, according to the Court, religion can exist in independence
from Christianity, theism, and all religious organizations and sects.
What, then, is the essence of religion? One suggestion, as we have already seen in our review of the conscientious objector cases (*Seeger* and
Welsh) is that religion is essentially a matter of a person's ultimate concern. But there are problems with this. For example, my family and I
regularly (though not invariably) perform on Friday evenings some Jewish ceremonies that welcome the sabbath. Almost anyone would consider these to be religious ceremonies. But neither the performance of
these ceremonies nor Judaism in general is an ultimate concern for me

in Tillich's sense. I do not associate them with the depth of my life, the source of my being, or what I take seriously without any reservation. I have many concerns. Judaism and its ceremonies are among those concerns, but they are not more fundamental to my life than the others. I take my roles as husband, father, teacher, and scholar more seriously than I take my role as a Jew. Nevertheless, Judaism remains my religion even though it is not my ultimate concern. So being of ultimate concern is not a necessary characteristic of all that is religious.

Being of ultimate concern is not sufficient, either, to make something religious. Vince Lombardi reportedly said that winning is not everything, it's the only thing. Are we to conclude that winning football games was Lombardi's religion? If so, we will have to say the same of a drug addict whose ultimate concern is getting the next fix. The ultimate-concern notion of religion fails in part because it conflicts at too many points with what we ordinarily consider religious.

Jesse Choper has suggested that the essential mark of religion is the existence of "extratemporal consequences." Religions, according to Choper, are systems of belief that include reference to consequences that extend beyond life on earth, as, for example, rewards in heaven or punishment in hell. Choper writes: "The 'extratemporal consequences' criterion . . . probably conforms more than the 'ultimate concerns' approach with the conventional, average-person conception of religion which, although largely intuitive, would generally conclude that a belief in God is religious but a belief in the Republican party is not, no matter how strongly held either of the beliefs might be."[121]

Choper may be correct about the comparison with "ultimate concern," but the extratemporal-consequences criterion fares poorly nevertheless. In fact, with candor that is hard to beat, Choper himself gives examples sufficient to discourage almost anyone from accepting his extratemporal-consequences criterion:

> Even within the Christian tradition, there are many articles of faith that
> do not relate directly to any rewards or punishments after death. Belief
> in the possibility of divine intervention on earth is one example: faith
> healing, retribution, and answered prayers. Another is the precept,
> which many find in the teachings of such persons as Saint Augustine and
> John Calvin, that salvation is the gift of God to his chosen, and is not to
> be earned by such behavior as good works during life.[122]

Surely we can do better than adopt a view of religion that excludes faith healing and the teachings of Saint Augustine and John Calvin.

The problem here is not just that the concept of religion has become elusive. An inability adequately to define religion for free exercise purposes casts a shadow over the adequacy of the Court-imposed evolution of the concept. The discussion earlier of methodologies (Original Understanding and Moderate view) showed that, *in general*, it is legitimate for our understanding of constitutional clauses and terms to evolve. But any *particular* evolutionary change that results in some kind of incoherence must be rejected, not because it is evolution, but because it is evolution that leads to conceptual problems.

Conclusion

The inability adequately to define "religion" as it is understood to be protected by the Free Exercise Clause is certainly a problem. How can it be known when the state is denying to someone free exercise of religion when there is no longer a widely accepted, and acceptable, definition of religion? The constitutional guarantee is liable to become a blank check. Without clearer guidance from the Constitution, judges are left to substitute their values regarding religious freedom for those of democratically elected representatives.

Fortunately, there is a viable definition of religion which is consistent with Supreme Court decisions. I present and defend it in the next two chapters. Chapter 6 then shows that according to this definition, beliefs about the personhood of fetuses younger than twenty-one weeks are religious. So antiabortion laws predicated on such beliefs amount to the unconstitutional establishment of religion.

The Definition of "Religion"

T HE FIRST AMENDMENT BEGINS, "Congress shall make no law respecting an establishment of religion, or prohibiting the free exercise thereof." We saw in the last chapter that the Court's understanding of these Religion Clauses has evolved considerably during the past one hundred years. But uncertainties attend the results of this evolution. The present chapter proposes and defends a unified, consistent, and satisfactory definition of "religion" that expresses the concept currently used by the Court.

Some judges and commentators deny the possibility of any unified and consistent definition. They maintain that "religion," though appearing only once in the First Amendment, has two different meanings, one for the Establishment Clause and another for the Free Exercise Clause. Another commentator notes that "the scope of religious pluralism in the United States . . . has resulted in such a multiplicity and diversity of ideas about what is a 'religion' or a 'religious belief' that no simple formula seems able to accommodate them all."[1] A third is more categorical: "No single characteristic should be regarded as essential to religiousness."[2] The chief justice of the Supreme Court wrote: "Candor compels acknowledgement . . . that we can only dimly perceive the lines of demarcation in this extraordinarily sensitive area of constitutional law."[3]

Yet the definition of religion remains important in many legal disputes, making the absence of a clear definition at least regrettable. As one appellate judge put it:

> Though litigation of the question whether a given group or set of beliefs
> is or is not religious is a delicate business, our legal system sometimes

111

requires it so that secular enterprises may not unjustly enjoy the immunities granted the sacred. When tax exemptions are granted to churches, litigation concerning what is or is not a church will follow. When exemption from military service is granted to those who object on religious grounds, there is similar litigation.[4]

According to the same judge, however, the "doctrines and definitions . . . the law has provided [are] unsatisfactory."[5] The present chapter remedies this situation by providing a definition of religion that is clear, that expresses the concept *employed by the Court*, and that applies equally to both Religion Clauses.

This chapter first argues that for constitutional purposes it is not the noun "religion" but the adjective "religious" that needs to be defined, and that all things religious can be defined in terms of religious belief. The next two sections explain the contrast between secular (nonreligious) beliefs and religious beliefs as these are judicially understood in First Amendment contexts. Judicial decisions that classify texts, activities, doctrines, groups, and so forth as either religious or nonreligious are shown to reflect the proposed definition.

Here is a preliminary account of that proposed definition. Religious beliefs are those that cannot be established by appeal merely to secular premises and methodologies. Secular premises and methodologies include what passes for common-sense knowledge in our society (e.g., fire burns people, punishment deters crime), the scientific beliefs that underlie our technology (e.g., electrons and bacteria exist), the methodology accepted in our society for the generation of scientific and technological knowledge (e.g., observation, microscopes, carbon dating, and mathematical calculations can be useful), and the values considered essential to society (e.g., peaceful coexistence among its members, limits on assault and murder) or essential to our type of society (e.g., individual liberty, private property, pluralism, and hard work). More generally, secular premises are drawn from secular beliefs. I term "secular beliefs" all those agreements of belief, thought, and practice that are the basis of the cooperation and mutual understanding needed among people to maintain and perpetuate our society.

Religious beliefs are those that cannot be supported cogently with arguments or demonstrations whose premises include only secular beliefs. What is more, for First Amendment purposes, all religious matters are religious because of their relationship to religious beliefs. For example, "creation science" is religious because it results from an interpretation of the Bible. The Bible is a religious text because of its relationship to belief in the existence of God, whose actions in history it is supposed to record. Belief in the existence of God cannot be supported cogently by the use of common sense, science, technology, or accepted scientific methodologies, so it is a religious belief.

I call this the *epistemological definition* of religion because religion is defined in terms of how we gain knowledge and how we support our claims to knowledge. Epistemology is the branch of philosophy that concentrates exclusively on explaining, distinguishing, and evaluating knowledge claims.

This chapter concludes by summarizing major theses and reiterating the epistemological understanding of "religion." The chapter to follow deals with objections and adds supporting considerations.

A word of caution is in order at the start. The present chapter presents a definition of religion that conforms to the Supreme Court's interpretation of the Religion Clauses of the First Amendment. There is no claim that this definition would serve the purposes of, for example, a minister preparing a sermon on the nature of religion, or an anthropologist deciding how to characterize the religion of the group she is studying. There may be many definitions of religion, each of which helps clarify the nature of religion in different contexts. The definition of religion offered here is meant to clarify the nature of religion only in the context of the Constitution's First Amendment.

The definition is further limited to clarifying the concept *as understood by the Supreme Court during the past fifty years.* I do not support every detail of the concept that I find implicit in the Court's work. For example, I find implicit in the Court's work belief in a sharp distinction between facts and values, and belief that all secular matters of fact can, in principle, be established to the satisfaction of society's reasonable members. I accept neither belief without qualification. But I maintain that judicial interpretations of the First Amendment are clarified by attributing these beliefs to the judiciary and that the resulting concept of religion is adequate for constitutional purposes. This is not to say, nor to deny, however, that the Court's concept of religion is the *best* one for constitutional purposes. Such a determination is beyond the scope of the present work. In sum, I make only two claims: The definition given here reflects best the concept that the Court does, in fact, employ; and the Court's concept is adequate for purposes of constitutional law.

The Adjectival Sense of Religion

The meaning of the constitutional guarantees contained in the First Amendment's Religion Clauses can be understood by recognizing, first, that legal controversies seldom, if ever, need to be framed in terms of "religion," a noun that seems to refer to a "thing" of some sort. Instead, (almost) all controversies involving the Religion Clauses can be thought of as involving something (allegedly) religious. In other words, where the meaning of "religion" seems to be at issue, the matter can be viewed most helpfully as concerning not the noun "religion" but the adjective "religious." I maintain that for constitutional purposes, instead of asking whether or not something is a religion, one should ask whether or not a given belief is religious; whether or not a ceremony, practice, or rite is religious; whether or not a text, symbol, or artifact used in a ceremony is religious, or is being employed with religious significance; whether or not a group is religious. This section explains and illustrates this thesis by showing that religion can be conceived adjectivally in all the cases considered in Chapter 3.

I argue also that religious belief is the cornerstone of the edifice of things judged religious. From a constitutional perspective, everything religious is religious because it is a religious belief or because it is essentially related to a religious belief. Ceremonies, rites, practices, texts, symbols, artifacts, and groups are religious by virtue of their relationship to one or more beliefs that are religious. So everything classified as "religion" for First Amendment purposes is adjectivally religious and is related to religious belief.

RELIGIOUS BELIEFS INDEPENDENT OF ORGANIZED RELIGIONS

In some cases, the Court recognizes religious belief to exist independently of any belief system constituting a religion. In other cases, the individual belief is part of a system constituting a religion, but the religion in question is personal or idiosyncratic, rather than organized. Cases of these two sorts are discussed in this part, beginning with those falling under the Free Exercise Clause.

Some free exercise cases considered earlier turn directly on whether or not a certain belief should be classified as religious. For example, in *Thomas v. Review Board*,[6] Thomas's eligibility for unemployment benefits turned on whether or not his quitting work to avoid participating in the production of gun turrets was motivated by a religious belief. If it was, then the state's denial of unemployment benefits constituted an unconstitutional burden on the free exercise of Thomas's religion. In *Bowen v. Roy*,[7] the Court considered Roy's refusal to place his daughter's social security number on forms used to apply for public assistance. The Court determined that if Roy's refusal was based on a religious belief, that refusal could not be the basis for the state's denial of benefits to Roy's daughter.

In both cases, the Court ruled in favor of the party claiming protection of the Free Exercise Clause. But in neither case was the belief system of an organized religion at issue. Thomas was a Jehovah's Witness; however, the doctrine of pacifism maintained by the Witnesses does not forbid participation in the manufacture of military weapons. Thomas was granted protection of the Free Exercise Clause as a result of the nature of his particular belief, rather than the tenets of the organized religion with which he was affiliated. The case is clearer in *Bowen v. Roy* because the record contains no evidence that any religion has as a tenet the belief that the use of a uniquely designating social security number jeopardizes a person's spirit. Roy was protected by the Free Exercise Clause because his belief was judged to be religious. This is the only sense in which religion was involved in the case.

Kolbeck v. Kramer[8] (1964) is another case in which "religion" means "religious belief." A young man had been expelled from a state university because, believing on religious grounds that one should avoid all recourse to medical treatment, he had refused to receive medical vaccinations required of all students except Christian Scientists. The young man was not a Christian Scientist, nor was he affiliated with any other religious group. Nevertheless, the Court required the state to grant an exemption in his case. Religion was involved, and the young man was protected by the Free Exercise Clause since the belief in question was deemed religious.

Cases of conscientious objection to military service illustrate the point in the context of statutory interpretation. Seeger, whose claim to conscientious objector status was upheld in *United States v. Seeger*[9] (1965), was a Catholic whose organized religion did not forbid participation in just wars. Seeger was nevertheless a complete pacifist, and the Court deemed his pacifism to be "by religious training and belief." This decision rested not on Seeger's religion, which did not officially require pacifism, but on Seeger's particular beliefs regarding pacifism, which the Court accepted as religious. The other conscientious objector case that we have reviewed, *Welsh v. United States*[10] (1970), presents the clearest case. Welsh lacked affiliation with any religious group and did not originally associate his pacifism with religion in any way at all. Nevertheless, after examining the nature of his belief, the Court declared it to be religious and ordered on this basis that Welsh be accepted as a conscientious objector.

The primacy of religious belief can be seen in Establishment Clause cases as well. In *Engel v. Vitale* (1962), for example, the Court invalidated a New York statute requiring a nonsectarian prayer to be recited in public schools. This nonsectarian prayer was not associated with any particular religion, or religious group. Nevertheless, the Court declared that "the State of New York has adopted a practice wholly inconsistent with the Establishment Clause." The "invocation of God's blessings as prescribed in the Regent's prayer is a religious activity."[11] The prayer unconstitutionally establishes religion, not because any particular religion is involved, but because "prayer is a religious activity."[12] Religion is involved here adjectivally as qualifying an activity. And why is that activity deemed religious? Because "it is a solemn avowal of divine faith and supplication for the blessings of the Almighty."[13] In other words, prayer is a religious activity because it presupposes and avows a religious belief (i.e., in the existence, benevolence, and responsiveness of God).

The ruling in *Wallace v. Jaffree* (1985) is similar. The Court invalidated a state law requiring in public schools a moment of silence "for meditation or voluntary prayer."[14] This law superseded a nearly identical statute that made no reference to prayer. The Court found constitutionally objectionable the newer statute simply because it added a reference to prayer. No particular religion or religious group was singled out for special treatment. Prayer is religious, all the same, because it presupposes religious beliefs without which it makes no sense. A statute endorsing prayer unconstitutionally establishes religion because it unavoidably conveys official endorsement of those underlying religious beliefs.

Religious Belief as Fundamental to Organized Religion

This part shows that organized groups and associated texts, symbols, and activities are also designated religious on the basis of judgments about their beliefs. (Apparent exceptions are discussed in "Secular Religions" in Chapter 5.)

In *Founding Church of Scientology v. United States*[15] (1969) an appellate court examined the belief system of the Scientology movement and determined that its claims should be given the constitutional protections reserved for religious doctrines. The movement is religious because its principal beliefs are religious. The same procedure was used in *Malnak v. Yogi*[16] (1977) where the group in question claimed to be nonreligious. They claimed that Transcendental Meditation (TM) was secular, so its inclusion in a public school curriculum did not violate the Establishment Clause. After examining the beliefs associated with TM, the appellate court disagreed. Transcendental Meditation was designated a religion, or a religious activity, and was banned from the public school curriculum.

In *Africa v. Commonwealth of Pennsylvania*[17] (1981) an appellate court was called upon to determine whether or not an organization called MOVE was a religious organization. Appellant Frank Africa maintained that membership in MOVE gave him religious grounds for a special diet during incarceration. His petition was denied. After examining the organization's belief system, the Court concluded that MOVE was secular, not religious.

Controversies surrounding the teaching of evolution in public schools turn similarly on which beliefs are considered religious. Courts have concluded in recent decades that the theory of biological evolution is secular. But the theory of creationism, or "creation science," as its proponents now call it, is a religious belief, or a set of religious beliefs, because it derives from an interpretation of the biblical account of creation. So the state cannot prohibit teaching the theory of biological evolution in the public schools.[18] In a later case the Court determined that the state may not require that "balanced treatment" be given in public schools to "creation science" and the theory of evolution whenever either is taught.[19]

These cases concerning instruction in the theory of biological evolution rest on the assumption that the Bible is a religious document, so any laws designed to promote its teachings are impermissible establishments of religion. This view of the Bible was stated explicitly in another case, *Abington School District v. Schempp* (1963), where the Court wrote: "Surely the place of the Bible as an instrument of religion cannot be gainsaid."[20] Accordingly, the Court found unconstitutional a law requiring that the Lord's Prayer or passages from the Bible be read at the beginning of each day in public schools. The Court conceded that the Bible could be taught "for its literary and historic qualities . . . when presented objectively as part of a secular program of education. . . . But the exercises here do not fall into these categories. They are religious exercises."[21]

The adjectival sense of religion is prominent here. The state's requirement is unconstitutional because it amounts to requiring a "religious exercise." It is a religious exercise because it employs the Bible as "an instrument of religion." The Bible lends itself readily to being used as an instrument of religion because it is the holy book of Christianity, and Christianity is a religion. We are so used to the classification of Christianity as a religion—indeed, it is the paradigm case of religion in our society—that we seldom wonder about the basis for this classification. On reflection, the basis must be the beliefs that Christianity contains and espouses. Just as Scientology and Transcendental Meditation were declared by courts to be religions because their beliefs were religious, whereas MOVE was declared not a religion because its beliefs were found to be secular, Christianity is, at least for First Amendment purposes, a religion because religious beliefs are integral to Christianity. These beliefs make Christianity a religion. The Republican Party, by contrast, is not a religion because its beliefs are secular.

Because Christianity is a religion, its basic text, the Bible, is religious. A ceremony or exercise employing the Bible (other than "for its literary or historical qualities") is therefore a religious exercise. A state law that requires such an exercise in public schools violates the Establishment Clause.

A similar chain of reasoning can be seen in cases concerning government sponsorship of nativity scenes during the winter holiday season. In *Allegheny County v. ACLU* (1989), the Supreme Court held that under the Establishment Clause, "the government's use of religious symbolism is unconstitutional if it has the effect of endorsing religious beliefs."[22] Accordingly, a creche standing alone on government property is unconstitutional because it contains purely religious symbolism. It depicts an event central to the Christian faith, the birth of Jesus, the nature and significance of which are matters of religious belief. Thus, a creche standing alone on public property "has the effect of endorsing religious beliefs." The Court seems to assume here what I have just maintained: Christianity is a religion, and its symbols are religious, because its distinctive and central beliefs are religious.

In sum, controversies regarding the Religion Clauses can all be viewed as concerning what is religious, but they cannot all be viewed as resting on determinations of what constitutes a religion. Some free exercise cases reviewed earlier in this section (*Thomas* and *Bowen*) rest on religious beliefs apart from any relationship of those beliefs to the doctrines of a religion. And determinations that Scientology and Transcendental Meditation are religions, whereas MOVE is not, rest on judicial determinations that the beliefs of the former, but not of the latter, are religious. So in constitutional law, "religious" is more basic than "religion."

Belief is the bottom line in determining what is religious. All judicial classifications of groups, symbols, texts, ceremonies, exercises, and the like as religious rest on, and are justified by, the relationship that those groups, symbols, texts, and so forth bear to beliefs that are judicially recognized as religious. No other adjectival use of "religious" is similarly basic. Roy's belief that spiritual damage can be done by using a social security number was accepted by the Court as religious, but it was unrelated to any religious group, text, rite, ceremony, exercise, or symbol. Thus, according to the Supreme Court, a belief can be recognized as religious without reference to anything else religious. But other matters are recognized as religious only by virtue of their relationship to religious beliefs. Prayer is inherently religious because it presupposes religious beliefs. A creche is a religious symbol because it symbolizes religious beliefs. The Bible is a religious text because it expresses beliefs that are distinctive of Christianity, and Christianity is a religion because its central beliefs are religious. "Creation science" is religious because it rests on biblical (religious) beliefs, and so forth.

In conclusion, understanding the meaning that the Court attaches to "religious belief" reveals the way the Court establishes the denotation of "religion" in the First Amendment. The sections to follow clarify the meaning of "religious belief."

Secular (Nonreligious) Belief

The present section explains the nature of "secular belief" (which I also call "nonreligious belief"). This explanation elucidates, by contrast, the nature of "religious belief." The section's last part, and the two sections that follow, show that this account corresponds to the Supreme Court's understanding of these concepts in its interpretations of the First Amendment. The explanations of "secular belief" and "religious belief" are intended, in other words, to be general characterizations of these concepts as they are employed and understood by the Court. I am making explicit what is implicit in the *Court's* opinions and views.

Each way of life involves agreements among the people sharing that way of life. In truly theocentric societies, these agreements may all be religious. Or, more likely, in such societies the distinction between religion and nonreligion may have little application. In other societies, however, including our own, a distinction is made between the religious and the secular. In such societies, what I term secular beliefs include all the agreements in belief, thought, and practice that enable people within the society to interact with that degree of mutual understanding and cooperation necessary to maintain and (largely) perpetuate that society's way of life. Many of these agreements are implicit, including those entailed by use of a common language.

Whether implicit or explicit, the agreements involved in one way of life are not entirely the same as those involved in a different way of life because no single way of life characterizes all human groups. For example, fifty years ago !Kung bushmen in the Kalahari Desert of southwest Africa gathered fruits, vegetables, and nuts for most of their dietary needs, and hunted wild game with spears, small arrows, and traps for the rest. They had no permanent residences, no money, no government, no taxes, no mortgage, no police, no cars, and no literacy. By contrast, contemporary life in the United States and other industrialized nations includes all these elements, and many more, which are lacking in the traditional !Kung way of life.

Corresponding to these different ways of life are different agreements among the societies' members. For example, it is important to our way of life that we (generally) agree that people should stop at red lights, pay their taxes, and learn to read and write. We believe also that inoculations are effective means of reducing the incidence of some serious diseases and that the rate of savings can affect interest rates. The traditional !Kung way of life, in contrast, involved no such agreements, as they had neither traffic lights, taxes, interest rates, monetary savings, or inoculations. Nor did they have any need for literacy. Instead, it was important to them that people be free to take up residence at any water hole expecting that the water hole's current occupants would grant them permission to stay. It was also important that a certain plant could be used to make a poison that would help them to kill animals. Equally important was the belief that the meat of animals so killed was safe for people to eat. Contemporary Americans, by contrast, have no need of such a poison or of the beliefs and practices associated with it. What is more, our system of residential property rights precludes a rational expectation that people can, simply by asking, gain permission to live wherever they choose.

I call "secular" all those agreements in belief, thought, and practice that enable people (in nontheocentric cultures) to interact with sufficient mutual understanding and cooperation to maintain and (largely) perpetuate their way of life. As the above examples suggest, such agreements are not all, strictly speaking, matters of belief. Practices are not always described in statements that are then believed. But such practices presuppose at least implicit beliefs. These are beliefs that people engaged in the practices would subscribe to if asked whether their involvement in the practice can be taken as an indication that they hold the beliefs in question. So, rather than use the phrase "belief, thought, and practice" I refer in what follows to "secular beliefs." The remainder of this section illustrates and explains the various types of secular beliefs in our society.

A word of caution is necessary before beginning. Because I am discussing *our* society, I must explain in a preliminary way my use of "our" and "we" in such expressions as "our belief" and "we believe." I do not mean to imply that all contemporary Americans share the belief in question. I mean merely that the belief is one of those whose *general* (but not unanimous or uniform) acceptance is vital to our way of life. In fact, the existence among us of exceptions is part of my thesis. The nature of secular belief is here explained in order to clarify the nature of religious belief. Religious beliefs are, in the first instance, those that cannot be established by appeal to secular beliefs alone. What is more, these initial religious beliefs are sometimes used by religiously motivated people in our society as premises for further religious beliefs that contradict some secular beliefs. So when I refer to a secular belief as one that "we" hold, I do not mean to imply unanimous or uniform acceptance of that belief. A contradictory belief may be held on religious, or other, grounds by people who are nonetheless members of our society.

I turn now to an account of secular beliefs, which I have divided into four parts: (1) secular beliefs of fact and value related to material reality; (2) secular beliefs related to social interaction; (3) contrasts between secular beliefs about facts and secular beliefs about values; and (4) the relationship of the above to the Supreme Court's general characterizations of secular beliefs.

SECULAR BELIEFS RELATED TO MATERIAL REALITY

We interact with material reality to secure food, shelter, transportation, safety, and other necessities. We base our interactions with material reality partly on common-sense beliefs that we verify in our own experience. Fire is painful and destructive when it comes in contact with the body. Eating certain things as food relieves hunger. And so forth. We rely also on common-sense values. Other things being equal, for example, illness and hunger are bad, and to be avoided where possible, whereas literacy, efficiency, and convenience are good, and to be promoted where possible.

But our interactions with material reality are not guided entirely by personal experience and common sense because in our society we are highly dependent on the use of technological devices to secure life's necessities. Most of us are relatively ignorant of the way this technology works, of the science on which it is based, and of the methodology appropriate to scientific study and technological innovation. Nevertheless, by employing this technology, we live in a manner that presupposes acceptance of beliefs about science and technology, as well as beliefs about appropriate methods of inquiry in science and technology. For example, every time I drive my car across a bridge (without suicidal intent), my actions depend on many beliefs that I could not state, much less prove. My use of the bridge is evidence of the acceptance in our society of myriad beliefs about matters in physics and metallurgy. At one further remove, my use of the bridge constitutes implicit acceptance of the method employed in the generation and justification of such beliefs. Others in our society are in the same situation as I. So, considering our reliance on cars, refrigerators, airplanes, elevators, and scores of other machines and appliances, our society's implicit acceptance extends to most matters of science and technology, regardless of whether or not we are as individuals even aware of the specific beliefs involved. Because these beliefs about physical reality are implicated in activities that secure food, clothing, shelter, safety, transportation, health, and other physical needs and conveniences, they are all secular (nonreligious) beliefs.

Secular beliefs related to material reality are not immune from error. Those based on personal experience and contained in common sense can be wrong. For example, I may become allergic to a food, such as apples, rendering erroneous my belief, based on past experience, that apples are a healthful way for me to relieve my hunger. I may believe on the basis of personal experience that Buicks are more reliable than Toyotas, but statistics related to customer complaints may suggest that I am wrong. Until recently, what passed for common sense suggested that girls' health would be maintained optimally by less physical activity than was optimal for boys. This, too, may be an error. But whether erroneous or not, beliefs such as these are nevertheless secular beliefs.

So, too, are the common-sense values that guide our interactions with material reality. For example, though we are unlikely to renounce the value currently placed on physical health, we may come in time to reassess the value currently placed on personal convenience. We may qualify our commitment to that value through increased emphasis on the competing value of hard work. Regardless of any such change in emphasis, however, both personal convenience and hard work are likely to remain secular values in our society. In other cases, society may evolve so as to replace one secular value with another. For example, early in this century the vast majority valued the human domination of nature. Today people value increasingly living in harmony with nature, which may eventually eclipse the value of human domination.

The possibilities within secular thought of recognizing error and making revisions exist also with regard to the myriad beliefs whose acceptance is implied by our reliance on modern technology. Some of these beliefs, too, may be erroneous. Bridges on which people rely sometimes collapse. Methods of generating electricity may prove more dangerous to people's health than was earlier thought. Beliefs about such matters are secular, even though they are fallible, because they are implicit in the ways that we in our society commonly deal with material reality as we attempt to secure physical necessities and attain what we value.

Whether matters of personal experience, common sense, or science and technology, these beliefs are secular because the processes of thought, investigation, and argument that support them are secular. These processes are commonly held in our society to yield information that is helpful in and basic to the pursuit of physical necessities and valued outcomes. These processes include, but are not limited to, scientific methods of discovery. Commonly accepted processes of thought, investigation, and argument include also beliefs about when to trust one's own experience and when to defer to experts, when to believe one's perceptions and when to assume that they are illusions, when to accept common sense and when to reject common sense as embodying out-of-date prejudice, and so forth. Like the secular beliefs that they are used to generate and defend, our processes of thought, investigation, and argument are fallible. The methods that we use may be less reliable or complete than we believe. Western methods of medical investigation, for example, may lack the ability to attain insights regarding human health that Oriental methods of investigation have secured. Also, we may formulate inaccurately our methods, or the beliefs that are implicit in the use of those methods. For example, we may think that a branch of science relies primarily on observation, whereas it actually relies more heavily on mathematical calculations. Nevertheless, because our way of life is inextricably bound to acceptance of these methods and beliefs, they are secular.

This account of why and when beliefs about material reality are secular illuminates the evolutionism–creationism controversy. The methods of investigation used to support the theory of biological evolution are the same as those used generally in the geological, archeological, and biological disciplines that we depend on for useful information about topics as diverse as where we are likely to find natural oil reserves and which animals are the best subjects for experiments designed to find a cure for acquired immunodeficiency syndrome (AIDS). The theory of evolution is incomplete all the same, and any one scientist's account may be inaccurate at many points, but it is a belief of a piece with those on which we stake our lives and hopes every day. Creation science, however, does not employ the same methodology. So, for constitutional purposes, the one is secular and the other religious. The appellate court in *McLean v. Arkansas* (1982) correctly stressed this point in its rejection of the claim that evolutionism and creationism are equally religious views.[23] Because of differences in the methodologies used to support them, evolutionism is a secular belief, whereas creationism is not. The next section contains a fuller characterization of religious belief.

SECULAR BELIEFS RELATED TO SOCIAL INTERACTION

Many secular beliefs concern social interaction. Here, too, beliefs regarding matters of fact are based on individual perception or insight, common sense, and the expertise of specialists. Some beliefs are supported by all three. For example, many people would say that all three support the claim that individual monetary reward is a good way to motivate people in our society to work. There is general agreement, also, that punishment is necessary to deter crime. To be secular, however, a belief does not have to command general assent. For example, there is disagreement concerning the effectiveness of the death penalty as a deterrent to crime. Both the belief that the death penalty deters crime and that it does not are secular beliefs because, as in the case of beliefs about material reality, there are generally accepted methods of investigation that can, in principle, be applied to the matter. So people on both sides of the controversy can agree that certain research results would count powerfully for one conclusion, whereas certain other results would support the opposite conclusion. The debate continues largely because our values place severe limits on social research, especially where human lives are at stake.

In other cases, generally accepted factual beliefs about social interaction have proven to be mistaken or seriously incomplete. The famous Hawthorne Studies, for example, suggested hitherto unrecognized limitations on the generalization that individual monetary reward is the best way to promote worker productivity.[24] But even if beliefs about the efficacy of monetary rewards were somewhat erroneous, they were nevertheless secular beliefs. There are socially accepted methods of supporting any given view about the responsiveness of workers to different kinds of rewards and incentives.

Our secular beliefs about social interaction include beliefs about values as well as about facts. We believe that people have certain individual rights that others should respect. Some of these are embodied in the Constitution and its amendments. Other things being equal, we also value peace, harmony, and cooperation among people. Stated in this general way, these secular values are uncontroversial.

Controversies arise when these general values are applied to specific kinds of situations where respect for one of these values compromises respect for another such value. For example, we believe that children should not be abused but that parents have special prerogatives regarding the way that they rear their children. What one person considers abuse, another may consider a parental prerogative. In such a situation, at least one of these values may have to be compromised in order to accommodate respect for the other value. The same situation can arise regarding the value of free speech and the value of protecting children from pornography; the value of a free press and the value of protecting people's privacy; the value of religious freedom and the value of reducing disease (e.g., through programs of required inoculation); and so forth.

Though the settlement of any particular controversy in any of these areas can (usually) be criticized, the (usually continuing) controversy and the (provisional) settlement remain secular because the general values stressed by the competing parties are accepted in their general form by almost everyone in our society. Almost everyone values the freedoms of speech, press, and religion, but also the protection of children, privacy, and public health. Cultural leaders, including Supreme Court justices, protect and further these values as vital to our way of life. In addition, almost everyone values the settlement of controversies by peaceful, legal means. Much legislation and adjudication is therefore designed to effect peaceful, legal settlements of controversies arising from conflicts among general secular values.

General secular values regarding social interaction are not static or eternal. In our society, the rights of children to be free of parental abuse was not recognized much more than a hundred years ago. The value of religious and social pluralism was recognized by the Supreme Court in 1970 as it approved state-mandated tax exemptions for religious groups.[25] The toleration of great religious diversity is now one of our secular values. But in 1892, as we saw in Chapter 3, the Court saw no value in accommodating the needs of non-Christians. Perhaps the most dramatic changes in generally accepted values regarding social interaction concern race relations. Segregation by race was widely regarded with favor until relatively recently. Racial segregation is now widely viewed with disfavor. Many laws and public policies are designed to discourage it. In *Bob Jones University v. United States* (1983), the Court placed such importance on the value of combating racial segregation that it refused to honor a contrary claim of religious freedom. Bob Jones University was refused tax-exempt status by the Internal Revenue Service (IRS) because the university code of conduct forbade interracial dating and marriage. The university claimed that this aspect of its code was dictated by the religious beliefs of the religious sect that founded and continued to support the institution. The Court ruled that notwithstanding this religious motivation, the support of segregation could be properly interpreted by the IRS as "contrary to public policy."[26] The Court stated also that, "there can no longer be any doubt that racial discrimination in education violates deeply and widely accepted views of elementary justice."[27]

SECULAR FACTS VERSUS SECULAR VALUES

Supreme Court opinions suggest that in the *Court's* view, secular beliefs about values differ in some respects from secular beliefs about matters of fact. Whether concerning physical or social reality, controversies concerning secular beliefs about matters of fact can all be settled, at least in principle. Our secular beliefs include methodologies of science and common sense that enable people to design, or at least to imagine, tests or experiments whose results could settle disagreements about secular matters of fact.

This is not to say that all such disagreements can be settled in practice. As we have seen, disagreements about the deterrent effect of the death penalty may persist indefinitely because value constraints preclude our conducting the experiments that our methodologies indicate are appropriate. Other disagreements about matters of fact persist because we lack the time, money, or physical means of conducting the experiment. People may disagree, for example, about the chemical composition of the material a thousand meters below the surface of Venus. We can imagine actions and results that would settle the disagreement, but we may never be able, or sufficiently motivated, actually to undertake the actions in question. And even when appropriate actions are undertaken, the results may not settle the particular disagreement at hand. The results that (it was imagined) would settle the controversy may not materialize, leaving the matter unsettled unless and until more definitive results are obtained. Still, the matter is settleable in principle because we can *imagine* having obtained, or obtaining in the future, *through the application of secular methodologies*, results that would settle the matter one way or the other.

Secular methodologies are methods of obtaining information and settling disagreements that are integral to, and supportive of, society's way of life. In our society, as noted, secular methodologies include individual perception or insight, common sense, scientific experimentation, and deductive reasoning. Where secular matters of *fact* are at issue, whether about social or physical reality, these secular methodologies suffice in principle to settle matters. Beliefs of secular fact secured in this way can then (in principle) be combined with one another, and with additional applications of secular methodologies, to settle additional matters of secular fact.

This is not an entirely satisfactory account of secular beliefs about matters of fact. Some matters, generally thought to be matters of secular fact, cannot even in principle be settled one way or the other through the application of secular methodologies. For example, since time travel is not, even in principle, an available method of secular investigation, many matters of historical fact cannot be determined. Thus, if there were a dispute about Homer's height or weight, we would not be able, even in principle, to settle the dispute one way or the other. Yet Homer surely had some particular height and weight at any given time of his life, and his height and weight seem to be matters of secular fact. Again, there are controversies in cosmological theory about the origins of the universe. These controversies *may* be unsettleable, even in principle, through the application of secular methodologies. Yet we usually consider the issue to be one of secular fact.

It is important to remember at this point that the concepts explained in this chapter, and applied subsequently to the issue of abortion, are those implicit in the Supreme Court's interpretations and applications of the Religion Clauses of the First Amendment. They are not my views, and they may not be the best views on these matters, but they are the *Court's* views. Regarding their merit, I claim merely that they are adequate for judicial interpretations of the First Amendment.

It should come as no surprise, and should occasion no reproach, that the Court's concepts of secular and religious belief are inadequate to handle appropriately such matters as Homer's height and weight or competing cosmological theories about the origins of the universe. Unless and until such matters are the subject of legislation, the Court has no need of a theory that classifies them appropriately as secular or religious. So, its theoretical incompleteness notwithstanding, the Court's concepts are adequate to its needs. According to those concepts, matters of secular fact can in principle be settled through application of secular methodologies of discovery and investigation. Of course, (almost) all such settlements are merely provisional, as new experiences, events, and technologies can usually be applied eventually to cast doubt on, or justify replacement of, settlements made at an earlier time. According to the concept implicit in the Court's First Amendment decisions, then, matters of secular fact can in principle be settled through the application of secular methodologies, but not infallibly, nor for all time.

Matters of secular value are not always settleable in the same way, even in principle and provisionally. Where values are concerned, we rely on certain generally accepted value premises. These value premises are combined with one another and with relevant premises concerning secular facts in chains of reasoning that meet publicly accepted standards of argumentation. The results are justifications for legislative initiatives designed to secure such secular values as public health and general literacy. Legislation designed to ameliorate such disvalues as fraud, assault, and toxic pollution are justified in a similar manner.

But in many situations, generally accepted value premises support opposite conclusions. Thus, for example, the values of a free press and of personal privacy can point to opposite conclusions concerning the liability of the press in civil litigation. The question is not which value is important, a free press or personal privacy. It is agreed that both are important in our secular scheme of values. But which value should be accorded more *weight* in the specific kind of situation under review? Factual uncertainty may complicate resolution of the issue because matters of secular fact are settleable in principle, but not always in practice. Even when factual uncertainty is eliminated, however, the issue may still be one on which reasonable people may differ. So where the resolution of a controversy turns on the relative weights to be assigned different values as they apply to a specific kind of situation, the matter may not be settleable, even in principle. Matters of secular value differ in this respect from matters of secular fact.

The Court's Characterizations of Secular Beliefs

Some general statements by members of the Court suggest that the foregoing account of secular beliefs accords with judicial conceptions. More important than these general statements, however, are the decisions made by the Court in First Amendment contexts. The section following this one and a section early in Chapter 5 show that the Court's applications of the Religion Clauses support the present chapter's characterizations of secular and religious beliefs.

According to the Court, beliefs can be secular even though their origin or original acceptance was influenced by religion. As Justice Brennan pointed out in *Abington School District v. Schempp,* "nearly every criminal law on the books can be traced to some religious principle or inspiration."[28] Yet the protection of people from assault, murder, and theft is a secular matter because the belief that people should be so protected is a secular belief.

Beliefs are secular, according to Brennan, when they are "interwoven . . . deeply into the fabric of our civil polity."[29] Chief Justice Burger used the same language in support of tax exemptions for religious organizations. "Few concepts," he wrote, "are more embedded in the fabric of our national life."[30] Years later, in *Marsh v. Chambers,* Burger maintained again that a government practice, originally of religious inspiration, becomes secular, and so does not violate the Establishment Clause, when it "has become part of the fabric of society."[31] The same can be said of all beliefs that are properly considered secular. They are secular because they are part of the social fabric that holds society together. They are interwoven in the manner of our interaction with one another, with physical reality, or with both. They are contained or implied in our way of getting through life, that is, in our common way of life. They enable us to act with enough cooperation and mutual understanding to maintain and (largely) perpetuate our society. Thus the values of physical health, individual liberty, and equal opportunity regardless of race, to name but a few, are part of the warp and woof of this society. So, too, are myriad propositions of science, technology, and scientific methodology presupposed in the development of the machines and the materials that pervade and structure our lives.

Beliefs *about* religion are part of the essential fabric of our society, just as are many beliefs of religious origin or inspiration. For example, we generally believe that, all other things being equal, people should not repress the religious side of their nature. Thus we encourage people through public service advertisements to engage in religious worship. More integral to the fabric of our society is belief that religion should be and remain a matter of voluntary choice. Voluntarism in matters of religion is one of the secular values underlying the Establishment Clause (the state should not force a particular religion on people) and the Free Exercise Clause (the state should accommodate, where reasonable and practical, people's voluntary religious practices). These secular beliefs about religion are discussed in Chapter 5.

Religious beliefs per se, however, are not essential parts of the fabric of our society. They are not part of the warp and woof that holds the social fabric together. People can differ on such strictly religious matters as whether or not God exists, whether or not there is a life after death, and whether or not baptism is valuable, without impairing the cooperation and mutual understanding needed for a way of life that is common in society. These beliefs may be compared, as I interpret the Court's metaphor, to optional threads that are unnecessary to maintain the social fabric's strength and endurance. They are not essential parts of the social fabric. Their loss would not endanger our way of life.

It follows that a belief may be secular in one society but not in another because people in the two societies live differently. People in North Korea may see little value in individual liberty, and those in South Korea may, on Confucian principle, value nepotism rather than equal opportunity in employment. Foraging people whose technology is simple generally do not, and certainly need not, believe, as is presupposed in our way of life, that scientific methodology is capable of discovering microorganisms and objects invisible to the naked eye.

The secular nature of a belief is relative not only to the society but also to the era in which it is entertained. A belief that is secular in a given society at one time may no longer be so at a later time. We have seen that our society was at one time built around the assumption that racial segregation is proper. We no longer make that assumption. As there are changes in the science and technology integral to our way of life, there are corresponding changes in the beliefs presupposed by our way of life. Two hundred years ago, nothing in our way of life suggested that the earth must be millions of years old. Now, our use of petroleum products, and our use of the geological sciences that aid discovery of oil reserves, make secular the belief, which is integral to the geological sciences, that the earth is millions of years old. That belief is now integral to our way of life. It underpins many of our agreements of belief, thought, and practice. These agreements enable us to act with such cooperation and understanding as is needed for our way of life to be maintained and perpetuated.

Not every society has a political constitution or a commitment to the separation of church and state. So not every society has the same reasons that we have to care about the distinction between the religious and the secular. Because we do have a Constitution, and its First Amendment contains guarantees of religious freedom, we do need to distinguish religious from secular beliefs. Since the job of interpreting the Constitution falls in the final analysis on the Supreme Court, they must make this distinction. But they are required to do so only for our society. They need to decide what beliefs are protected as religious by our Constitution at this time. Their inquiry is limited to our society (our way of life) and our time. Of course, an understanding of our time requires the placement of contemporary concerns in the context of our distinctive history and traditions.

We have seen that the Court considers secular the belief that human beings evolved from other types of organisms and that racial segregation is unjust. We have seen also that according to the Court's metaphor, those beliefs are secular that are embedded deeply in the fabric of society and are interwoven in our common way of life. We now turn to a direct consideration of the kinds of beliefs that the Court considers religious. These are beliefs not built into the fabric of society or interwoven in our common way of life. Examples and a general characterization of such beliefs are given in the next section.

The Epistemological Standard for Distinguishing Religious from Secular Belief

Epistemology is the branch of philosophy that concerns the theory of knowledge. It concerns how we know, and how we could have come to know, what we claim to know. Using belief in the existence of God as the primary (but not the only) example of a religious belief, this section shows that according to the Supreme Court, religious and secular beliefs are distinguished from one another *for constitutional purposes* primarily by epistemological considerations. Secular beliefs are those that are integral to our way of life or that can be established entirely by premises and methods of argumentation that are integral to our way of life. Religious beliefs about matters of fact either cannot be established entirely by secular premises and methods of argumentation or else, as a result of features inherent in the subject matter, arguments based on secular premises can be used both for and against such beliefs in roughly equal measure. Consequently, the accuracy of religious beliefs about matters of fact can never be established, even in principle, on secular grounds alone.

The present section is divided into two parts. The first documents the Supreme Court's acceptance of certain beliefs as religious. The sec-

ond part shows that these beliefs conform to the epistemological standard for distinguishing the religious from the secular.

Judicial Examples of Religious Beliefs

Belief in the existence of God is clearly classified by the Supreme Court
as a religious belief. A Maryland statute requiring those who hold public office to declare their belief in the existence of God was found unconstitutional in *Torcaso v. Watkins* (1961). The Supreme Court found
the statute to establish a religion.[32] The following year, as we have seen,
the Court struck down in *Engel v. Vitale* (1962) the New York law that
required the day in public schools to begin with prayer. The Court supported its contention that prayer is a religious activity by pointing out
that prayer "is a solemn avowal of divine faith."[33] Faith (belief) in the
existence of God is religious. The Court has more recently reaffirmed
this view. The Court struck down in *Edwards v. Aguillard* (1987) a
Louisiana law that required "creation science" to be taught in public
schools on an equal basis with the theory of biological evolution. The
statute mandated "that public schools present the scientific evidence to
support a theory of divine creation whenever they present the scientific
evidence to support the theory of evolution."[34] Justice Powell found this
mandate to establish religion because "concepts concerning God or a
supreme being of some sort are manifestly religious."[35] From a constitutional perspective, then, belief in the existence of God is a religious
belief and is sufficient to render religious those requirements (oath of
public office in *Torcaso*), activities (Regent's prayer in *Engel*), and theories (creation science in *Edwards*) that are tied inextricably to belief in
the existence of God.

Courts have found other beliefs to be religious as well. As we have
seen, an appellate court found Scientology to be a religion. "The fact
that it postulates no deity in the conventional sense does not preclude
its status as a religion."[36] The Court examined the theory of Dianetics
that Scientology postulates.

> The basic theory of Dianetics is that man possesses both a reactive mind
> and an analytic mind. Social problems and much human suffering . . .
> are traceable . . . to the reactive mind, which is made up of "engrams,"
> or patterns imprinted on the nervous system in moments of pain, stress
> or unconsciousness. . . . The goal of Dianetics is to make persons
> "clear," thus freeing the rational and infallible analytic mind. . . . A pro-
> cess of working toward "clear" is described as "auditing."[37]

As characterized so far, Scientology could be a secular theory of psychology and mental therapy. But the founder of Scientology considered integral to these beliefs certain claims about a person's immortal spirit. He also considered his views to be similar to those of certain Eastern religions. The Court brought these points out clearly, writing that Scientology's founder, L. Ron Hubbard, "has claimed kinship between his theories and those espoused by Eastern Religions, especially Hinduism and Buddhism. He argues that man is essentially a free and immortal spirit (a 'thetan' in Scientological terminology) which merely inhabits the 'mest body' ('mest' is an acronym of the words matter, energy, space, time)."[38] In spite of Hubbard's disavowal of all "mysticism and supernaturalism,"[39] the Court was convinced of Scientology's religious nature by the similarity between Scientology and certain Eastern religions, and by Scientology's references to the "immortal spirit" of "man."

In declaring Scientology to be a religion, the Court noted that some "curative techniques or powers are . . . religious," rather than medical. "Established religions claim for their practices the power to treat or prevent disease, or include within their hagiologies accounts of miraculous cures." Because the Court found Scientology's curative practices to be related to religious beliefs, it found those practices to be religious. "In the circumstances of this case we must conclude that the literature setting forth the theory of auditing, including the claims for curative efficacy contained therein, is religious doctrine of scientology."[40]

Malnak v. Yogi (1977) is another case in which an appellate court found a doctrine to be religious despite the absence in that doctrine of belief in the existence of God. Over the protests of its proponents, the Court found Transcendental Meditation to be based on religious beliefs. According to the Court, TM "clearly teaches and assumes that there exists and has existed eternally an unmanifested or uncreated field of life which is unbounded or infinite . . . , permeates everything . . . and is the ultimate reality of everything in the universe. This field of life . . . has unlimited power, and encompasses all knowledge."[41] Because these are religious ideas, according to the Court, they could not be taught in a public school.

We have seen, too, that the Supreme Court has more recently accepted as religious the claim that using a person's social security number can deprive that person of spiritual power and purity.[42] This belief was unrelated to any belief in the existence of God or to the belief system of any organized religion, but was nevertheless judicially recognized as religious. What concept of religious belief is guiding courts when they make decisions in this area?

GENERAL CHARACTERISTICS OF RELIGIOUS BELIEFS

Courts have on occasion provided general characterizations of religious beliefs. In *United States v. Kauten* (1943) an appellate court reviewed the statutory requirement that conscientious objection to military service be based on "religious training and belief." Writing for the court, Judge Augustus Hand maintained: "Religious belief arises from a sense of the inadequacy of reason as a means of relating the individual to his fellow-men and to his universe."[43] Within months, this view was quoted with approval by Supreme Court Justice Felix Frankfurter.[44]

The following year, Justice Douglas adopted a similar view of religious belief. Writing for the majority in *United States v. Ballard* (1944), he wrote: "Men may believe what they cannot prove. They may not be put to the proof of their religious doctrines or beliefs. Religious experiences which are as real as life to some may be incomprehensible to others. Yet the fact that they may be beyond the ken of mortals does not mean that they can be made suspect before the law."[45] Here, too, "religious belief" is associated with the "inadequacy of reason." If a belief is religious, there is no requirement that others find the belief reasonable or even comprehensible.

Religious beliefs, in other words, are those that cannot be established by publicly accepted standards of evidence and argumentation. This is the sense in which they are beyond the adequacy of reason. Reason enables people to explore, and often narrow, the areas and/or the extent of their disagreements. But this process of reasoning presupposes common ground among those who are reasoning together. They must hold in common some premises and/or some assumptions of methodology that will enable them, at least in principle, to attain agreement about premises. With sufficient commonality of premises, methodologies, or both, people can use reason to prove things to one another.

Where religious beliefs are concerned, the required commonality exists (where it exists) only among members of certain social subgroups. Within each religious subgroup (where there is commonality of premises, methodologies, or both), reasoning can occur and valid proofs can be offered. Matters remain religious, however, because the premises, methodologies, or both, that are common within the religious subgroup are not secular beliefs. They are not among the fundamental premises of fact, value, methodology, or argumentation that foster the mutual understanding and cooperation needed to sustain our society's way of life. The assumptions common among members of a religious subgroup, then, while enabling members of that subgroup to reason with one another, do not enable members of that subgroup to reason with other members of society because other members of society do not share requisite religious assumptions.

This is how religious belief is related to "the inadequacy of reason,"[46] and why people "may not be put to the proof of their religious doctrines or beliefs."[47] Reason is inadequate, and proofs cannot be required, where religious beliefs are concerned because the premises, methodologies, or both, used to reason about and prove propositions of religion are not vital for understanding and cooperation in society at large. They are matters about which people in society at large may agree to disagree. Disagreement on matters fundamental to the proof of religious propositions undercuts the adequacy of reason to establish religious beliefs.

Consider, for example, belief in the existence of God. As a paradigm of religious belief, it illustrates that a belief can be widely held and remain religious. When polled, most Americans profess belief in the existence of God. So religious beliefs are not merely those of eccentrics and very small minorities. Belief in the existence of God illustrates also that a belief can remain religious even though contrary considerations are put forward as evidence by believers and nonbelievers. "Proofs" and "disproofs" regarding the existence of gods, spirits, and a separate heavenly reality are at least as old as ancient Greek philosophy. So people can reason, and have been reasoning, about these matters, but they remain religious.

Belief in the existence of God is religious notwithstanding its popularity and a long tradition of attempted proofs, because the proofs are *inherently inconclusive* on secular grounds. The proofs are inconclusive by nature of the subject matter. Given the definition of God in the Western religious tradition, God's existence is thought by most people to be a question of fact. We saw earlier in this chapter that, in principle, disagreements about secular matters of fact can be settled. God's existence is not a secular matter of fact, then, because it is impossible in principle to prove on secular premises alone that, as a matter of fact, God does or does not exist. Our society's commonly accepted canons of evidence and argumentation cannot be used to convince someone reasoning logically from secular premises alone that God does or does not exist, as they can be used to convince people that, for example, bacteria and electrons exist, whereas Martians do not. So belief in the existence of God is religious, not secular.

There are secular beliefs of fact, too, on which there is widespread and long-standing disagreement. Earlier in the chapter we discussed belief in the deterrent effect of capital punishment. Though the controversy may never be settled, we know how publicly convincing evidence could be gathered. So our publicly accepted theory of knowledge deems the controversy amenable in principle to settlement. It is not amenable in practice because our values prohibit the kind of social experiments that thorough testing would require. The matter of God's existence, in contrast, is not amenable to settlement even in principle, according to our prevailing theories of knowledge. Regardless of value constraints, there is nothing that people could do or say to make a case for the existence of God that can withstand the force of competing considerations.

Belief in the existence of God is religious also because disagreement about it does not impair the cooperation needed to maintain our society. In our society, atheists, agnostics, and theists are co-actors in the social drama without their different beliefs about ultimate reality disturbing to a socially threatening degree their peaceful coexistence or productive cooperation. The same is true in our society of other disagreements on matters of religion. Secular matters, in contrast, are those on which agreement is more important for society's maintenance.

In sum, two general characteristics can be distilled from judicial discussions concerning the nature of religious beliefs. Such beliefs cannot be established solely by appeals to generally accepted methods of coming to know what is true and right. This is the epistemological standard for distinguishing religious from secular belief. Additionally, religious beliefs are those on which agreement is unnecessary for the cooperation required to sustain our society. They are matters on which people sharing our current way of life can agree permanently to disagree. They are not among the threads needed to hold our social fabric together. They are matters on which our society can afford to be tolerant of differences.

These two aspects of religious belief are related to one another. Where agreement is vital for social survival, people in a successful society cannot agree to disagree. So they foster agreement by adopting common fundamental premises and by employing shared canons of evidence and argumentation. They use these fundamental premises and canons of evidence and argumentation to construct experiments and arguments that provide bases in reason for common agreement. For example, because measures of public health are matters on which people must generally be able to settle disagreements, we have developed the means of arriving at such settlements. These means include common acceptance of expert judgments about, to mention just a few, the germ theory of disease, the theory of optics employed in the construction of microscopes, and statistical theories used in evaluating the effects of public health measures. In principle, expert adoption of such beliefs (and methods) enables people who generally rely on such experts to settle disagreements so that such measures as inoculation programs can proceed without major social disruption. It is no coincidence, then, that secular beliefs, defined as those on which general agreement is required for vital social cooperation, are also those that can be established by what the society considers cogent argumentation.

Religious beliefs are nonsecular. Defined epistemologically as those for which cogent argumentation based solely on secular premises is inherently unavailable, religious beliefs are, essentially, those on which agreement is unnecessary for vital social cooperation and the mutual understanding that it requires.

Controversies regarding the teaching of evolution in the public schools reveal another aspect of religious beliefs. In the first instance, religious beliefs are those *for and against* which convincing arguments based solely on secular premises are unavailable. Such, for example, are belief in the existence of God, belief that God is the author of the Bible, belief that everything in the Bible is true, and belief that the words of the Bible are to be interpreted literally. Because these beliefs are, on the epistemological standard, religious beliefs, beliefs derived from them are considered religious even when the derived beliefs diverge from the epistemological standard as stated above.

Creation science illustrates the point. It is derived from the four religious beliefs just mentioned. But it does not itself conform to the epistemological standard. According to that standard, religious beliefs are those *for and against* which there are no cogent secular arguments. They are beyond secular reason, but not opposed to it. Nevertheless, while creation science cannot be supported by secular reason, secular reason can be used in cogent arguments against it. The theory of biological evolution, which is the major alternative to the account given by creation science, is supported by the ways that our society considers appropriate for arriving at knowledge of natural history. So creation science does not, strictly speaking, conform to the epistemological standard of religious belief. Like a religious belief, it cannot be cogently supported by arguments drawn from secular premises. Unlike a religious belief, however, cogent arguments drawn from secular premises can be used against it. It is less beyond secular reason than opposed to it. Creation science is properly classified as a religious belief nevertheless, because of its close dependence on beliefs that clearly conform to the epistemological standard.

It follows that the same belief can be either a religious belief or an erroneous secular belief. The difference is made by the other beliefs on which it depends. Consider, for example, the belief that blacks are morally inferior to whites. Like the beliefs included in creation science, this belief runs counter to secular views. But if it is maintained on the basis of biblical interpretation, it is a religious belief because one or more of its essential premises are religious. If, however, it is maintained on the basis of personal observation, income statistics, and crime rates, it is an erroneous secular belief. Personal observations, income statistics and crime rates are appropriate elements in secular inquiries. So the individual's premises are secular, not religious. But secular canons of reasoning and argumentation preclude valid derivation of the conclusion from the premises. Thus the belief is secular, but erroneous.

A more complete characterization of the judicial interpretation of "religious belief," then, is the following: Religious beliefs are, for reasons inherent in the belief, incapable of being established or refuted by appeal to secular premises alone, or else they can be refuted, but are religious because of their dependence on beliefs that cannot be established or refuted. I call this "the extended epistemological standard." Because formulation of the extended standard is cumbersome, I use the ordinary standard in what follows, adverting to the extended standard only when necessary.

According to the ordinary epistemological standard, beliefs cannot be identified conclusively as religious until there is agreement about which beliefs are secular. Only after secular premises have been identified can it be determined that arguments based solely on such premises are inadequate to either establish or refute a given belief. Where secular premises are inadequate, the belief is religious.

Summary

In First Amendment contexts the Supreme Court understands the noun "religion" through its understanding of the adjective "religious." It applies the religion guarantees to groups, activities, ceremonies, practices, texts, symbols, artifacts, and beliefs that it classifies as religious. The

Court's classification rests on its definition of "religious belief" because it deems religious only religious beliefs and whatever is related to religious belief.

Religious beliefs are understood by the Court through contrast with secular beliefs. Secular beliefs are all those agreements in belief, thought, and practice necessary for the mutual understanding and cooperative interaction among people required for the society's way of life to be maintained and perpetuated. The Court divides secular beliefs into two types: beliefs about facts and beliefs about values. Controversies concerning factual beliefs are, at least in principle, settleable. We can in every case imagine, even when we do not or cannot actually perform, tests or investigations using secular methodologies and forms of reasoning that would settle the factual dispute one way or the other. Controversies concerning beliefs about secular values cannot similarly be settled by appeal to tests or investigations.

Religious beliefs are, according to the Court, those that are not secular. Because secular beliefs are agreements needed for mutual understanding and cooperation, religious beliefs, by contrasts, are opinions on which agreement is not essential. The society's way of life can be maintained and perpetuated while people agree to disagree about the subject matter of religious beliefs.

A second manner of identifying what the Court considers religious belief is epistemological; it concerns the way we justify claims to knowledge. Religious beliefs cannot be established through reasoning whose methodologies and premises are entirely secular. This is the epistemological standard for distinguishing religious from secular belief. The standard applies to beliefs both of fact and of value. According to the *ordinary* epistemological standard, factual beliefs are classified as religious when secular beliefs and methodologies cannot, even in principle, show them to be either true or false. According to the *extended* epistemological standard, beliefs that can be refuted on secular grounds may be classified as religious when they are closely associated with ordinary religious beliefs.

The Court deems religious those ceremonies, activities, practices, symbols, texts, artifacts, and groups whose basic reason for being is tied inextricably to religious beliefs. For example, a group is religious if its central tenets prominently feature religious beliefs. A text is religious if it expresses religious beliefs. A symbol is religious if it symbolizes religious beliefs, and so forth. The Court protects the free exercise, and invalidates the establishment, of religion so understood. Thus, for example, activities, practices, and ceremonies expressive of religious belief are protected by the Court under the Free Exercise Clause. Government endorsements of religious beliefs, groups, symbols, or texts are invalidated by the Court under the Establishment Clause.

The present chapter attributes the views just summarized to the Supreme Court. The chapter to follow shows that these views are implicit in the Court's decisions regarding religion and that they are sufficient to solve puzzles and difficulties noted in Chapter 3.

"Religion" in Court

THE PRECEDING CHAPTER ATTRIBUTES to the Supreme Court a particular understanding of "religion" as it appears in the First
Amendment. That understanding is summarized at the end of
Chapter 4. Court opinions were used to illustrate several, but not all of
the views there attributed to the Court. Other views can be attributed
only indirectly. For example, in no opinion (that I am aware of) does
the Court maintain explicitly that beliefs of fact and beliefs of value are
epistemologically different, that secular beliefs are agreements needed
for vital social cooperation, or that religious beliefs can be neither refuted nor confirmed on secular grounds (except for those that can be
refuted on such grounds but are called religious because of their association with other beliefs that can be neither refuted nor confirmed).
These views are attributed to the Court not because the Court states
them, but primarily because attributing them to the Court helps make
sense of what the Court has stated and decided, much as attributing
gravitational attraction to physical mass helps make sense of lunar
movements and tidal changes.

The present chapter supports the analysis given in Chapter 4. First,
it provides additional examples of Court decisions and statements that
are explained well by attributing to the Court use of the epistemological
standard for distinguishing religious from secular belief. The next two
sections defend the epistemological understanding of religion against
objections. They show that this understanding does not blur unaccepta-
bly the distinction we need to make between fanatics and the mentally
ill, on the one hand, and religious believers, on the other. Then, an
apparent conflict is resolved between the epistemological understanding

of religion and judicial recognition of secular religions. The next section shows that the analysis of "religion" provided in Chapter 4 relieves whatever tension exists between the two Religion Clauses (see Chapter 3), so dual definitions are unnecessary. The chapter concludes by reiterating a unitary definition that makes sense of every interpretation of the Religion Clauses rendered by the Court during the past fifty years.

The Epistemological Standard Applied

As we saw in the preceding chapter, the analysis given here conforms to the Supreme Court's contrasting treatment of creation science as religious and the theory of evolution as secular. The same contrast between the religious and the secular can be seen in other areas of judicial concern. The present section shows, through examples, that what I call the extended epistemological standard is used by the Court in First Amendment contexts. Consider again, for example, programs of inoculation. The value judgment that physical health is generally good is a basic value premise or postulate in our society. From this and associated basic postulates one can legitimately derive the desirability of reducing the incidence of such diseases as polio and smallpox. Socially accepted methods of gaining knowledge about medicine and disease support the belief that inoculation programs are reasonable means of reducing the incidence of these diseases. So such inoculation programs are secular. They can be supported by public funds and can be conducted in public schools without compromising the constitutional prohibition regarding the establishment of religion.

Scientology, too, claims to promote the secular goal of human health. In the words of Circuit Judge J. Skelly Wright: "Though auditing is represented primarily as a method of improving the spiritual condition of man, rather explicit benefits to bodily health are promised as well. Hubbard has asserted that arthritis, dermatitis, asthma, . . . eye trouble . . . and sinusitis are psychosomatic and can be cured, and further that tuberculosis is 'perpetuated by engrams.'"[1] Nevertheless, the scientological theory that connects "auditing" and the reduction of "engrams" to these health benefits does not accord with canons of evidence commonly used in medical sciences. Because scientologists cannot show that their knowledge is based on publicly accepted standards of knowledge acquisition, their belief in the health benefits of auditing is religious, not secular.

Transcendental Meditation is similar. It promises improvements in mental health that accord with our society's fundamental value premises. But its account of how those results are achieved involves, according to the appellate court, belief in transcendental entities and a transcendental reality. By definition, transcendental reality is beyond mundane reality. Normal canons of knowledge acquisition apply only to mundane reality. So knowledge about transcendental matters is religious, not secular, and cannot be taught in the public schools. As Justice Frankfurter wrote years earlier in a different case: "The Establishment Clause withdrew from the sphere of legitimate legislative concern and competence . . . man's belief or disbelief in the verity of some transcendental idea and man's expression in action of that belief or disbelief."[2]

The epistemological standard of religious belief can be seen also in *Bowen v. Roy*. Roy believed that using a uniquely designating social security number would impair his daughter's spiritual development. This belief cannot be supported significantly through appeal to methods of argumentation and types of evidence normally relied on in our society to establish matters of fact. In other words, like Scientology and Transcendental Meditation, Roy's belief is out of the epistemological mainstream. Accordingly, the Court properly classified it, like the others, as religious.

The contrast that the epistemological standard establishes between religious and secular beliefs is reflected well in judicial treatments of conscientious objection to military service. In *United States v. Kauten* (1943), Justice Augustus Hand maintained that for conscientious objection to be "by . . . religious training and belief," it must involve "a general scruple against 'participation in war in any form' and not merely an objection to participation in this particular war."[3] Hand considered the latter, which we now call selective conscientious objection, to stem from "a course of reasoning resulting in a conviction that a particular war is inexpedient or disastrous."[4] The reasoning that leads to such a conviction may involve considerations regarding technology, military science, geographic distance, history, or the intentions of the enemy, to name but a few. These considerations can be debated and decided according to the normal canons of reasoning and evidence used to justify policies in most areas of government concern. On the epistemological standard, such considerations are secular because the canons of reasoning and evidence are the same as those we use in debates about such matters as the effectiveness of the death penalty, the advisability of strict drug laws, the need for regulation of the banking industry, and so forth. Judge Hand came to the same conclusion. He maintained that what we now call selective conscientious objection is not objection "by religious training and belief."

The Supreme Court agreed a generation and two wars later when it considered the issue of selective conscientious objection. In *Gillette v. United States* (1970), a would-be conscientious objector, Gillette, "had stated his willingness to participate in a war of national defense . . . but declared his opposition to American military operations in Vietnam, which he characterized as 'unjust.'"[5] Justice Marshall, writing for the Court, noted: "A war may be thought 'just' or not depending on one's assessment of . . . the character of the foe, or of allies; the place the war is fought; the likelihood that a military clash will issue in benefits, of various kinds, enough to override the inevitable costs of the conflict. And so forth."[6] Having noted this, Marshall maintained that "opposition to a particular war may more likely be political and nonconscientious, than otherwise." This agrees precisely with the epistemological standard and with the opinion of Judge Hand, which Marshall cited approvingly.

What, then, is conscientious objection? It is objection based on "a general scruple," to use Judge Hand's phrase, which epistemologically takes us beyond the ambit of political and policy judgements. It goes beyond this ambit because it does not rest entirely on, and cannot be meaningfully addressed solely on the basis of, the normal canons of reason and evidence. It rests essentially on a religious belief and, to quote Judge Hand again, "religious belief arises from a sense of the inadequacy of reason"[7] (that is, reason based solely on secular premises). This is exactly the basis on which the epistemological standard would classify "a general scruple" as "a religious belief."

The conscientious objector cases illustrate, too, that insofar as the courts are concerned, no reference to transcendental reality or to any other entities unknown to secular science is required for a belief to be religious. The courts in *Kauten* and *Gillette* consider beliefs to be religious on the basis of what they lack, convincing justifications on entirely secular grounds. A "general scruple" lacks such a justification, and so is religious (*Kauten*). The belief that a *particular* war is immoral, unwise, or improvident is justified, if at all, on secular (moral and political) grounds, and so it is not a religious belief (*Gillette*). Thus the distinction between religious and secular beliefs is epistemological. It does not turn ultimately, or in general, on the nature of entities referred to by beliefs.

Another case concerning military matters supports the epistemological standard. In 1983 some activists opposed to nuclear armaments vandalized a B-52 bomber. In their defense they claimed that "there has arisen a 'national religion of nuclearism . . . in which the bomb is the new source of salvation'"[8] and nuclear weapons are sacred objects. According to the activists, property-protection statutes designed to protect these sacred objects advance the religion of nuclearism. Because these laws support a religion, they are unconstitutional. They establish a religion, which the First Amendment prohibits. So acts of vandalism that contravene the property-protection statutes are legal, since the statutes they violate are unconstitutional. (The reader will please note that I did not make up the preposterous suggestion that the protection of religious property could constitute an establishment of religion.)

The appellate court that had the patience to hear this case pointed out that "many nuclear weapons proponents . . . believe that our nuclear weapons program is a means to prevent nuclear war."[9] Opponents of nuclear weapons make an opposite political judgement:

> In essence, then, antinuclear protesters . . . believe that nuclear weapons
> have no purpose but destruction, while pronuclear supporters believe
> that nuclear weapons help to keep the peace. The two sides in the nu-
> clear debate thus differ primarily in their perception of the way the
> world works, not necessarily in their ultimate concern for peace. This
> difference we hold to be one of political judgement, not religious belief.[10]

Again, because the claims on both sides are about "the way the world works," they can be debated according to the normal canons of argument and evidence that we apply to political matters. So according to the appellate court, the issue is secular, not religious, for reasons identical to those captured by the epistemological standard. (Perhaps for other purposes, in another context, nuclearism could be considered a religion. But that is outside the scope, and does not affect the claims, of the present work.)

The epistemological standard helps to explain also the Supreme Court decision in *Allegheny County v. ACLU.* The American Civil Liberties Union (ACLU) claimed that two holiday displays violated the Establishment Clause. The Court agreed with the ACLU that a creche placed on the Grand Staircase of the courthouse violated the Establishment Clause. Writing for the Court, Justice Blackmun contended: "There is no doubt . . . that the creche itself is capable of communicating a religious message. Indeed, the creche in this lawsuit uses words, as well as the picture of the nativity scene. . . . 'Glory to God in the Highest!' says the angel in the creche—Glory to God because of the birth of Jesus. This praise of God in Christian terms is indisputably religious."[11]

The majority ruled that "the government . . . may not observe . . . a Christian holy day by suggesting that people praise God for the birth of Jesus."[12] We can see implicit in this ruling the epistemological standard for distinguishing between the religious and the secular. The miraculous birth of Jesus and its relationship to God's plan for human salvation are matters whose truth cannot be established solely by appeal to canons of reasoning and evidence used in science, social science, or daily life.

The Court reached the opposite conclusion about the other holiday display. It consisted of a large Christmas tree, a large Chanukah menorah, and a sign that "states that during the holiday season the city salutes liberty."[13] The Court concluded that the "overall display must be understood as conveying the city's secular recognition of different traditions for celebrating the winter-holiday season."[14] Thus, according to the Court, the display's primary message is the endorsement of liberty and diversity. As noted in Chapter 4, those are secular values in our society. They are among the values that form the common ground for social interaction. According to the epistemological standard, therefore, they are secular. The Court agreed. So in *Allegheny County v. ACLU* the Court considered religious what the epistemological standard deems religious, and secular what the epistemological standard deems secular.

Cults and Crazies

I have now explained the epistemological standard and cited judicial opinions to show that it is actually used in constitutional law. My articulation of the standard simply makes explicit what has long been implicit in judicial opinions spanning nearly fifty years. But people may object that the standard yields absurd results in a variety of cases. In particular, people may object that the standard would afford to dangerous cults the protection of the religion guarantees, and would forbid protective, parentalistic government intervention in the lives of the mentally ill. The present section explains and responds to these two objections.

The first objection focuses on currently unpopular cults. According to the account given above, if a group's beliefs do not rest on premises or methodologies that form the epistemological mainstream in our society, those beliefs are religious, and the group is a religious group. So a group can ensure that it enjoys the protections of the religion guarantees merely by making central to its doctrines beliefs whose truth cannot be cogently supported or refuted by appeal to secular premises. Then it can attach to these religious beliefs any number of absurd claims. According to the extended epistemological standard, these absurd claims are religious by virtue of their dependence on religious beliefs. Finally, under cover of the First Amendment, the group can take people's money under the guise of providing miracle cures, or get people to work for little or no wages on communes while some self-styled guru gets rich.

This unflattering characterization of the implications of the epistemological and extended epistemological standards is largely correct. But in fact those standards have been our law for nearly fifty years, and for good reason. The reason was well expressed by Justice Douglas in *United States v. Ballard*. That case arose because Guy Ballard had established the "I Am" movement. He claimed that he "had been selected and thereby designated by the alleged 'ascertained masters,' [including] Saint Germain, as a divine messenger."[15] He maintained that he and two relatives "had, by reason of supernatural attainments, the power to heal persons of ailments and diseases."[16] Prosecutors skeptical of the truth of these claims charged Ballard with fraudulent use of the mail.

Justice Douglas maintained for the Supreme Court that the truth of these religious claims was beyond the purview of any court or government body. An official inquiry into their truth would amount to a heresy trial, and "heresy trials are foreign to our Constitution."[17] They must remain so. Douglas wrote: "The miracle of the New Testament, the Divinity of Christ, life after death, the power of prayer are deep in the religious convictions of many. If one could be sent to jail because a jury in a hostile environment found those teachings false, little indeed would be left of religious freedom."[18] Thus it is constitutional law, and must remain so if religious liberty is to be maintained, that people may believe whatever they want, and may sacrifice time and money pursuant to their beliefs. The only limits are those justified by secular considerations, including considerations regarding public health, child welfare, property rights and interpersonal violence. These are secular values, and values of such importance in our secular culture as to justify limiting the freedom to act on religious belief. So, for example, regardless of religious motivation, people are not allowed literally to steal from others or to assault them. These protections, which apply generally, cannot be escaped under cover of the First Amendment's Religion Clauses.

In sum, the clauses' protection of religious cults maintains religious freedom, which includes the freedom to give away time and money voluntarily, but does not include the freedom to jeopardize significantly the safety and well-being of the general public. This is the implication of the epistemological standards (i.e., the epistemological standard combined with the extended epistemological standard) of religious belief. It accords with Supreme Court decisions and with our tradition of tolerating religious pluralism.

The other criticism considered in this section concerns the mentally ill. It may be objected that according to the epistemological standards of religious belief, mentally ill people may be denied the help and protection they need. Consider a person who believes that he is acting under divine inspiration, or that he is the reincarnation of Moses or Jesus. According to the epistemological standard of religious belief, such beliefs are religious precisely because they are so outlandish. The person's activities are thus protected by the First Amendment's Religion Clauses. The Free Exercise Clause gives people freedom from some constraints that are applicable to most other people. For example, as we saw in *Thomas v. Review Board*,[19] a person who is led by religious conviction to quit his job must be given unemployment benefits. Others who quit work are usually denied such benefits. In *Bowen v. Roy*,[20] we saw that people who refuse for religious reasons to supply the government with an appropriate social security number may not be denied government benefits, whereas some others who refuse to supply such a number may be denied benefits. The objector worries that such unusual deference to the wishes of those acting out of religious conviction will hamper the efforts of people whose job it is to ameliorate the effects of mental illness.

This worry is unfounded. People's freedoms of speech and association, for example, are as vigorously protected by the Constitution (as currently interpreted) as is freedom of religion. Yet the Constitution does not cripple efforts to help the mentally ill, even though these constitutional guarantees, like the religion guarantees, afford to people special protections against government interference. The reason is that all such special protections apply in full force only to competent adults. They generally apply to minors in lesser degree, and to the severely mentally ill only through a guardian. Legal powers associated with guardianship enable guardians of the severely mentally ill to ensure that the ill receive proper help even if their illness includes religious belief (such as belief that one is Jesus reincarnate). Of course, it is not always easy to determine whose condition conforms to society's concept of mental illness or when the degree of illness warrants assigning guardianship to another person. But these problems are no greater with regard to the religion guarantees than with regard to other constitutional guarantees, and they are no greater on the epistemological standard of religious belief than on any other definition of what is for constitutional purposes considered a religion.

Secular Religions

Another ground for rejecting the epistemological standard is the claim that the standard does not reflect accurately judicial determinations of what constitutes a religion. According to the epistemological standard, the Court's use of the term "religion" depends fundamentally on the religious nature of the tenets involved. A religion contains beliefs, and those beliefs include some, of central importance, which are religious. Religious beliefs are those that are not secular. They do not rest on, or conform to, what passes in our society for common sense, scientific truth, or commonly accepted basic moral values. Religious beliefs thus go beyond the bounds of what we in our society accept as knowledge.

According to the objector, this account is a deficient explication of the *constitutional* concept of religion for two reasons. First, courts sometimes consider such factors as organizational structure and typical behavior patterns, as well as belief system, when determining whether or not a group is religious. My account, according to the objector, has improperly excluded all considerations except those related to belief systems. Second, the objector maintains, my account requires that a religion feature as centrally important one or more beliefs that do not conform to ordinary epistemological standards. The objector claims that there are important exceptions. In particular, Ethical Culture and Secular Humanism have been recognized by courts, including the Supreme Court, as religions. But these groups reject all epistemologically odd beliefs. So my account is wrong when it says that such beliefs characterize all groups that the courts consider religious.

I begin by addressing the second objection. It stems originally from two decisions made in 1957 by appellate courts. In both cases, the issue before the court was the eligibility of a group for tax-exempt status as a religious organization. Neither the Washington Ethical Society nor the Fellowship of Humanity was committed doctrinally to belief in the existence of God, and it was on this ground that taxing bodies sought to deny them tax-exempt status. Both appellate courts ruled that the organizations qualify for the tax exemption even though neither adhered doctrinally to any belief that is religious on the epistemological standard. So two appellate decisions run counter to my claim that courts classify as religious only those groups whose doctrines feature epistemologically religious beliefs.

But the Washington Ethical Society, the Fellowship of Humanity, and similar secular humanist organizations are accepted judicially as religious for tax purposes only, and only because they meet two conditions: Their good works make them assets to the community, and their organizational structure and typical patterns of member interaction resemble those of undoubtedly religious groups. These points were well expressed by then Judge (later chief justice of the Supreme Court) Warren Burger in *Washington Ethical Society v. District of Columbia.* His short opinion points to the fact that the Ethical Society holds regular Sunday services and Sunday school classes for children, it has "Leaders" who preach and minister to the members, conducting services for naming, marrying and burying members. "The services of the organization held at regular hours each Sunday have the forms of worship service with Bible readings, sermons, singing, and meditation familiar in services of many formal or traditional church organizations."[21] Thus the organizational structure and typical patterns of member interaction are like those of traditional religious groups.

These factors alone would not necessarily be sufficient, according to Burger, to justify concluding that the Ethical Society "is in an ecclesiastical sense a religious society or a church." But that broader issue was not before the Court. The Court was called on to decide whether the society qualified for a tax exemption under a statute designed "to grant support to elements in the community regarded as good for the community. . . . The exemption of buildings belonging to 'religious corporations or societies' is in a context of exemption to art galleries, libraries, public charities, hospitals, schools and colleges, and many named organizations."[22] The Ethical Society qualifies for an exemption, then, primarily because it is dedicated to good work. Just as an art gallery or library can qualify for the exemption without being religious in its belief system, the Ethical Society can qualify, regardless of its secular belief system. Its organization and activities are like that of a church, making it an asset to the community in the same manner as a church. And, like libraries and art galleries, churches serve the public good in ways that the legislature decided to reward with a tax exemption.

Burger carefully avoids suggesting that the Ethical Society is a religious organization within the meaning of the First Amendment's Religion Clauses. That is the point of his concluding observation: "The question before us now is not broadly whether petitioner is in an ecclesiastical sense a religious society or a church, but narrowly whether under this particular statute it is qualified for tax exemption."[23]

Burger's opinion is not unique in its separation of tax-exemption issues from First Amendment issues. *Founding Church of Scientology v. United States* also separates these issues. In that case, however, the belief system was held to be religious (as we have seen), but the organization was denied tax-exempt status. "The Commissioner found that a large part of the activities of the Founding Church was profit making in nature, and that some of its net earnings enured to the benefit of L. Ron Hubbard."[24] So, even though members of the church "are entitled to the protection of the free exercise clause,"[25] the church itself is not tax exempt as a religious organization.

The same view was held by the Supreme Court in *Bob Jones University v. United States*.[26] The beliefs of the group supporting the university were held to be religious, but the university was denied the tax exemption available to most religious groups. The denial was predicated on the university's segregationist rules, which were held to be against public policy. The opinion in the case, also written by Burger, underlines the point that he made nearly a quarter of a century earlier in the *Washington Ethical Society* case. Religious groups are granted tax exempt status not because they are religious in the epistemological sense but because, without seeking private profit, they do work that is considered good for the community. This is what qualifying religious groups have in common, for tax purposes, with not-for-profit hospitals, libraries, and art galleries. Their tax-exempt status is not related to their qualification for First Amendment protection under the Religion Clauses. Groups may qualify for First Amendment protection as religious groups and fail to be tax exempt as religious groups (the Founding Church of Scientology and Bob Jones University), and they may be tax exempt as religious organizations without necessarily enjoying First Amendment protection as religious groups (Washington Ethical Society and Fellowship of Humanity). So the distinction urged here between the question of tax exemption and that of religious freedom is anchored firmly in judicial opinions.

This distinction is essential where organizations of Ethical Culture and Secular Humanism are concerned. These organizations receive tax exemptions as religious groups, but they cannot be considered religions for purposes of the First Amendment. I next demonstrate this with regard to each of the two Religion Clauses, beginning with the Establishment Clause.

The discussion in Chapter 3 of *Grove v. Mead School District* showed that problems of establishment arise when Secular Humanism is considered a religion for Establishment Clause purposes. The same is true of any group, such as an Ethical Culture society, whose doctrines are composed exclusively of secular beliefs. If these secular beliefs are considered religious for Establishment Clause purposes, then they cannot be taught in public schools. This would decimate the content of the public school curriculum.

In order to avoid this intolerable result, the appellate court that decided the *Grove* case proposed two different meanings for the term "religion" as it appears in the First Amendment. A restrictive meaning would be applied to issues of establishment. Secular Humanism, Ethical Culture, and other entirely secular belief systems would be excluded from the definition of religion where establishment is at issue, thereby avoiding a conflict between the Establishment Clause and the presentation of secular subjects in public schools. Public school instruction in secular subjects would not constitute an impermissible establishment of religion because, where the Establishment Clause is concerned, such subjects would not be religious. But some of these same subjects could still be religious where the Free Exercise Clause is concerned. The *Grove* Court maintained "a generous functional (even idiosyncratic) definition best serves free exercise values."[27] Secular Humanism, the court suggests, could be a religion under this broader definition that is used in free exercise cases.

The appellate court failed to see that equally insuperable problems result from allowing secular beliefs to be deemed religious for free exercise purposes. Consider, for example, the secular belief that a certain war is unwise or unjust. This secular view may be propounded from the pulpit of an Ethical Culture society. If the view were on that ground designated religious for free exercise purposes, someone opposed on grounds of national policy to participation in a particular war would have to be considered a religiously motivated conscientious objector. Thus, in general, selective conscientious objectors would have to be considered, as currently they are not, to have religious motivation second to none. The Constitution would require that selective conscientious objection be allowed if any conscientious objection is allowed. We saw earlier in this chapter that this does not accord with the prevailing interpretation of the Constitution.

More important, absurdities would result if secular beliefs, insofar as they enter into moral judgments, were to receive the protection that the Free Exercise Clause affords to religious beliefs. Consider the person who quits work at the Hostess Cupcake factory pursuant to a secular belief that the chemicals used as preservatives in the cupcakes are harmful to people's health. Though she quit work on moral grounds pursuant to a secular belief, she would be as entitled to state unemployment benefits as was the man who quit work because his pacifist views conflicted with the requirement that he make gun turrets, and the woman who quit because her religion forbade work on Saturday. States would be hard pressed to meet the demands for unemployment compensation of all those who could come up with a secular belief to justify quitting their jobs. And consider the Social Security Administration. We have seen that Mr. Roy could refuse on grounds of religious belief to fill in his daughter's social security number on applications for public assistance. If secular beliefs were accorded the same free exercise protection as are religious beliefs, people who believe, for example, that the social security system is unnecessary, harmful, or wasteful would be able, like Roy, to refuse cooperation with the system. The Free Exercise Clause would afford constitutional protection for failure to conform to many legal requirements related to social security.

The general point is this. The Free Exercise Clause often allows people with religious views that conflict with legal requirements to be exempted from those requirements. If secular beliefs are considered religious in free exercise contexts, the class of people with beliefs entitling them to exemption will be so large as to make such exemptions impractical. So continued use of the Free Exercise Clause requires distinguishing secular from religious beliefs and affording the protection of the Free Exercise Clause to religious beliefs only. This accords with judicial practice. So the secular beliefs of the Washington Ethical Society, the Fellowship of Humanity, and similar organizations are not religious in any First Amendment context. They do not fall within the purview of either the Establishment Clause or the Free Exercise Clause. Such organizations are religious, if at all, only within the meaning of certain tax laws.

I pointed out in the introductory chapter that no interpretation of the Constitution can agree with everything that the Supreme Court justices have said, since some Court opinions contradict others. It is for this reason that I must disagree with Justice Black's statement in *Torcaso v. Watkins* (discussed in Chapter 3 or 4) that Ethical Culture and Secular Humanism are religions. Writing in 1961, he referred to the tax-exemption cases of 1957 and seemed to be unaware of the need to confine the results of those decisions to tax law.[28] He seemed to be unaware of the insuperable difficulties attendant upon the application of the First Amendment Religion Clauses to the secular beliefs associated with these groups. But anyone can make a mistake. This error is all the more to be excused as it is contained in a dictum, not in the ratio of his decision. (The ratio is the part of a decision that explains the essential steps in reasoning that justify the conclusion reached. Any additional comments in the opinion are dicta.) The case in which Black referred to Ethical Culture and Secular Humanism as religions concerned a Maryland law that required holders of public office to declare belief in the existence of God. No pronouncement about Ethical Culture or Secular Humanism was needed to determine the invalidity of Maryland's requirement. So Black's comment was dictum, not ratio. In fact, Black's dictum appears in a footnote. It is best ignored.

So far, we have considered one of the objections introduced (long ago) at the beginning of this section. I now turn to the other objection. It is objected that in *First Amendment contexts* courts do sometimes consider such factors as organizational structure and typical behavior patterns, as well as belief system, when determining whether or not a group should be considered religious. The appellate courts in *Malnak v. Yogi*[29] and *Africa v. Commonwealth of Pennsylvania*,[30] for example, do treat organizational structure as relevant in First Amendment contexts. But I maintain that these courts failed to recognize the Supreme Court's use of the epistemological standard. Beliefs are fundamental to Supreme Court determinations regarding the application of the Religion Clauses. The courts in *Malnak* and *Africa* do not entirely disagree, as their decisions are based entirely (*Malnak*) or primarily (*Africa*) on the belief systems, not the organizational structures, of the groups in question. But the courts in these cases maintained that organizational structure could be relevant to a determination that a group is religious, and I regard this as deviating from Supreme Court precedents. I believe that, like Justice Black, these courts were influenced by tax-exemption cases and overlooked the important distinction between the meaning of "religion" in the First Amendment and in *statutes* granting *tax exemptions*.

Tensions between the Religion Clauses

The preceding section cleared away a few apparent difficulties. The problem of secular religions was dealt with by distinguishing between "religion" in tax laws and "religion" in the First Amendment. Only the former can have belief systems that are entirely secular. Failure to observe the distinction between tax exemption and First Amendment contexts accounts also for courts sometimes thinking that a group's organizational structure is relevant in First Amendment contexts to its classification as religious.

When secular belief systems are excluded from First Amendment protection, only one problem stands in the way of a unitary definition of First Amendment "religion." This is the tension some people believe to exist between the two Religion Clauses. The remainder of this section reviews the argument given in Chapter 3 that this tension exists. The dual definition approach to dealing with this tension is then explained and criticized. Finally, the accommodation approach, which eliminates the problem, is explained and shown to reflect the Court's longstanding position.

It was argued in Chapter 3 that a tension exists between the two Religion Clauses. The Free Exercise Clause mandates that special treatment be given to those who act pursuant to religious beliefs. For example, people who refuse on religious grounds to work on Saturday may not be denied state unemployment benefits if they are fired as a result of their refusal.[31] But, people fired because they refused on grounds of personal preference or convenience to work on Saturday may be denied state unemployment benefits. Children who refuse on religious grounds to say the Pledge of Allegiance in public schools must be excused, but those who wish to miss the Pledge so they can sleep longer in the morning may not be excused.[32] In many ways, then, the Free Exercise Clause works in favor of those whose actions are pursuant to religious beliefs. But how can such favoritism be reconciled with the Establishment Clause? Every government concession to free exercise of religion would seem to violate the neutrality between religion and nonreligion required by the Establishment Clause.

As explained in Chapter 3, one approach to solving this problem involves attributing two different meanings to "religion" in the First Amendment, a restricted meaning for establishment purposes and a more expansive meaning in free exercise contexts. This approach has just been discussed, and rejected, as a solution to the problem of allegedly secular religions. We found that insuperable difficulties attend the classification of secular belief systems as religious, regardless of the Religion Clause in question. But the dual definition approach has been advanced also to address the problem of the alleged tension between the two Religion Clauses. Because this is a different problem, it is worth reviewing the dual definition approach to show that here, too, the approach does not work and is not necessary.

According to the dual definition approach, when a person like Mr. Roy refuses out of religious belief to cooperate with the Social Security

Administration, his daughter should continue to receive government benefits. Roy is thus guaranteed free exercise of his religion. This concession on the part of the government does not constitute an impermissible establishment of religion because, on the approach we are now exploring, "religion" has a narrower meaning in establishment contexts. According to this narrower meaning, "religion" refers only to organized religions. This establishment meaning is so narrow that it excludes Roy's belief, since his belief was not a tenet of any organized religion. If Roy's belief is not religious from the establishment point of view, then concessions to that belief cannot constitute an establishment of religion. Thus, according to this line of thought, the tensions that exist between the two Religion Clauses can be eliminated by assuming that religion has a narrower meaning in establishment than in free exercise contexts.

I now show that this dual definition approach does not relieve tension between the Religion Clauses. It does not work because concessions to religious belief that are mandated by the Free Exercise Clause often concern beliefs undoubtedly religious for Establishment Clause purposes as well. Jehovah's Witnesses can quit work in order to avoid violating their Saturday sabbath and still receive unemployment benefits. Most others who quit work have no constitutional right to receive unemployment benefits. Surely we cannot deny the religious nature of Jehovah's Witness' belief that God forbids work on Saturday. Surely this belief is religious for purposes of the Establishment Clause. We would not let a Jehovah's Witness teacher instruct public school students in this belief. The same can be said of the Jehovah's Witness belief that interferes with their participation in the Pledge of Allegiance. It follows from their interpretation of the Bible.[33] Beliefs having no warrant other than biblical authority are clearly religious, and they are religious in establishment contexts no less than in free exercise contexts. For example, public school instruction in creation science violates the Establishment Clause because the only warrant for belief in creation science is biblical. Thus the tension between the Religion Clauses is not resolved by saying that concessions made to religion for free exercise purposes concern what does not count as religion in establishment contexts. In many cases, the belief to which free exercise concession is made is also a religious belief for Establishment Clause purposes. Can these concessions be made without the government violating the neutrality between religion and nonreligion that is (usually thought by the Court to be) required by the Establishment Clause?

Fortunately, the Supreme Court has a ready solution to this problem. The required government neutrality between religion and non-religion (the Establishment Clause) either incorporates or is qualified by the (Free Exercise Clause) requirement that religious beliefs be *accommodated*. This is the accommodation analysis championed most recently by Justice O'Connor, but endorsed for some decades in nearly identical terms by other Supreme Court justices.

The general idea is this: Government neutrality with regard to religion does not mean hostility toward religion. Failure to accommodate those whose religious needs are jeopardized by government actions would constitute government hostility to religion, which is not true neutrality. True (Establishment Clause) neutrality requires, rather than forbids, the accommodation of religious beliefs.

The requirement of such accommodation can be read into the Establishment Clause because that clause is conjoined with the Free Exercise Clause. The latter clearly requires the government to treat those with religious claims in some ways more favorably than those whose claims are based on other kinds of considerations. Because we are guaranteed free exercise specifically of religion, but, say, not of our preferred sleep patterns, the Constitution requires that children with religious objections be excused from the morning Pledge of Allegiance, but not those who wish merely to sleep longer in the morning. Similarly, people who refuse on religious grounds to work on Saturdays should be treated more favorably than those who refuse to work because they like to go hiking on Saturdays. The Constitution guarantees free exercise of religion, not of recreation. Regardless of the particular meaning attached to "religion," then, special accommodation of religious beliefs (whatever they may be) is inherent in the Free Exercise Clause. Since that clause is conjoined with the Establishment Clause, to say that such accommodation violates the Establishment Clause is to say that the two Religion Clauses are inherently contradictory. Any such reading of the First Amendment is uncharitable to the point of perversity. Interpretations that make sense of a document are generally to be preferred to those that render it self-contradictory. So there is excellent reason to interpret the Establishment Clause as requiring or allowing, rather than precluding, the government's accommodation of religious belief.

Some of these ideas were expounded by Justice Douglas in 1952 in *Zorach v. Clauson*, where the Establishment Clause was alone at issue. Writing for the Court, Douglas was defending the constitutionality of a New York law that permitted schools, upon parental request, to release students from regular classes so they could participate in religious instruction away from school. Douglas admitted that this law "encourages religious instruction." It "accommodates the public service to . . . spiritual needs."[34] But the state may do this. "To hold that it may not would be to find in the Constitution a requirement that the government show a callous indifference to religious groups. That would be preferring those who believe in no religion over those who do believe." This, he maintained, is not required by the Constitution. "We find no constitutional requirement which makes it necessary for government to be hostile to religion."[35]

This accommodation analysis was applied in 1963 by Justice Brennan to the relationship between the two Religion Clauses. He wrote, "Nothing in the Establishment Clause forbids the application of legislation having purely secular ends in such a way as to alleviate burdens upon the free exercise of an individual's religious beliefs." He calls this "accommodation," which he justified by noting that "the First Amendment commands not official hostility toward religion, but only a strict neutrality in matters of religion."[36]

In a different case, decided the same day, Justice Stewart conveyed the same message. He wrote: "I think that the guarantee of religious liberty embodied in the Free Exercise Clause affirmatively requires government to create an atmosphere of hospitality and accommodation to individual belief or disbelief."[37] Writing for the Court in 1970, Chief Justice Burger maintained: "Adherence to the policy of neutrality that derives from an accommodation of the Establishment and Free Exercise Clauses has prevented the kind of involvement that would tip the balance toward government control of churches or government restraint on religious practice."[38]

Justice O'Connor is of the same opinion. She wrote in 1985: "Government pursues Free Exercise Clause values when it lifts a government-imposed burden on the free exercise of religion. If a statute falls within this category, then the standard Establishment Clause test should be modified accordingly."[39] O'Connor differs from the others only in the meaning that she attached to the word "neutrality." Whereas Douglas, Brennan, and Stewart consider the religious neutrality required by the Establishment Clause to incorporate the accommodation required by the Free Exercise Clause, O'Connor thinks that true religious neutrality precludes such accommodation. So, in order to make the two Religion Clauses consistent with one another, she maintains that the Establishment Clause does not require complete neutrality. "The standard Establishment Clause test should be modified" away from complete neutrality in order to allow for the kind of accommodation required by the Free Exercise Clause. The end result is exactly the same. The Establishment Clause is consistent with the accommodation of specifically religious beliefs. Some say this is inherent in the meaning of Establishment Clause neutrality (Douglas, Brennan and Stewart). O'Connor considers this inherent in the Establishment Clause, which should not be interpreted to require complete neutrality. The difference concerns the meaning of "neutrality," not the meaning of the First Amendment.

The Unitary Definition of "Religion"

Having dispelled the appearance of tension between the two Religion Clauses, the way is now clear for a unitary definition of religion in the First Amendment. I have argued that First Amendment contexts require adjectival determinations regarding religion. Courts must determine whether or not a given activity, text, symbol, group, and so forth is religious. These determinations rest ultimately on decisions about which beliefs are religious, since all religious activities, ceremonies, texts, symbols, groups, and the like are religious because of their connection to beliefs that are religious.

Beliefs are designated religious on epistemological grounds. Religious beliefs regarding matters of fact are those that do not conform either to common sense or to the methodologies that underlie accomplishments in science, social science, and technology. Religious beliefs regarding matters of value are those that do not accord with the major values on which our society, and government legislation, generally rest. Religious beliefs are thus defined by contrast with secular beliefs. Secular beliefs are agreements needed for the cooperation and mutual understanding required to maintain and (largely) perpetuate our society. Religious beliefs are those whose truth cannot be established or refuted by arguments or demonstrations that employ only secular beliefs as premises. By extension, beliefs that can be refuted on secular grounds but are associated with religious beliefs are also deemed religious.

There is no limit to religious beliefs except that they be epistemologically distinct from secular beliefs. So beliefs do not have to concern God, a Supreme Being, an afterlife, extratemporal consequences, a transcendental reality, or ultimate concerns to be religious. Neither content nor function makes a belief religious. Beliefs are religious when, and only when, they can derive little or no support from our society's secular belief system (which includes many values of religious origin).

This understanding of religious belief, and consequently of religion, is the same for the Establishment and Free Exercise Clauses. The Establishment Clause forbids government sponsorship or adoption of a religious belief. So far as sponsorship is concerned, the government must be neutral in its treatment of competing religious beliefs, and in its treatment of religious beliefs versus agnosticism, skepticism, or rejection of those beliefs. The government's required neutrality must be displayed in its treatment of groups, activities, symbols, texts, claims, ceremonies, and so forth related to religious beliefs.

The Free Exercise Clause forbids undue government interference with activities related to religious beliefs. The government must especially accommodate such activities. This is either part of the meaning of Establishment Clause neutrality (because to accommodate is not to sponsor, adopt, or endorse) or a deviation from neutrality imbedded in the Establishment Clause. In any case, the religious beliefs of which the Free Exercise Clause requires accommodation are the same as those among which the Establishment Clause (generally) requires neutrality. Of course, only relatively popular religious beliefs, such as those concerning the Bible or belief in the existence of God, are likely to be embodied in legislation, which, for this reason, violates the Establishment Clause. A very unusual belief, such as one concerning the spiritual dangers of using social security numbers, is unlikely to be incorporated in legislation, and so is unlikely to be involved in Establishment Clause controversies. But whether popular or unusual, and regardless of the Religion Clause at issue, all beliefs that the Court considers religious are so considered because they meet the same epistemological standard for distinguishing the religious from the secular.

Using this unitary definition of religion, the next chapter argues that legislation aimed at preserving the lives of fetuses younger than twenty-one weeks violates the Establishment Clause.

CHAPTER 6

Fetal Personhood as Religious Belief

WE HAVE SEEN that according to the Supreme Court, "religion" in the First Amendment refers primarily to religious belief, and religious belief is identified through an epistemological standard. This chapter maintains that only on the basis of such religious belief can personhood, a right to life, intrinsic value, or inherent worth be attributed to fetuses twenty weeks or younger (which I refer to as "young fetuses"). So laws whose purpose or primary effect is protecting the lives of young fetuses violate the Establishment Clause of the First Amendment. By officially endorsing, and enforcing, a religious belief, such laws constitute what the Supreme Court considers an establishment of religion.

In order to sustain this thesis I examine the structure and epistemology of arguments about the existence of God, when God's existence is viewed as a matter of fact. The structure of such arguments rests on the interplay of considerations favoring and disfavoring belief that God exists. Epistemologically, the belief is religious because the issue cannot be resolved through recourse to secular considerations alone. The next section shows that arguments about the personhood and right to life of young fetuses are structurally and epistemologically identical to arguments about the existence of God. So beliefs about the personhood and right to life of young fetuses are religious beliefs.

In the following sections I consider and then reply to three different kinds of objections. I answer Justice White's worry that if beliefs about young fetuses are religious, beliefs about the personhood of fetuses at any stage of gestation are equally religious. If such beliefs were religious, then fetuses on the eve of birth could not be officially declared persons and given legal protection. I show that this worry is groundless because there are secular reasons for attributing personhood and a right to life to twenty-eight week fetuses.

Next, I address the following concern. If the humanity of young fetuses cannot be determined *one way or the other* on secular grounds alone, then such fetuses *may* be persons (just as God *may* exist, even though this cannot be established on secular grounds alone). Where there is uncertainty, the objection continues, caution is appropriate. Abortion should be illegal because it may be murder. I argue, however, that laws violate the Establishment Clause when their goal is the reduction of risks, such as the risk of murder in the case of abortion, that exist only on religious premises.

Finally, I argue against a view put forward by Kent Greenawalt. Greenawalt assimilates issues regarding the intrinsic value or inherent worth of young fetuses to issues regarding environmental preservation and animal protection. He maintains that although religious beliefs influence judgments on these matters, they are all proper subjects for legislation. I maintain that Greenawalt has confused issues where religion may matter, such as those concerning environmental preservation and animal protection, with issues that are purely a matter of religion, such as those concerning the humanity of the fetus and the existence of God. Political judgments about many secular concerns may properly be influenced by religious beliefs. These include judgments about the value or worth of animals and the environment. But where young fetuses are concerned, there is no secular issue to begin with, so laws reflecting religiously inspired judgments about the intrinsic value or inherent worth of young fetuses violate the Establishment Clause.

Before beginning the chapter's main argument, I redeem a pledge made in Chapter 1. I there promised to provide an alternative to the privacy rationale that the Court employed in its review of anti-contraception statutes. Accordingly, I now explain the Court's understanding of the Establishment Clause and relate that understanding to laws prohibiting the use or distribution of contraceptives. I maintain that such laws violate the Establishment Clause because, like laws promoting "creation science," they exist primarily to reconcile the law with an interpretation of the Bible.

Anti-Contraception Laws and the Establishment Clause

I argued in Chapter 1 that the Supreme Court provided inadequate rationales for its decisions in leading cases concerning the use and sale of contraceptives. This section reviews those rationales and the reasons for their inadequacy before providing firmer foundations in the Establishment Clause for the results reached in those cases. I support the results reached by the Court, but on different rationales.

In *Griswold v. Connecticut* (1965) the Court struck down a law that prohibited the use of contraceptives. Justice Douglas argued that the law infringed unduly on people's right of privacy in "the sacred precincts of marital bedrooms."[1] This rationale is suspect because it employs a Liberal view of constitutional interpretation. It interprets the Constitution as guaranteeing a general right of privacy, whereas no such general right is announced in the document. This weakness is compounded in *Eisenstadt v. Baird* (1972)[2] where the Court invalidated a law prohibiting the sale of contraceptives. The sale of a commodity is a public transaction, not a private act. Invalidating the law on grounds of a general constitutional right of privacy is defective, first, because there is no such general right in the Constitution, and second, even if privacy in some sense is constitutionally protected, the invalidated law did not concern privacy in any such sense.

The statutes invalidated in these cases were nevertheless unconstitutional, I maintain, because they contravened the First Amendment prohibition of laws "respecting an establishment of religion." I begin by explaining the standards applied by the Supreme Court to cases involving the Establishment Clause.

In *Abington School District v. Schempp* (1963) the Court struck down a law that required the day in public schools to begin with a reading of "at least ten verses from the Holy Bible."[3] Justice Clark, writing for the Court, offered a general test to be applied when determining whether or not a statute violates the Establishment Clause: "The test may be stated as follows: what are the purpose and primary effect of the enactment? If either is the advancement of religion then the enactment exceeds the scope of legislative power as circumscribed by the Constitution. That is to say that to withstand the strictures of the Establishment Clause there must be a secular legislative purpose and a primary effect that neither advances nor inhibits religion."[4]

The state contended that it had secular purposes in requiring readings from the Bible: "Included within its secular purposes, it says, are the promotion of moral values, the contradiction to the materialistic trends of our times, the perpetuation of our institutions and the teaching of literature."[5] The Court concluded that "even if its purpose is not strictly religious, it is sought to be accomplished through readings, without comment, from the Bible. Surely the Bible as an instrument of religion cannot be gainsaid."[6] A secular purpose is not enough. That purpose must be accomplished through means whose "primary effect . . . neither advances nor inhibits religion."[7]

Justice Brennan, concurring in *Schempp*, maintained that states run afoul of the Establishment Clause when they choose religious means to secure secular purposes where secular means would do. He wrote that the Constitution forbids "those involvements of religious with secular institutions which . . . use essentially religious means to serve governmental ends where secular means would suffice."[8] The secular purposes of promoting moral values, combating materialism, perpetuating our institutions, and teaching literature can be secured by means other than readings from the Bible, means that do not so clearly resemble a religious ceremony. Brennan's point could have been that the choice of religious means where secular means would do raises questions about the state's sincerity in its announcement of a secular purpose, or he may have meant that the use of religious means in these circumstances results in a primary effect that unconstitutionally advances religion. Alternatively, Brennan may have been proposing a requirement in addition to those of "a secular legislative purpose and a primary effect that neither advances nor inhibits religion."[9] In any case, Brennan's requirement is often referred to as "the alternate means test." Religious means may not be used when secular means would suffice.

In *Lemon v. Kurtzman* (1971) Chief Justice Burger added a different item to the two-part test announced eight years earlier by Justice Clark. Burger wrote: "Three such tests may be gleaned from our cases. First, the statute must have a legislative purpose; second, its principal or primary effect must be one that neither advances nor inhibits religion; finally, the statute must not foster 'an excessive government entanglement with religion.'"[10] This three-part test has been used by the Court almost invariably since its announcement by Burger.

In 1984, however, Justice O'Connor proposed a useful refinement. Referring to the requirements that a statute have a secular purpose and that its "principal or primary effect . . . be one that neither advances nor inhibits religion," O'Connor saw endorsement as the key. The Establishment Clause forbids "government endorsement or disapproval of religion. Endorsement sends a message to nonadherents that they are outsiders, not full members of the political community, and an accompanying message to adherents that they are insiders, favored members of the political community. Disapproval sends the opposite message."[11] She reiterated this view a year later: "*Lemon*'s inquiry as to the purpose and effect of a statute requires courts to examine whether government's purpose is to endorse religion and whether the statute actually conveys a message of endorsement."[12] She added: "The relevant issue is whether an objective observer . . . would perceive it as a state endorsement" of religion.[13] Again: "In assessing the effect of . . . a statute—that is, in determining whether the statute conveys the message of endorsement of religion or a particular religious belief—courts should assume" the perspective of an "objective observer."[14]

The foregoing can be summarized as follows: The Establishment Clause forbids laws whose purpose, primary effect or both, are religious. According to O'Connor, a religious purpose or primary effect may be taken to inhere in legislation that an "objective observer" would consider to convey "the message of endorsement of religion or a particular religious belief."[15] Another sign that the Establishment Clause has been violated is the state's use of "essentially religious means to serve governmental ends where secular means would suffice."[16] Finally, recalling from Chapter 4 the necessity of interpreting the Establishment Clause so as to render it consistent with the Free Exercise Clause, accommodations made by the government to meet free exercise requirements should not be seen as establishments of religion. Though, in a sense, the purpose and primary effect of such accommodations are religious, they are not endorsements of religion. They are needed to avoid government hostility to religion, and no entirely secular means is available for this purpose.

With this understanding of the Establishment Clause in mind, I return to consider the constitutionality of laws proscribing the use or restricting severely the distribution of contraceptives. What is the purpose of such laws? At a minimum, the purpose is to prevent or discourage the use of contraceptives. But why?

In *Griswold v. Connecticut* (1965) the state advanced the purpose of "discouraging . . . extramarital relations." This rationale made little sense because the statute prohibited the use of contraceptives in marital, as well as extramarital, relations. Also, the statute did not diminish the availability of contraceptives to either married or unmarried people when the intended use was prevention of disease. Justice Goldberg emphasized these points. The state, he wrote,

> says that preventing the use of birth control devices by married persons helps prevent the indulgence by some in extra-marital relations. The rationality of this justification is dubious, particularly in light of the admitted widespread availability to all persons in the State of Connecticut, unmarried as well as married, of birth-control devices for the prevention of disease, as distinguished from the prevention of conception.[17]

The Massachusetts law restricting the sale of contraceptives, invalidated in *Eisenstadt v. Baird* (1972), was defended similarly by the state as a measure aimed at discouraging "extramarital and premarital sexual relations." But, Justice Brennan stated for the Court, "we cannot agree that the deterrence of premarital sex may reasonably be regarded as the purpose of the Massachusetts law."[18] As in the case of Connecticut's law, the statute's provisions "do not at all regulate the distribution of contraceptives when they are used to prevent, not pregnancy, but the spread of disease."[19] Because contraceptives are thus widely available, "it is abundantly clear that the effect of the ban on distribution of contraceptives to unmarried persons has at best a marginal relation to the proffered objective" (of discouraging extramarital sex).[20] What is more, Brennan noted: "It would be plainly unreasonable to assume that Massachusetts has prescribed pregnancy and the birth of an unwanted child as punishment for fornication, which is a misdemeanor under Massachusetts General Laws."[21] Thus, the anti-contraception laws invalidated in *Griswold* and *Eisenstadt* lacked a credible secular purpose.

Because the Court believed, erroneously in my view, that people have a fundamental (constitutional) right of privacy that these statutes interfered with, it should have subjected the statutes to strict scrutiny. It should have required that the burdens the statutes place on this fundamental right be necessary to meet a compelling public need. In *Eisenstadt*, however, the Court indicated clearly that it considered neither law to pass even the relatively relaxed standard of being rationally related to a legitimate (secular) public purpose. Writing for the Court, Justice Brennan indicated twice that purported justifications of the Massachusetts law are unreasonable. He referred in this connection to *Williamson v. Lee Optical*[22] where the weak rational relationship standard is explained. He also applied this view to *Griswold* through reference to Justice Goldberg's concurrence in that case. So the Court did not find in either statute a rational relationship to a legitimate (secular) public purpose. This implies that the Court's references to a fundamental right of privacy were unnecessary. Even if people have no such right, the statutes are unconstitutional because they bear no rational relationship to a legitimate public purpose.

We must suppose, however, that the statutes had *some* purpose. We must assume that the legislators were conscious and purposeful when they drafted and passed these statutes. So what was the purpose? The only purpose to which the statutes were at all rationally related was that of expressing public disapproval of contraception. This purpose, however, was not even mentioned because it is illegitimate, as all the reasons for disapproving contraception per se are biblically based. They rest on an interpretation of Genesis 1:28, "God said . . . Be fruitful, and multiply, and replenish the earth." Hence, like the creation science laws that the Court considered unconstitutional establishments of religion,[23] the anti-contraception statutes embody some people's interpretation of the Bible. Since the statutes seem to have no other reason for being, they clearly contravene the Establishment Clause. Thus, recourse to a general right of privacy (which is not in the Constitution) or to substantive due process (which places inordinate power in judicial hands) is unnecessary.

I maintain later in this chapter and in Chapters 7 and 8 that most antiabortion statutes are similarly unconstitutional establishments of religion. Their invalidity does not rest on any problematic general right of privacy or on substantive due process. They are invalid because they lack a legitimate purpose. Their major goal, the protection of young fetuses, is predicated on a religious belief.

The anti-contraception statutes contravene the Establishment Clause in a second way as well. Their primary effect advances religion. As Justice O'Connor explains it, a statute unconstitutionally advances religion if an objective observer thought "the statute conveys the message of endorsement of religion or a particular religious belief."[24] I maintain that an objective observer who is well acquainted with American culture, way of life, and religious traditions could not fail to see in the anti-contraception statutes the endorsement of a religious belief, namely, the belief that God proscribes the use of contraceptives. This is the primary effect of the statutes. According to the Court's current understanding of the Establishment Clause, the statutes are, again, unconstitutional establishments of religion. They are invalid apart from any considerations of privacy or substantive due process.

Belief in the Existence of God

In the section following this one I turn to legislation that restricts access to abortion. Such legislation is often predicated on the belief that a fetus younger than twenty-one weeks old is a person entitled to the same right to life as other people. I argue that this belief is similar to belief in the existence of God (when both are viewed as beliefs about matters of *fact*.) Though reasons can be given both for and against the beliefs that young fetuses are persons and that God exists, neither belief can be established through recourse to purely secular considerations.

Chapter 4 explains conceptions of secular and religious beliefs about matters of fact. According to that explanation, secular beliefs about matters of fact can be established (though only provisionally) solely by recourse to secular methodologies, beliefs and forms of argumentation. Religious beliefs about matters of fact differ in this regard. They are beliefs that cannot be established (even provisionally) solely by recourse to secular methodologies, beliefs, and forms of argumentation. In Chapters 4 and 5 I argue that these conceptions of "secular belief" and "religious belief" accord with the Supreme Court's general statements and particular decisions involving interpretations of the First Amendment's Religion Clauses.

Since neither belief in the existence of God nor belief in the personhood of young fetuses can be established through recourse to purely secular considerations, both are religious beliefs. Accordingly, laws whose purpose or primary effect is to promote belief in God or to protect young fetuses as persons violate the Establishment Clause. I begin this line of argument by explaining in the present section the nature of arguments for and against belief in the existence of God.

The philosopher John Wisdom maintained that, according to a common view, the controversy over God's existence resembles the following situation:

> Two people return to their long neglected garden and find among the weeds a few of the old plants surprisingly vigorous. One says to the other, "It must be that a gardener has been coming and doing something about these plants." Upon inquiry they find that no neighbor has ever seen anyone at work in their garden. The first man says to the other, "He must have worked while people slept." The other says, "No, someone would have heard him and besides, anybody who cared about the plants would have kept down these weeds." The first man says, "Look at the way these are arranged. There is purpose and feeling for beauty here. I believe that someone comes, someone invisible to mortal eyes."[25]

The two study both the garden and "what happens to gardens left without attention. Each learns all the other learns." Neither directly perceives or expects to directly perceive something different from what the other perceives or expects.

"At this stage, in this context, the gardener hypothesis has ceased to be experimental" because the two people perceive, and expect to perceive, the same things. So when one affirms and the other denies the existence of a gardener whom no one can see directly, the difference is primarily "in how they feel toward the garden."[26] But "the disputants speak *as if* they are concerned with a matter of scientific fact, or of trans-sensual, trans-scientific and metaphysical fact, but still of fact and still a matter about which reasons for and against may be offered, although no scientific reasons in the sense of field surveys for fossils or experiments on delinquents are to the point."[27]

Wisdom compared this situation to people believing, or disbelieving, in the existence of God on the basis of their direct perceptions of, and expectations concerning, the natural world. One person believes that life is a miracle and could not exist without a divine creator. The other believes that life could have come into existence by chemical accident. The first one notes, however, that the chances against such an accident are astronomical. The second maintains that given enough time and trials, the astronomically unlikely is not so unlikely. The first points out as evidence of intelligent design that living things form biotic communities characterized by intricate interdependencies. The second person believes the theory of evolution provides an impersonal, unintelligent, biochemical explanation for these interdependencies. But then, asks the first, how do we account for the appearance of human intelligence, except as a gift from a benevolent, intelligent God? Why should evolution have taken such a turn unless an intelligent God wanted to place intelligent life on earth? The skeptic replies that it was all a matter of chance and that a truly benevolent, intelligent God would have created a world containing less suffering. The believer places responsibility for this suffering on people, not God. But does this account for children born with grave defects or killed in tornados? And so the conversation goes.

In this conversation, the existence of God is treated as "a matter of . . . trans-sensual, trans-scientific and metaphysical *fact* . . . and . . . a matter about which reasons for and against may be offered, although no scientific reasons . . . are to the point."[28] There is no way that purely secular premises or perceptions can settle the issue because every consideration raised on one side can be countered with a respectable consideration on the other. There is no possible experiment that people can run that will tend to settle the matter. What is more, the disputants about God, like Wisdom's disputants about the gardener, may agree completely on secular matters concerning the state of the world and the probable course of natural events during their lifetimes. What, then, do they disagree about? One sees in the world evidence of God, whereas the other does not. They place the world in different contexts, and this affects their feelings about the world, (and I would add, may affect their systems of value). But, as Wisdom points out, their differences in feeling (and values) stem from differences in what they regard as factual beliefs. These are not differences about common-sense facts or scientific facts. If they are facts at all, Wisdom notes, they are best called "trans-sensual, trans-scientific and metaphysical." Since they can only be the sorts of facts that our secular belief system is inherently incapable of establishing, they are "religious" according to the epistemological standard explained in Chapter 4. They are what the Supreme Court considers religious facts. They can only be, therefore, the sorts of facts that the law may not assume or presuppose. Thus, on the epistemological standard that the Court employs in First Amendment contexts to determine which beliefs are religious, belief in the existence of God is a religious belief. No laws may be predicated on this belief.

Belief in the Personhood of Young Fetuses

Similarly religious is the belief that fetuses younger than twenty-one weeks old are human persons with a right to life. (For reasons of brevity I refer to this as "belief in the personhood of young fetuses" or "belief in the right to life of young fetuses.") As with belief in the existence of God, there are reasonable considerations that can be offered for and against this belief, and the two sides do not differ about any significant matters of fact. But the facts and considerations are inherently incapable of resolving the dispute. Yet the difference is often perceived by the two sides as being in some sense *factual*, not merely attitudinal. The present section illustrates the structural identity between disputes about the existence of God and disputes about the personhood (and right to life) of young fetuses. It shows that when they are viewed as matters of fact, both sorts of disputed beliefs are epistemologically religious and therefore religious for First Amendment purposes.

I begin with reasons for believing in the personhood of young fetuses. Dr. E. Blechschmidt argues:

A human being does not *become* a human being but rather *is* such from the instant of the fertilization. During the entire ontogenesis, no single break can be demonstrated, either in the sense of a leap from the lifeless to the live, or of a transition from the vegetative to the instinctive or to characteristically human behavior. It may be considered today a fundamental law of human ontogenesis . . . that only the appearance of the individual being changes in the course of its ontogenesis.[29]

These are the considerations discussed in Chapter 2 in connection with Justice White's dissent in *Thornburgh v. American College of Obstetricians and Gynecologists* (1986).[30] The earlier discussion revealed that such considerations are inconclusive. Conceptual, practical, and legal difficulties attend the attribution, which Blechschmidt advocates, of full personhood to newly fertilized ova. Also, the view is defended by a fallacious form of reasoning. It is argued that the zygote is a person because the newborn is a person, and the newborn develops from the zygote by a continuous process. This argument is fallacious because, according to our secular forms of reasoning, continuous processes of change can alter fundamentally what is undergoing change, so that what exists at the end is not the same sort of being as existed at the beginning. Acorns develop through a continuous process into oak trees, but we do not conclude that "acorn" and "oak tree" are different words for the same thing. The possibility of fundamental change cannot be ruled out in the case of the transition from fertilized ovum to newborn child.

The opposite possibility cannot be ruled out either. Defenders of the personhood of young fetuses can point out that gradual change does not always produce a change in essence. Furthermore, there is reason to think that no change in essence takes place in human gestation. Consider the following question: "Why a human ovum always results in a human being, while any other ovum always results in another organism. For instance, no human being originates from a duck's egg. The answer is because in each ovum the essence has already been fixed; only the appearance changes in development. It is characteristic for every ontogenesis that only that develops which is essentially already there."[31]

This consideration is far from conclusive, however. What is present from the beginning in the fertilized ovum's genetic code may be the *potentiality for the development* of a person, not the essence of personhood. Those who agree completely on the scientific details of ontogenesis may thus disagree about the essence of the newly fertilized egg. This is characteristic of disagreements about matters of fact in areas of religious belief. All relevant secular facts of science and common sense can be held in common by people whose attitudes differ and who justify their different attitudes by appeal to "facts" of some other kind. One "sees" the essence of personhood in the fertilized ovum, while the other "sees" merely the potential for personhood.

Reasons against identifying personhood with the presence of a human genetic code are drawn from medicine and science fiction. Consider, first, what I call the common sense of science fiction. Beings who lack a human genetic code are presented in science fiction as persons. They include at the moment Mr. Spock, E.T., and Alf. Common sense accepts these characters as persons, suggesting that, according to our normal concept, the essence of personhood rests on what persons can do, not on what they are biochemically composed of. More specifically, the public acceptance of these characters as persons suggests that a human genetic code is *not necessary* for personhood.

But this does not settle the issue of greatest importance for the classification of the fetus. The fetus has a human genetic code, and the issue is whether the presence of that code is *sufficient*, not whether it is necessary, to make the fetus a person. This is where people in a persistant vegetative state come in. They have a functioning spinal cord and brain stem, but not a functioning cortex. Apart from fictional examples, cortical activity is (believed) necessary for all the distinctively human abilities of thought, imagination, and will. So people in a persistent vegetative state, though they are alive and have a human genetic code, lack all distinctively human abilities. If, as the science fiction cases show, such abilities are sufficient for personhood, perhaps they are necessary as well.

The necessity of such abilities for personhood is implied in the treatment of those in a persistent vegetative state. Life-threatening infections and coronary problems that it would be literally criminal to leave untreated in patients with normally functioning brains are often left untreated in persistently vegetative individuals. Life-threatening conditions are left untreated precisely so that the patients can be allowed to die. Such patients are not, then, accorded the right to life that normally accompanies personhood. Few people are troubled by this. Since young fetuses are similarly incapable of the activities that distinguish persons from others, they should be classified with those in a persistent vegetative state. Despite their human genetic code, they should be denied the status of personhood and the accompanying right to life.

Defenders of the young fetus's right to life have two cogent replies to this reasoning. First, nothing is proven by the fact that few people are troubled by common medical practices that violate the right to life of permanently vegetative individuals. Defenders of the fetus can condemn indifference toward the lives of those in a persistent vegetative state just as they condemn indifference toward fetal life. In neither case is common acceptance a proof of moral acceptability. If it were, the treatment of Native Americans during our country's westward expansion, of slaves before the Civil War, and of Jews in Nazi Germany would have been morally acceptable, because they also enjoyed widespread acceptance.

Second, even if indifference were acceptable in the case of persistently vegetative individuals, the same would not follow for the fetus. Characteristically, the fetus is temporarily, not permanently, incapable of engaging in distinctively human activities. Allow it to develop and its activities will be distinctively human. Thus a fetus is more like a person who is temporarily unconscious than one who is persistently vegetative. Just as we do not deny personhood and the right to life to the temporarily unconscious, we should not deny personhood and the right to life to the temporarily immature.

Critics of fetal personhood object to the analogy between young fetuses and normal, but unconscious, children and adults. The latter have already engaged in characteristically human activities and are able, typically, to resume such activities on a moment's notice. They are in what Aristotle calls the state of second potentiality. They have already developed and displayed their abilities, but happen not to be displaying them at the moment. They are like car mechanics who are not currently fixing cars. We call them car mechanics in honor of the abilities that they have developed and displayed, ignoring the fact that they are temporarily asleep or on lunch break.

The young fetus, in contrast, has never yet developed or displayed the abilities distinctive of human beings. The young fetus is in a state of first potentiality, as it has to develop further before it can ever act like a person. Normally, beings in first potentiality are denied the rights associated with the state of being for which they are in a state of first potentiality. For example, those who are not already trained to be doctors may not act as doctors, even those who, because they could acquire such training, are in a state of first potentiality for a medical degree. Similarly, the young fetus is reasonably denied a person's right to life because it is in merely first potentiality for personhood, unlike most unconscious people, who are in a state of second potentiality.

Defenders of the young fetus point out, however, that the fetal potential for personhood is very different from a young person's potential for a medical degree. The young person does not have to become a physician to live. She could follow a different career path. The young fetus has no alternative but death to the development of distinctively human traits and activities. Also, the young person becomes a physician only through conscious choices about the expenditure of time and energy. The young fetus develops personhood automatically, without any choice at all. So its potentiality is based on, and flows naturally from, its actuality. Thus "the potential of a human conceptus to think and talk is an actuality."[32]

The same author points out in this context that "every potential is itself an actuality. . . . A woman's potential to give birth to a baby is an actuality that a man does not have."[33] This example shows, however, apparently contrary to its author's intention, that potentiality and actuality (in the meanings that are important for his argument) are *not* the same thing. A woman's uterus is part of her actuality that underlies her potential for giving birth. Even if a uterus were necessary and sufficient for giving birth, however, a uterus and a birth are different. More generally, an actuality that *underlies* a potentiality (as the uterus is an actuality that underlies the potential for giving birth) is different from the actuality that *fulfills* the potentiality (in this case, giving birth). Analogously, the genetic code is an actuality that underlies the young fetus's potential for personhood, but for that very reason it is not the fulfillment of that potentiality. By secular standards, the young fetus is not yet a person. Furthermore, it is logically impossible for the same thing to be at the same time and in the same respect both potential and actual.[34] So if the young fetus is a potential person, it cannot be at the same time and in the same respect an actual person.

Defenders of the young fetus reply that it is an actual, not a potential, person. But how can it be an actual person when it lacks the current ability to engage in distinctively human pursuits? Advocates for the young fetus point out that newborns are no more able than are young fetuses to engage in distinctively human pursuits. Typically, people "can understand things and reason about them, make plans, and act; they can . . . argue, negotiate, express themselves, make agreements, honor commitments, and stand in relationships of mutual trust."[35] Newborns cannot engage in these activities much better than young fetuses can. So if young fetuses are not actually persons with a right to life, newborns are not either, and infanticide would be morally acceptable. Since infanticide is not morally (or legally) acceptable, newborns must be considered actual persons with a right to life. Young fetuses must for the same reasons be included among persons with a right to life.

The reply is that newborns are significantly closer than are young fetuses to being able to engage in distinctively human pursuits. Unlike young fetuses, typical newborns have already developed all the physiological specializations necessary for human life. They have a heart, liver, kidneys, and lungs that can actually function. Depending on its age, a young fetus may have some of these, but it does not have all of them, since the lungs do not become functional until after twenty weeks, and young fetuses are here defined as those twenty weeks or younger. Also, distinctively human pursuits are directed by the neocortical functions of the brain, and it is only at twenty-two to twenty-four weeks of gestation that neocortical brain functions appear.[36] So it is reasonable to maintain that newborns and fetuses somewhat older than twenty weeks are persons with a right to life, but young fetuses are not.

Defenders of young fetuses point out, however, that the significance of these particular physiological developments is in the eye of the beholder. Someone who finds the heartbeat to be the most significant development could, with equal logic, locate the onset of personhood at five weeks of gestation. Others, more impressed with the similarity of fetal to infant facial features, could justify a few different cutoffs before twenty weeks, depending on how much similarity is believed necessary for the similarity to be significant. Still others, who consider learning to be the most fundamental human trait, could locate personhood at six weeks, when the first reflex occurs, eight weeks, when the head turns toward a source of stimulation, twelve weeks, when swallowing accompanies the "turning toward" reflex, and so forth.[37]

Much more can be, and has been, said on both sides of the debate about the personhood of young fetuses. I think the forgoing sufficient, however, to illustrate my point. The debate is structurally and epistemologically identical to debates about the existence of God. Relevant, secular facts can be used in respectable arguments to address the issue. But the arguments are inconclusive because every argument on one side can be countered with an effective argument on the other. This is inherent in the subject matter, as we have no method of resolving the dispute even in principle. So the issue is not one of ordinary secular fact. Yet it is believed by both sides to be more than an issue of attitude. It seems to be about some "trans-sensual, trans-scientific and metaphysical fact." Thus, like belief in the existence of God, belief in the personhood of young fetuses is, on the epistemological standard, a religious belief.

Since the epistemological standard of religious belief is fundamental to the Court's understanding of "religion" in the First Amendment, the personhood of young fetuses is, for First Amendment purposes, a religious matter. Any state endorsement of a view on this matter and any state law predicated on such a view are unconstitutional establishments of religion.

Distinguishing Religious from Secular Determinations of Fetal Personhood

The present section and the two that follow state and then reply to objections to the position I have taken. The present section is inspired by Justice White's disagreement with Justice Stevens in *Thornburgh v. American College of Obstetricians and Gynecologists*. Stevens maintained what I have just argued, namely, that attributing personhood "during the entire period from the moment of conception until the moment of birth" rests on "a . . . theological argument." It is essentially religious. Stevens added, "I believe our jurisdiction is limited to the evaluation of secular state interests."[38] So enactments that reflect any such theological position would unconstitutionally establish religion.

White replied that attributing personhood from conception onward "is no more a 'theological' position than is the Court's own judgment that viability is the point at which the state interest becomes compelling. (Interestingly, Justice Stevens omits any real effort to defend this judgment.)"[39] White suggests here that if one position on the beginning of personhood is religious, all such positions are equally religious. If this were the case, the religious freedom argument that I have employed would be embarrassed by an unwelcome consequence—abortions could never be restricted in the interests of the unborn, even on the eve of birth. If attributing personhood to a fetus, regardless of its stage of development, is a religious judgment, this would apply to a fetus on the eve of birth. Restricting abortions to save the life of that fetus would be no more constitutional than denying first-trimester abortions because all restrictions aimed at protecting a fetus would unconstitutionally establish a religious belief. This is an embarrassing result because most people believe that the older fetus is a person with a right to life and that restrictions on late abortions are justified by this fact.

This section justifies the distinction that Stevens makes between younger and older fetuses. I argue that while the personhood of young fetuses is inherently a matter of religious belief, the personhood of older fetuses is a secular matter.

I do not base my argument on considerations of secular fact. As shown in the preceding section, when personhood is viewed as a matter of fact, considerations of secular fact and of secular methodologies employed in the determination of secular facts are insufficient. Such considerations cannot establish that a fetus (at any stage of development) *or even a newborn* is a person. In order to address White's concern, then, I treat the issue as a question of value, not a question of fact. Viewed as an issue of fact, the question is posed: "Is, in fact, a fetus (or a newborn) a person?" Viewed as an issue of value, however, the question becomes: "Should we apply the concept of personhood to a fetus (or a newborn)?" Here we are concerned with a matter of choice. We must choose an application of the concept of personhood. Since choice is involved, it is appropriate to consult our values. Since we are concerned with legislation and constitutional interpretation, the values must be secular.

Basing my argument on secular values, I do not maintain in this section that the acquisition of personhood should be placed at a particular week in the gestational process. Instead, I argue that personhood becomes a secular matter, and so a fit subject for legislation, sometime between twenty and twenty-eight weeks. This allows the Court to avoid the embarrassing result, suggested by White's dissent, that the Establishment Clause prohibits legislation designed to save the lives of fetuses on the eve of birth. Because the personhood of such fetuses is a secular matter, the Establishment Clause is no bar to legislation designed to save their lives.

The preceding section showed that arguments can be given for and against the personhood not only of the fetus (at any stage of gestation) but even of the newborn. If the abilities to reason, argue, make compromises, and keep agreements are essential characteristics of persons, then newborns are not, as a matter of fact, persons. Some philosophers have adopted this position and concluded that newborns do not have a right to life.[40] These same philosophers are quick to add, however, that there remain secular reasons to protect newborns *as if* they had a right to life. The details of their reasoning need not detain us. The point is that in our society the protection of newborns, either *because* they have a right to life or *as if* they have a right to life, is *an accepted secular value*. Indeed, few values that legislation embodies or fosters are as central to our commonly accepted way of life as the value of protecting (healthy) newborns. That value is woven into the fabric of our society as surely and securely as, for example, the values of general literacy, public health, and national defense.

In none of these cases do I attempt to explain *why* our society adheres to the secular value in question. That kind of sociological inquiry is beyond the scope of the present work. I take secular values as I find them and begin reasoning from that point. I recognize that a different society would likely differ somewhat in the secular values to which it is committed and that our society's value commitments vary over time. Nevertheless, it can be safely maintained that one of our society's secular values at this time is the protection of newborns as (or as if they were) persons.

Chapter 2 notes that we do not believe our right to life to vary with our physical location. One's right to life is the same, according to our values, at home, while out shopping, and during a visit to a foreign country. Also, we do not believe that temporary dependency on external life-support systems affects one's right to life. For example, other things being equal, people in temporary need of a respirator have the same right to life as other people. Finally (not mentioned in Chapter 2), our secular concepts make size and strength irrelevant to attributions of a right to life. Other things being equal, we do not attribute a right to life more readily to the strong than to the weak, or to the big than to the small.

These secular beliefs can be combined with the secular view that newborns are persons with a right to life to yield the view that fetuses late in the gestational process are persons with a right to life. Fetuses late in the gestational process, eight-month fetuses, for example, differ from newborns primarily in their location, size, strength, and temporary need for support external to themselves. (From the perspective of the fetus, maternal support is external.) Since these features are generally irrelevant to attributions of personhood and a right to life, eight-month fetuses have the same personhood and right to life as newborns. Because all the values employed in this reasoning are secular, this judgment about eight-month fetuses is secular, not religious. The Establishment Clause notwithstanding, states may constitutionally pass laws designed to protect the lives and health of eight-month fetuses. Generally speaking, states may constitutionally forbid late abortions (except to save the life of the mother) where such abortions jeopardize the life or health of the fetus-would-be-newborn. This allows states to rule out most late, elective abortions. Even when steps are taken to preserve the life and health of the fetus-would-be-newborn, premature delivery (which is what such abortions amount to) jeopardizes the life and health of the prematurely delivered infant.

To what part of the gestational process does this reasoning apply? The reasoning turns on the secular value of respecting newborns as (or as if they were) persons. So the reasoning applies to all those fetuses who differ from newborns primarily in location, size, strength, and temporary dependency (on their mothers). By week twenty-eight, a normal fetus has already developed all the basic physiological systems that characterize newborns and other people. Such fetuses are much smaller and weaker than healthy newborns, so they require special care if they are delivered at this time, and their life prospects on delivery are much worse than normal. Nevertheless, they have already developed all the basic physiological systems needed to sustain human life. They differ from newborns only in location, size, strength, and temporary dependency (on their mothers). But these factors are not usually regarded in our secular culture as relevant to the attribution of a right to life. So the twenty-eight-week fetus can, on purely secular grounds, be treated by the state as a person with a right to life.

The twenty-week fetus cannot. The twenty-week fetus has not yet developed all the physiological systems that are necessary to sustain human life. It differs significantly, therefore, from the twenty-eight-week fetus. It is not yet just like a newborn except in location, temporary dependency, size, and strength. It lacks one or more basic systems that newborns have and use.

Since the personhood and right to life of the (healthy) newborn is what anchors abortion legislation in secular concepts (and secures their constitutionality), the absence in twenty-week fetuses of what newborns have and use makes their personhood problematic. Secular concepts regarding the irrelevance of location, temporary dependency, size and strength no longer suffice to justify protecting twenty-week fetuses, as such fetuses differ from newborns in other ways as well. As we saw in the previous section, the significance of these other differences cannot be decided by reference to secular concepts. Where secular concepts leave off, religious ideas take over. But legislation must not be predicated on religious ideas, so abortion legislation designed to protect the lives of fetuses twenty weeks or younger are unconstitutional establishments of religion.

I have argued so far in the present section that considerations of secular value require extension of the concept of personhood to older, but not to younger, fetuses. Combined with the argument of the preceding section, this is sufficient for First Amendment purposes. Lacking secular justification as a matter of fact (preceding section) or value (present section), the attribution of personhood to young fetuses is left, by default, in the realm of religion. I now go further, however. Not only are secular values insufficient to justify attributing personhood to young fetuses, such values argue powerfully against attributing personhood to the youngest among the unborn: newly fertilized ova. Attributing personhood to newly fertilized ova (which are medically termed "zygotes") runs counter to, and so would require significant modifications of, our secular values. The attribution is, from the perspective of secular values, a radical proposal. Several considerations supporting this contention were explained in Chapter 2. I briefly review a few of those considerations.

Since nearly one-half of fertilized ova die early as a result of failure to implant on the uterine wall, failure of implantation would be the gravest medical problem facing humanity if the concept of personhood or humanity were extended to include zygotes. Unprecedented expenditures of resources on medical research would be justified, even if the most favorable result, saving the lives of these "people," increased by

800 percent or more the number of infants born with severe genetic defects. Our society's practices do not reflect, and most people's values do not require, any such commitment to the personhood of zygotes.

Other consequences of attributing personhood to fertilized ova are equally at odds with social practices and secular values. Deliberate abortion at any stage of pregnancy would be murder and would have to be treated as severely as any other deliberate homicide. If the criminal law may be used as evidence of secular values, such treatment of abortion conflicts sharply with secular values. Abortion has never in our legal tradition been equated with murder or with homicide of any sort. So the decision to extend the concept of personhood to zygotes entails practices and values that conflict with those of our society.

The conflict is greatest when the deliberate termination of pregnancy occurs shortly after fertilization, as is the case, for example, with the IUD and the morning after pill. The use of such contraceptives would be murder if a fertilized ovum were thereby destroyed. Otherwise, the crime would be reckless endangerment. These conclusions, too, conflict with our criminal laws and secular values. But the matter gets worse. Since the crimes of murder and reckless endangerment differ significantly in their seriousness and in the severity of associated punishments, probable cause to believe that someone had used an IUD or morning-after pill would justify the examination of the woman's next menstrual flow to check for the presence of a fertilized ovum. Again, the conflict with our laws, practices, and values is manifest. Thus, the extension of the concept of personhood to include zygotes conflicts sharply with our secular values and with social practices expressive of those values.

More important for purposes of the present work, we saw earlier in this section that secular values fail to justify the choice of attributing personhood to fetuses twenty weeks or younger. We saw in the preceding section that no such attribution can be justified as a matter of secular fact. Having eliminated the bases of both secular fact and secular values, the only grounds for attributing personhood to fetuses twenty weeks or younger are religious. Such grounds may not form the basis for legislation.

But Justice White need not be concerned that if any view about the onset of personhood is deemed religious, all such views must be deemed religious. After twenty-eight weeks, as we have seen, there are grounds in secular values for attributing personhood to the fetus, so laws protecting the fetus at this point do not run afoul of the Establishment Clause.

I cannot say exactly where between twenty and twenty-eight weeks the matter of fetal personhood becomes secular. Those more expert than I must determine when the fetus differs from the newborn in no more than location, temporary dependency, size and strength. Even experts may not be able to agree on a particular week when the fetus differs from healthy newborns in no more than these four ways. Expert opinions may range from twenty to twenty-six weeks.

It is important to avoid confusing this issue with one about viability, which turns on the technological ability to foster the development of a fetus outside its mother. Even if, for example, a form of artificial oxygenation enables us to bring twenty-week fetuses to term outside their mothers, such fetuses still differ from newborns in ways whose significance is a religious matter. Even if such fetuses become viable, then, they are not considered persons on purely secular grounds.

Religious versus Secular Uncertainty

The objection considered in this section is expressed in the following reasoning: Fetuses twenty weeks and younger can be classified as persons only on religious, not on secular, grounds because secular concepts do not suffice to decide the matter one way or the other. On the epistemological standard, undecidability makes a matter religious. But if we cannot decide on secular grounds how to classify young fetuses, the objector continues, we should exercise caution. Feelings of uncertainty about whether abortions early in pregnancy kill a person (the fetus) should lead us to refrain from such abortions, just as uncertainty about whether a movement in the bushes is caused by a person or a deer should lead a hunter to refrain from shooting.

The objector notes also that the government often protects people where uncertainty leads to grave dangers. The government regulates the airline and nuclear power industries, for example, to protect people from such dangers. But there are few, if any, losses more tragic than the premature death of a healthy young person. Given uncertainties about the personhood of young fetuses, the objector concludes, the government has a responsibility to protect such fetuses. It can do this best by outlawing abortions.

Finally, the objector maintains, since all the steps in this reasoning are based on secular premises regarding prudence in the face of uncertainty, the antiabortion legislation promoted here does not establish a religious belief. Such legislation is constitutional and is required if the government is to fulfill its responsibility in situations of uncertainty to protect people against serious harm.

So much for the objection. Now the reply. The flaw in the objector's argument can be seen by first comparing the danger of killing a young fetus who may be a person with the danger of killing a fellow hunter who may be behind a bush. The existence of the danger in the second case does not rely in any way on religious beliefs, whereas in the first case the danger exists only because of uncertainty about the truth of a religious claim. The young fetus is a person according to a certain religious belief. To say that the young fetus may be a person is to say that this religious belief may be true. The objector maintains, then, that dangers implied by the possible truth of religious beliefs may for legal purposes be considered secular dangers. Since they are secular dangers, legislation addressing these dangers does not contravene the Establishment Clause.

The objector fails to appreciate that religious freedom could be suppressed entirely if legislation could be justified by dangers whose existence depends on uncertainty about the truth of religious claims. Consider baptism, for example. Many people believe it necessary for individuals to avoid eternal damnation and suffering when they die. The reduction of suffering is a secular value. We have laws to reduce the suffering even of animals. So, the argument goes, if baptism is necessary for the reduction of suffering, it should be required by law, or at least be promoted and paid for by the government. Of course, the belief that baptism is necessary for the reduction of suffering is a religious belief. From the government's point of view, therefore, its truth is uncertain. But the possibility of its truth, according to this line of reasoning, makes it dangerous for the government to ignore baptism. In sum, if a religiously claimed danger of secular harm (suffering in this case, killing a person in the case of abortion) constitutes a secular danger, then the danger of suffering due to lack of baptism is a secular danger. Like the danger of murder associated with abortion, the danger of suffering associated with failure to baptize would have to be considered a matter that legislation can legitimately address.

This result is clearly unacceptable. Legislation requiring, promoting, or granting public payment for baptism would obviously be an unconstitutional establishment of religion. Any line of reasoning that suggests such legislation would be constitutional is certainly flawed.

The flaw is apparent also from numerous other unacceptable results of this line of reasoning. These results follow from the fact that myriad secular dangers can be associated with religious beliefs. Some concern the welfare in this life of society in general. For example, according to the Old Testament, the world was inundated, two cities were later destroyed, and Egypt was visited with successive plagues, all because people failed to observe God's laws. The Old Testament is often interpreted to indicate continuing dangers from disobedience to God's laws. Chapter 28 of Deuteronomy, for example, is devoted to explaining the earthly rewards of obedience (1–14) and the earthly ruin that attends disobedience to the word of God (15–60). For disobedience: "The Lord shall make the pestilence cleave unto thee. . . . The Lord shall smite thee with a consumption, and with a fever." In addition, the rain will cease, the ground grow hard, and the harvest diminish. National enemies will prevail and enslave the people. In short, the problems associated with disobedience to God's will include secular matters of the utmost importance. Many people in our society hold this sort of belief, for example, those who view the AIDS epidemic as punishment from God for human transgression.

Consider someone who believes that God's law prohibits equality for women, use of contraceptives, or instruction in the theory of evolution. Biblical passages are often cited to justify these, and many similar, beliefs. Combine such beliefs with the view that secular ruin follows disobedience to God's will, and an argument is made for the legal subjugation of women, the prohibition of contraceptives, the suppression of the theory of evolution, and as many other legal restrictions and requirements as someone's religious convictions can justify. According to the type of argument being discussed in this section, uncertainty about the truth of the underlying religious premises means merely that the government's failure to act *risks* (rather than causes) social ruin. Surely the government should act, the argument continues, to reduce or eliminate these grave risks, just as it acts to combat the risks of cancer associated with certain chemicals and the risks of deforestation associated with acid rain. Thus, any number of legal prohibitions can be justified in this way.

But the resulting prohibitions clearly violate the Establishment Clause. The risks that the prohibitions are aimed at reducing or eliminating are risks of secular harm. The existence of these risks, however, is predicated on a religious belief, for example, belief that God requires the subordination of women or forbids the use of contraceptives. This is the crux of the problem. Because religious beliefs are so varied and numerous, any number of legal requirements, restrictions, and prohibitions could be justified if the government were permitted to respond to risks predicated on religious beliefs. The Establishment Clause protects us from this intolerable situation. Accordingly, the Establishment Clause rules out antiabortion statutes aimed at reducing or eliminating the risk of murder associated with aborting young fetuses, as the risk of murder is predicated in this case entirely on a religious belief about young fetuses.

Environmental Preservation and Animal Protection versus Fetal Value

This section presents and then replies to an objection raised by Kent Greenawalt in *Religious Convictions and Political Choice*. Greenawalt contends that religious beliefs properly and inevitably influence public policy. So even if beliefs about the personhood of young fetuses are religious, antiabortion legislation may appropriately rest on such beliefs. I contend to the contrary, that religious beliefs may appropriately affect political decisions only when they influence people's judgments about secular matters. Legislation may not appropriately rest on beliefs about the personhood of young fetuses because this is not a secular matter.

The present section is divided into three parts: The first part explains Greenawalt's argument; two major flaws in Greenawalt's reasoning are exposed and discussed in the second and third parts.

GREENAWALT'S ARGUMENT

Greenawalt begins his argument as follows: "Legislation must be justified in terms of secular objectives, but when people reasonably think that shared premises of justice and criteria for determining truth cannot resolve critical questions of fact, fundamental questions of value, or the weighing of competing benefits and harms, they do appropriately rely on religious convictions that help them answer these questions."[41] The abortion question is, in his opinion, a case in point because "commonly accessible reasons do not settle the status of the fetus at various stages."[42] This means, according to Greenawalt, that the issue must be settled by appeal to personal and idiosyncratic convictions: "If this is inevitable, the religious believer has a powerful argument that he should be able to rely on his religiously informed bases for judgment if others are relying on other bases of judgment that reach beyond common premises and forms of reasoning."[43] Thus, Greenawalt maintains, antiabortion legislation can be constitutional even if it reflects primarily the religious convictions of voters and legislators.

Greenawalt considers abortion to be in this respect like the issue of capital punishment. People differ on factual questions about the effect of capital punishment on the reduction of crime. They differ also on the propriety of returning evil for evil, as the retributive theory of punishment prescribes. These differences of opinion cannot be settled by appeal to secular reasons. "The ultimate premises . . . either are not in principle establishable by reasoned argument or rest on such fundamental and complex factual assumptions about human nature and social existence that convincing resolution between them on publicly accessible grounds is not practically possible for real human beings."[44] Where publicly accessible grounds are inadequate, other bases for judgment must be employed. If some people are influenced by the authority of revered teachers or political figures, Greenawalt maintains that others may legitimately be influenced by the authority of a religious teacher or doctrine. Thus, for example, someone who "belongs to a religious group that is extremely pessimistic about human nature"[45] may be especially skeptical about the possibility of reforming criminals. This may legitimately incline that person toward endorsing the death penalty. Someone else, whose "religion teaches that people are basically good, that love and mercy can draw out the best in them," may be more favorably disposed to efforts at reform in all cases.[46] This rules out the death penalty. In this way, religious convictions can legitimately influence legislation.

Indeed, Greenawalt argues, there is no practical alternative to the influence of religious convictions on political judgments about such matters as the death penalty. Few, if any, people are intellectually or psychologically able to sort out the various influences on their political judgments on such issues, isolate influences of recognizably religious origin, and alter their judgments so as to reflect what those judgments would be if recognizably religious influences had been absent from the start. Thus the exclusion of religious convictions would be not only unfair (since other nonrational influences are allowed) but impossible (because people are incapable of isolating and excluding religious influences).[47]

Greenawalt applies this reasoning to the abortion issue by maintaining, first, that "the nub of the question whether a restrictive abortion law can be justified turns on when a fetus warrants sufficient protection from society." He assumes, as I do, "that if the fetus as such does not warrant any protection, the legal permissibility of abortion follows."[48]

He next identifies judgments about the degree of protection the fetus warrants with judgments about the fetus's "intrinsic value"[49] or "inherent worth."[50] The more intrinsic value or inherent worth that a fetus has, the more it warrants protection, and the more easily justified are restrictive abortion laws. Publicly accessible reasons do not suffice, Greenawalt notes, to settle controversies regarding the intrinsic value or inherent worth of fetuses at various stages of the gestational process. So people are properly and inevitably influenced by their religious convictions where abortion is concerned, just as they are similarly influenced in their political judgments regarding the death penalty.

Greenawalt applies the same reasoning to issues of environmental concern and animal protection. Environmental legislation may rest in part on the intrinsic value or inherent worth that people attribute to wilderness areas or species diversity. Controversies about these value judgments cannot be settled on neutral, secular grounds, so people must have recourse to subjective evaluations. It is unfair and impossible to exclude religious conviction as a source of subjective evaluation in this area. The degree to which animals deserve protection from people's cruelty depends, similarly, on the inherent worth or intrinsic value of such animals. Again, this is a matter on which reasonable people may differ, so subjective evaluations are necessary. Religious convictions must be admitted alongside other determinants of these subjective evaluations.

I turn now to criticisms of Greenawalt's perspective. His reasoning about legislation concerning abortion, animal cruelty, and environmental protection is flawed by two related errors. First, he confuses issues where religious convictions matter with issues that are purely a matter of religious convictions. Second, he fails to recognize fully the importance and reach of secular considerations. I begin with the second problem.

THE REACH OF SECULAR CONSIDERATIONS

Greenawalt acknowledges that "our culture, in its struggles over the status of the fetus, starts with a relatively firm consensus . . . that, for most purposes and on most occasions, a newborn baby has a moral status equivalent to more developed human beings and should have equivalent legal protection of its life."[51] But Greenawalt fails to see (what I argued earlier in this chapter) that this kind of moral consensus is commonly considered sufficient to justify legislation that embodies a moral or value preference. Legislation designed to further general literacy, public health, and national defense rest on value claims that gain their legitimacy from this kind of consensus. Greenawalt may not consider consensus on such matters to constitute what he calls publicly accessible reasons. But this kind of consensus is certainly sufficient to make the relevant values secular, and that is the central issue where the Establishment Clause is concerned.

Thus the moral consensus that newborns have a right to life, or have inherent worth, provides a sufficient secular basis for legislation designed to protect newborns. Equally secular are the principles that, other things being equal, location, temporary dependency, size and strength do not affect a being's right to life. Through these principles the newborn's right to life can be extended to those among the unborn who differ from newborns only in location, temporary dependency, size, and strength. Some antiabortion legislation is justified in this way on entirely secular grounds. Greenawalt has underestimated the reach and power of secular reasons. Thinking that secular reasons are insufficient, he believes that idiosyncratic reasons must be employed and sees no reason why religious convictions should not be included among such idiosyncratic reasons. But from the constitutional point of view, secular reasons are required to justify legislation. What is more, secular reasons, reaching farther than Greenawalt's "publicly accessible reasons," are sufficient to justify the obviously necessary legislation in this area (legislation protecting older fetuses and newborns). No recourse to idiosyncratic reasons is needed. So there is no justification for recourse to religious convictions in rationales for abortion-related legislation.

Legislation aimed at preserving the environment or protecting animals is somewhat different in this regard. Such legislation can be justified on entirely secular grounds, so there is no *need* to employ religious convictions. But the influence of such convictions is constitutionally legitimate.

There is no need of religious justification for laws that protect the environment because preserving the environment for future generations of human beings is a secular value. In the light of our growing ignorance about how to preserve the environment, no one can rule out the possibility that, for example, preserving wilderness areas and endangered species is necessary for the earth's habitability in the long run for human beings. Nor can we rule out the possibility that steps needed to preserve wilderness areas and endangered species will be facilitated by some or many people attributing intrinsic value to species diversity in natural habitats. So secular reasons can be given for legislation aimed at preserving the environment. There is no need to employ religious convictions.

Legislation aimed at ameliorating cruelty to animals can also be justified by wholly secular reasons. Suffering is a secular disvalue wherever it occurs. Again, there is no need to employ religious convictions.

But religious convictions may legitimately (constitutionally) influence legislation designed to preserve the environment and protect animals. For example, legislation needed to protect the environment must be considered in the light of competing needs for affordable electricity and for employment opportunities. It is reasonable and inevitable, Greenawalt correctly maintains, for those weighing these competing considerations to include religious convictions among the factors that influence their judgment. Someone who believes that God has designated people stewards and caretakers of the earth may legitimately emphasize considerations of preservation more than would someone who believes that the earth was created by God solely for human exploitation. Similarly, those who believe that God wants people to care for other creatures may place more weight on considerations of animal suffering than would someone who thinks that animals were created solely for the benefit of human beings. These differing religious views legitimately affect people's judgment about anticruelty legislation.

I agree with this. I disagree however when Greenawalt applies these insights to the issue of abortion. The abortion issue is different. Laws regarding animals, the environment, the death penalty, and many other subjects concern secular issues where religious convictions may legitimately matter. The personhood or intrinsic value of young fetuses, in contrast, is a purely religious matter. Greenawalt confuses issues where religion matters with issues that are matters of religion.

Secular versus Religious Matters

We have seen that religion may legitimately matter where the death penalty, the environment, and animals are concerned. But these are secular issues because they concern problems where undoubtedly secular values are involved, and where legislative decisions, including decisions to refrain from legislating, affect the attainment of these values. For example, kidnapping, rape and murder occur in our society. They are secular disvalues. Whatever decision society makes regarding punishment for these crimes, including the decision to have no punishment at all, affects the attainment of thoroughly secular values. So in the death penalty debate, as Greenawalt acknowledges, people whose judgment is affected by religious convictions "do not introduce into the balance any new interests or values that a nonbeliever would not recognize; rather they have developed opinions about how to serve the values accepted by all."[52] Their religious convictions matter, but the issue of capital punishment is not inherently a matter of religion.

The same is true of issues regarding environmental preservation and animal protection. Heart disease caused by air pollution and deforestation caused by acid rain are secular disvalues, so laws designed to deal with these problems have a secular purpose. The issue does not become religious simply because religious convictions may affect people's judgments. As long as entirely secular premises are sufficient to justify the legislation, it is constitutional.

Protecting animals from cruelty rests, similarly, on a secular view, namely, that suffering is an evil. So anticruelty legislation addresses a secular matter. If it rested crucially on a belief in some "trans-sensual, trans-scientific and metaphysical" fact about the animals' possession of human souls, or about the *post mortem* transmigration of souls between people and animals, or about God's special concern for the welfare of certain sacred animals, then anticruelty legislation would be unconstitutional. It would establish a religious belief because religious belief would be fundamental to its reason for being. As things stand, however, anticruelty legislation is constitutional because it responds to the secular evaluation that suffering is bad.

Legislation aimed at eliminating the abortion of young fetuses has no secular justification. It makes no sense as a measure to protect maternal health, reduce medical expenses, or promote population growth. Nor is such legislation put forward as serving any secular goal. The legislation is put forward by its proponents as needed to protect the lives of young fetuses. But, as we have seen, the personhood and right to life of young fetuses is a religious matter. The view that such fetuses have intrinsic value or inherent worth amounts to the same thing. If these fetuses have intrinsic value or inherent worth, then they should be preserved for their own sakes, just as if they had a right to life. So the issue of the intrinsic value or inherent worth of young fetuses corresponds to the issues of their personhood and right to life. And whatever terms are used—personhood, intrinsic value, inherent worth or right to life—the issue is a religious matter. The Establishment Clause forbids legislation that addresses it.

Conclusion

The Establishment Clause forbids legislation "respecting an establishment of religion." The Supreme Court's interpretations of "religion" in the First Amendment make religious belief fundamental to religion, and the Court interprets religious belief in an epistemological way. On the epistemological standard, beliefs about the personhood, right to life, intrinsic value, and inherent worth of young fetuses are as religious as are beliefs about the existence of God. No legislation can be predicated on any such belief. We saw in Chapter 2 that young fetuses also lack significant instrumental value. So there is no constitutional justification for legislation whose purpose or primary effect is saving the lives of young fetuses.

This does not preclude all legislation regarding abortion. For example, it permits legislation designed to save the lives of older fetuses. In the two chapters to follow I discuss additional abortion-related legislation. This legislation concerns maternal health, the health of older fetuses, public funding, special consent requirements, spousal consent requirements (for married women), and parental consent and notification requirements (for minors).

CHAPTER 7

The Regulation of Abortion

C HAPTERS 4 AND 5 ARGUED that the Supreme Court interprets the First Amendment religion guarantees according to what I call the epistemological standard. Chapter 6 maintained that beliefs about the personhood or humanity of fetuses twenty weeks or younger are religious according to this epistemological standard. Thus, legislation bearing upon abortions performed before the twenty-first week of pregnancy touches significantly on a matter of religious belief. The religion guarantees therefore apply to all such legislation. Because the Establishment Clause is the religion guarantee of greater relevance to most such legislation, I call the approach employed here the "Establishment Clause approach." By this I mean the approach to abortion-related legislation that reflects a recognition of the religious dimension of abortion and, consequently, of the relevance of the religion guarantees to the constitutionality of such legislation.

The present chapter and the one to follow are devoted primarily to applying the Establishment Clause approach to selected areas of legislative concern. There is no attempt at completeness. In the present chapter some issues are discussed because their treatment helps explain the meaning, implications, and advantages of the Establishment Clause approach. These include issues surrounding required pathology reports, written consents and recordkeeping. The discussion of these issues shows that the Establishment Clause approach entails what I call the Neutrality Principle. This principle is sometimes acknowledged and employed by the Court and is, I maintain, superior to reliance on accepted medical practice, which is the Court's most common alternative. The Establishment Clause approach is also shown to be free of the defects that Justice O'Connor correctly attributes to *Roe*'s trimester framework. In addition, the chapter discusses state requirements designed to protect the life chances of older fetuses.

Chapter 8 discusses restrictions on public funding for abortions, information requirements, required spousal and parental consent, and required parental notification.

The Trimester Framework and Its Exceptions

Justice Blackmun, writing for the Court in *Roe v. Wade*, divided pregnancy into three roughly equal segments, or trimesters. In the first of these, "the abortion decision and its effectuation must be left to the medical judgement of the pregnant woman's attending physician."[1] In the second trimester, "the State . . . may, if it chooses, regulate the abortion procedure in ways that are reasonably related to maternal health."[2] Finally, in the last trimester, "the stage subsequent to viability, the State in promoting its interest in the potentiality of human life, may . . . regulate, and even proscribe, abortion except where it is necessary, in appropriate medical judgement, for the preservation of the life or health of the mother."[3]

While the Court continues to discuss abortion in terms of these trimesters, exceptions allowed by the majority and criticisms leveled by Justice O'Connor provide ample justification for abandoning this framework. The present chapter reviews reasons for abandoning the trimester framework and proposes an alternative. This alternative, which is based on the Establishment Clause analysis in Chapter 6, provides a principled basis for most of the Court's decisions concerning the state's regulation of abortion. It also answers the concerns expressed well by Justice O'Connor.

According to the trimester approach, state abortion regulations that are "reasonably related to maternal health" cannot be applied before the second trimester. The reason is that "abortion in early pregnancy, that is, prior to the end of the first trimester, although not without its risk, is now relatively safe. Mortality rates for women undergoing early abortions, where the procedure is legal, appear to be as low as or lower than the rates for normal childbirth."[4]

This restriction on state regulations generated confusion almost immediately. On the one hand, states could not regulate first-trimester abortions. On the other hand, such abortions were to be left to the medical judgment of physicians. Where does this leave a state requirement that first-trimester abortions be performed by licensed physicians? The Court seems to allow this requirement when it leaves first-trimester abortion decisions up to the medical judgment of the attending physician. But if a state allows only physicians to perform first-trimester abortions because the state is concerned about maternal health, then this physicians-only requirement is an exception to the rule that state regulations designed to protect maternal health may not be applied to abortions performed during the first trimester.

Faced with the choice, the Court had no difficulty accepting physicians-only requirements as exceptions to its rule against the regulation of first-trimester abortions. In *Connecticut v. Menillo* (1975), the Court upheld a Connecticut statute that made it a crime for nonphysicians to perform first-trimester abortions. The Court justified its decision in these words: "The insufficiency of the State's interest in maternal health [before the second trimester] is predicated upon the first trimester abortion's being as safe for the woman as normal childbirth at term, and that predicate holds true only if the abortion is performed by medically competent personnel under conditions insuring maximum safety for the woman."[5] So state requirements that only physicians perform first-trimester abortions are exceptions to the rule disallowing before the second-trimester state regulations designed to protect maternal health.

The following year, the Court added two more exceptions. In *Planned Parenthood of Missouri v. Danforth* (1976), the Court approved, first, Missouri's requirement that to undergo even a first-trimester abortion, a woman "must certify in writing her consent to the procedure and 'that her consent is informed and freely given and is not the result of coercion.'"[6] The Court considered this requirement to be reasonable because "the decision to abort . . . is an important, and often a stressful one, and it is desirable and imperative that it be made with full knowledge of its nature and consequences."[7]

The other state requirement concerning first-trimester abortions that the Court upheld in *Danforth* concerned reporting and recordkeeping. Even as applied to first-trimester abortions, the Court maintained, "recordkeeping and reporting requirements that are reasonably directed to the preservation of maternal health and that properly respect a patient's confidentiality and privacy are permissible."[8] The records so collected "may be a resource that is relevant to decisions involving medical experience and judgment," and have "no legally significant impact or consequence on the abortion decision or on the physician–patient relationship."[9]

A fourth exception to the trimester framework, made by the Court in *Akron v. Akron Center for Reproductive Health* (1983), concerns the state's application of a hospitalization requirement to the entire second trimester. Ohio required that all second-trimester abortions be performed in hospitals and disallowed abortions by the method of dilatation-and-evacuation (D and E). They claimed permission for these requirements in *Roe v. Wade*, where it is written that after the first trimester "examples of permissible state regulation . . . [include] requirements . . . as to the facility in which the procedure is to be performed, that is, whether it must be a hospital or may be a clinic . . . and the like."[10] In *Akron*, however, the Court stressed the condition that such state regulation is legitimate only "to the extent that the regulation reasonably relates to the preservation and protection of maternal health."[11] According to the Court, Ohio's regulations did not meet this standard. The Court cited evidence recognized by the court of appeals. During the first part of the second trimester (at least up to sixteen weeks of pregnancy) "D and E is the safest method of performing post-first-trimester abortions today."[12] In addition, the Court noted that the American College of Obstetrics and Gynecology (ACOG) "no longer suggests that all second-trimester abortions be performed in a hospital."

In sum, Ohio's requirements are unconstitutional because they "depart from accepted medical practice."[13] Where accepted medical practice divides pregnancy in ways that differ from the trimester approach, the state must follow suit. A state regulation that is reasonable with regard to one part of a trimester cannot be applied to the entire trimester if such application does not accord with accepted medical practice. "Rather, the State is obliged to make a reasonable effort to limit the effects of its regulations to the period in the trimester during which its health interest will be furthered."[14] Here the Court not only allows, but requires, departures from its original trimester approach.

O'Connor's Objections to the Trimester Framework

After noting these Court-endorsed exceptions to the trimester approach, Justice O'Connor presents cogent reasons for abandoning that approach altogether. First, as the Court's own exceptions suggest, the underlying rationales for the trimester divisions do not reliably correspond to those divisions. The rationale for restricting state regulations during the first trimester is "that until the end of the first trimester mortality in abortion may be less than mortality in normal childbirth."[15] But medical improvements move forward (to a time later in pregnancy) the point at which continuing a normal pregnancy is more dangerous to a woman than is abortion. So, on the Court's own rationale, the state should be prohibited from regulating not only first-trimester abortions but many (probably most) second-trimester abortions as well, since these abortions now pose a health risk to the pregnant woman that is less than that of continued pregnancy. Thus, the rationale for dividing the first from the second trimester conflicts irreconcilably with placement of the division in question between those two trimesters.

The same is true of the division between the second and third trimesters. The Court maintained in *Roe* that because third-trimester fetuses are viable, the state could go so far as to proscribe abortions altogether in the third trimester ("except where it is necessary . . . for the preservation of the life or health of the mother"[16]). The Court reasoned that when a fetus is viable, the state's interest in its "potential life" is great enough to permit such a proscription. In 1973, when *Roe* was decided, viability was at about twenty-eight weeks, which corresponds closely to the division between the second and third trimesters. But medical advances have moved the point of viability to some point during the second half of the second trimester. If viability remains the point at which the state's interest in "potential life" is sufficient to justify the proscription of abortion, then that point no longer corresponds to the division between the second and third trimesters.

Worse than this, O'Connor points out, is the following possibility: Because of advances in medicine, abortions may become safer than continued pregnancy so late in the gestational process, and viability may come so early in pregnancy, that the abortion of a viable fetus will pose a smaller health risk to a pregnant woman than would continuation of a normal pregnancy. Should this be the case, *Roe*'s trimester approach would disallow any state regulation of, or interference with, such abortions (because they are safer than continued pregnancy) and at the same time would allow states to proscribe such abortions (in the interest of preserving "the potential life"). This is the contradiction that O'Connor foresees. She writes:

> The *Roe* framework, then, is clearly on a collision course with itself. As the medical risks of various abortion procedures decrease, the point at which the State may regulate for reasons of maternal health is moved further forward to actual childbirth. As medical science becomes better able to provide for the separate existence of the fetus, the point of viability is moved further back toward conception.[17]

A deeper problem in the *Roe* framework, O'Connor contends, is largely responsible for this regrettable result. In *Roe* the Court tied constitutional guarantees to "accepted medical practice." This means, according to O'Connor, that

> the State must continuously and conscientiously study contemporary medical and scientific literature in order to determine whether the effect of a particular regulation is to "depart from accepted medical practice."
> . . . Assuming that legislative bodies are able to engage in this exacting task, it is difficult to believe that our Constitution *requires* that they do it as a prelude to protecting the health of their citizens. It is even more difficult to believe that this Court . . . believes itself competent to make these inquiries.[18]

In short, the *Roe* framework misallocates institutional responsibilities regarding the adjustments needed for health care to correspond to "accepted medical practice." This is primarily the responsibility of the medical profession. It can also be the responsibility of the legislature, but only insofar as the legislature so chooses. It certainly is not the responsibility of the courts.

Finally, O'Connor correctly questions the rationale that the Court used in *Roe* to distinguish first- from second-trimester abortions. The rationale is that when abortion is at least as safe as continuing a normal pregnancy, the state may not regulate abortion in the interest of maternal health. We have seen that this rationale does not justify a division between the first and second trimesters. The point here is that it makes no sense in the first place to attach constitutional importance to the distinction between abortions that are, and those that are not, safer than continued pregnancy. The state's legitimate interest in fostering the health of its citizens justifies regulations rationally related to improving medical practice. Abortion at a certain state of pregnancy may be safer than childbirth, yet state regulation may make it safer still. In these circumstances, O'Connor reasons, the state is properly doing its job when it mandates the regulation in question. The Court should not stand in its way. She writes: "The fallacy inherent in the *Roe* framework is apparent: just because the State has a compelling interest in ensuring maternal safety once an abortion may be more dangerous than childbirth, it simply does not follow that the State has *no* interest before that point that justifies state regulation to ensure that first-trimester abortions are performed as safely as possible."[19]

Justice O'Connor went on to criticize the Court for attaching importance in *Roe* to the advent of viability. She maintained that "*potential* life is no less potential in the first weeks of pregnancy than it is at viability or afterward." She concluded on this basis that "the choice of viability as the point at which the state interest in *potential* life becomes compelling is no less arbitrary than choosing any point before viability or any point afterward."[20]

Chapter 2 maintained that O'Connor's argument at this point is fallacious. It fails to observe the distinction between first and second potentiality that was implicit in the Court's *Roe* decision. Nevertheless, there are different reasons for agreeing with O'Connor that the viability standard should be replaced by the standard of similarity to newborns. Chapter 6 argued that fetuses twenty weeks or younger are so dissimilar to newborns that attributions to them of personhood, a right to life, inherent worth, or intrinsic value are epistemologically religious. State laws predicated on such attributions violate the Establishment Clause of the First Amendment because the epistemological standard corresponds to the meaning that the Court attaches to "religion" in First Amendment contexts.

I turn now to applications of the above Establishment Clause analysis to state regulations of the abortion procedure. I argue, first, that the Establishment Clause provides a basis for constitutional limitations in this area. The resulting limitations do not fall prey to the objections that O'Connor has justly leveled against *Roe*'s trimester framework.

Superiority of the Establishment Clause Approach to the Trimester Framework

The First Amendment analysis given in Chapter 6 divides pregnancy into two parts, from fertilization through the twentieth week of pregnancy (when the unborn's humanity is a matter of religious belief), and from the twenty-first week (or so) through birth (during which the unborn's humanity becomes a secular matter). In some respects this account resembles the Uniform Abortion Act of 1972 that the American Bar Association (ABA) recommended for adoption by state legislatures. That act, too, divided pregnancy into two parts, and suggested that the twentieth week was a reasonable time for more stringent legal requirements to be applied. It did not, however, justify that division as constitutionally required, much less as resting on the First Amendment's Establishment Clause.[21] The analysis given in Chapter 6 may be viewed as a justification for the result that the ABA endorsed, but did not support with adequate constitutional arguments.

The two-part Establishment Clause analysis offered here does not suffer from the defects noted in the previous section to bedevil the

Court's trimester framework. For example, we saw in the previous section that there is conflict in the Court's trimester framework between the rationales for the divisions between trimesters and the location of those divisions at the points of trimester transition. In addition, the rationales for tripartite division justify continued movement of the points of division. States and courts must keep abreast of, and adjust quickly to, rapidly evolving standards of accepted medical practice.

The standard proposed here does not suffer from either of these problems. The point of division corresponds to the rationale for that division. Through at least the twentieth week of gestation, the unborn differs from newborns in ways whose significance for the attribution of personhood is, in our secular conceptual framework, inherently problematic. Through at least the twentieth week of gestation, then, attributions of personhood, a right to life, inherent worth, and intrinsic value are properly treated as religious beliefs. The Establishment Clause disallows legislation that lacks a secular purpose or whose primary effect is to advance or inhibit the acceptance of such a belief.[22] So there are constitutional limitations, discussed at greater length below and in Chapter 8, on legislation concerning abortions performed before the twenty-first week of gestation. The rationale for these constitutional limitations accords exactly with the gestational period to which the limitations apply, that is, the first twenty weeks of pregnancy.

What is more, due to the nature of the underlying rationale, the period to which the limitations apply will not vary with the state of medical technology or with evolving standards of accepted medical practice. Of course, as explained in Chapter 6, the cutoff is left somewhat indeterminate in the present work. Rather than place the division between the twentieth and twenty-first week, the Court may place it at some other point before the twenty-eighth week. But this complication does not affect the contention made here (or any other matter of substance in the present work). The cutoff point will be no less stable if it is placed by the Court at twenty-three or twenty-four, rather than at twenty or twenty-one, weeks. There is, in any case, no way that advances in medical technology or changes in standards of accepted medical practice can alter the differences between typical newborns and the unborn during the first twenty (or twenty-three) weeks of gestation. Thus the point of transition will remain stable as long as we retain relevant secular concepts.

In the long run, it is true, advances in medicine affect some of our secular concepts. An example is the replacement of heartbeat with brain activity as the standard for distinguishing between life and death. But such changes are much slower than, for example, changes in the point at which abortion is safer than childbirth, changes in the probability of continued development outside its mother of a twenty-six week fetus, changes in the safest method of mid-second-trimester abortion, or changes in the availability of that method in Missouri.[23] So conceptual changes, even those associated with medical advance, are many fewer and much slower than are medical advances themselves.

Equally important, conceptual changes, unlike changes in medicine, are matters within the competence of courts. Thus the standard proposed here does not suffer from the problem, correctly attributed by O'Connor to the Court's trimester framework, of misallocating institutional responsibilities for responding to technological change. Such responsibility rests on the profession involved, and on legislatures to the extent that they so choose. The courts, lacking popular mandates and adequate powers of investigation, should not be primarily or often in the forefront of responding to changes in medicine and technology. Courts properly deal primarily in concepts—those employed in the Constitution, in statutes, and in the common law. The Establishment Clause approach proposed here, unlike the Court's trimester framework, confines courts to their proper role. Courts would have to decide when, between the twenty-first and twenty-eighth week of gestation, a fetus resembles a newborn sufficiently to make its treatment as a human being a secular, rather than a religious, matter. This is properly the responsibility of a court whose mandate includes ensuring the constitutionality of legislation. In view of the provisions of the Constitution, and of its amendments, the Supreme Court's task inevitably includes interpretation of such concepts as "religion" and "person."

The Establishment Clause approach is free, also, of the remaining defects that O'Connor noted in the trimester framework. Because the Establishment Clause approach does not maintain that viability is constitutionally relevant, it is free of the defects peculiar to the trimester framework's use of viability. Because the Establishment Clause approach employs only one major conceptual distinction, rather than two, it cannot possibly be on "a collision course with itself," as O'Connor predicts for the trimester framework. As explained in the preceding section, that collision would result if viability, supposedly the second cutoff point, ever occurred before, rather than after, normal childbirth became safer than abortion, which is supposed to be the first cutoff. In this situation of transposed cutoff points, states would be both disallowed regulations that interfere with certain abortions (because those abortions are safe) and allowed to outlaw almost all of those very same abortions (because the fetuses in question are viable). Having only one cutoff point, the Establishment Clause approach is free of any such defect.

Required Efforts to Save the Fetus

Chapter 6 argued that Justice Stevens was correct in *Webster v. Reproductive Health Services*. Abortion-related legislation should be tested against the guarantee contained in the Establishment Clause. The result is what I now call the Establishment Clause approach. The present section applies this approach to state requirements designed to improve the chances for survival of aborted fetuses.

Because secular concepts are insufficient to justify the claim that fetuses twenty weeks or younger are persons with a right to life, any legislation predicated on that belief is an unconstitutional establishment of religion. The same restrictions do not apply to legislative efforts to preserve the life or health of somewhat older fetuses because they can be unproblematically classified as human beings.

The two-part division advocated here differs significantly from the viability standard used by the Court in *Roe v. Wade*. Medical technology may someday make possible the continued development outside its mother of an eighteen-week fetus. Such a fetus would then be viable. According to the Establishment Clause approach, it would still be unconstitutional for a state to *require* that provision be made to save the life of such a fetus. The requirement would lack a *secular* public purpose. For what purpose would be served by the requirement except to respect the human rights that some people (religiously) attribute to the fetus in question?

Suppose that a state cited needed population growth as the reason for its requirement that efforts be made to save the lives of young fetuses. Any such justification would probably fall prey to the alternate means test. A secular goal may not be served by religious means when secular means would suffice. This is why the Bible may not be used as the text to teach reading in public schools. Other books, unrelated to religion, could serve as well, and so must be used instead of the Bible. By the same token, population growth may not be fostered through means that suggest state endorsement of religious beliefs about the personhood of young fetuses when alternate means will do. In this case, the state could encourage population growth through special subsidies to families with three or more children, as is done in France. Or it could establish free day care so as to lessen the childrearing burden on parents, thereby encouraging more people to have more children. Until such means as these are demonstrably exhausted, a state that claimed a need for more population would not be able, according to the Establishment Clause approach, to meet that need by requiring efforts to save the lives of fetuses whose humanity is a matter of problematic religious belief.

This does not mean that I disagree at all with the Court's decision in *Planned Parenthood Association v. Ashcroft* (1983) to uphold Missouri's requirement that a second physician attend postviability abortions. The second physician is supposed to "take all reasonable steps in keeping with good medical practice . . . to preserve the life and health of the viable unborn child; provided that it does not pose an increased risk to the life or health of the woman."[24] At the time when Missouri passed this statute, viability was at about twenty-eight weeks, and the state is, according to the Establishment Clause approach, free to treat fetuses of that age as people with rights. The state is free, also, to suppose that a physician whose job it is to perform an abortion may be less able than one whose specialty is the delivery of premature infants, to minister to the complex needs of a barely viable fetus. So, even though "Missouri does not require two physicians in attendance for any other medical or surgical procedure, including childbirth or delivery of a premature infant,"[25] an exceptional requirement seems justified in this kind of case.

Again, however, Missouri's requirement is justified not by the fact that the fetus is viable but by the fact that the fetus can be viewed *through secular concepts* as a *person*. Should viability occur at twenty weeks or earlier, when the personhood of the fetus is a matter of religious belief, a second-physician requirement designed to save the lives of such young but viable fetuses would be an unconstitutional establishment of a religious belief.

The Neutrality Principle

This section explains and illustrates a general principle regarding statutes designed to protect the health of pregnant women undergoing abortions. From the Establishment Clause perspective, as we saw earlier in the chapter, state regulations to promote the medical well-being of pregnant women can be validly applied to abortions performed during all stages of pregnancy, including the earliest stages. The present section is devoted to considering the additional general principle that regulations regarding the abortion of young fetuses (twenty weeks or younger) should not differ from state regulations pertaining to medical procedures of comparable difficulty or danger. I call this the Neutrality Principle.

This principle can be illustrated by considering its operation in a more common Establishment Clause context. Consider, for example, city fire regulations. They generally apply to buildings regardless of whether those buildings are used for religious purposes, and regardless of which religion is involved. The fire code classifies buildings according to such factors as the materials from which the buildings are constructed, their height, their age, the number of their exits, and the number of people expected to occupy them. It would contravene the Establishment Clause for a municipality, without justifications based on secular considerations of fire prevention and human safety, to apply more stringent (or lax) fire regulations to buildings used for religious purposes, or to buildings used by members of a disfavored (or especially favored) religious sect.

The Establishment Clause applies in the same way to the state regulation of abortions performed before (at least) the twenty-first week of pregnancy. If these regulations are justified by the need to protect the pregnant woman's health, then protections afforded such women must be neither more nor less stringent than those afforded by the state to patients undergoing procedures of comparable complexity or risk. In other words, before at least the twenty-first week, the Establishment Clause approach requires the Court to adopt Establishment Clause neutrality with regard to the state regulation of abortion procedures.

At times, the Court seems to employ the Neutrality Principle. In *Doe v. Bolton* (1973), for example, the Court invalidated a Georgia requirement that abortions be performed only in hospitals accredited by the Joint Commission on Accreditation of Hospitals (JCAH). The Court noted that

> In Georgia, there is no restriction on the performance of non-abortion surgery in a hospital not yet accredited by the JCAH so long as other requirements imposed by the State, such as licensing of the hospital and of the operating surgeon, are met.[26]
>
> We hold that the JCAH-accreditation requirement does not withstand judicial scrutiny in the present context. It is a requirement that simply is not "based on differences that are reasonably related to the purposes of the Act in which it is found."[27]

The purpose of the act was purportedly protection of patients' health. If operations of comparable or greater medical difficulty or risk than abortion are legally permitted in certain facilities, then it is unconstitutional for the state to prohibit abortions in those facilities. The state is committed to the view that the facilities in question meet its standards of patient care. In short, it is unconstitutional to make an exception of abortion (before the twenty-first week) in a statute designed to protect the health of patients when the exception is unrelated to patients' health.

In the same case, the Court invalidated on similar reasoning Georgia's requirement that before an abortion is performed "the performing physician's judgment be confirmed by the independent examinations of the patient by two other licensed physicians."[28] The Court noted: "Again, no other voluntary medical or surgical procedure for which Georgia requires confirmation by two other physicians has been cited to us. . . . Required acquiescence by co-practitioners has no rational connection with a patient's needs."[29] Without good reason, abortion may not be made an exception to the state's general requirements for medical care.

The Court employed the same principle thirteen years later. In *Thornburgh v. American College of Obstetrics and Gynecology* (1986), the Court rejected Pennsylvania's requirement that all patients be informed of certain medical complications that abortion may involve. Among their reasons was the observation that "the Commonwealth does not, and surely would not, compel similar disclosure of every possible peril of necessary surgery or of simple vaccination."[30] Here, again, it seems to be the state's lack of neutrality that bothers the Court. The state should not, without justification, treat abortion in an exceptional manner.

On one point of contention in *Ashcroft*, both the majority and dissent seem to base their reasoning on this kind of neutrality. Missouri law required that tissues removed during all abortion procedures be examined by a trained pathologist. The majority upheld this provision of Missouri's abortion statute, noting that "Missouri requires a pathologist—not the performing physician—to examine tissue after almost every type of surgery."[31]

The dissent pointed out, however, that most abortions are performed in clinics, not hospitals, and Missouri's general requirement that removed tissues be examined by a trained pathologist applies, except in the case of abortion, only to tissues removed in a hospital. "Missouri does not require pathologists' reports for any other surgical procedure performed in clinics, or for minor surgery performed in hospitals."[32] So it should not require such reports in cases where abortions are performed in clinics, the dissent concluded.

The majority replied that there were relevant health-related differences between abortions and other minor surgical procedures, and these differences justified Missouri's special treatment of abortion. "The Sun-Times of Chicago . . . disclosed widespread questionable practices in abortion clinics in Chicago, including failures to obtain proper pathology reports. . . . It is clear, therefore, that a State reasonably could conclude that a pathology requirement is necessary in abortion clinics as well as in general hospitals."[33]

The point of greatest importance for our purposes concerns the agreement, rather than the disagreement, between the majority and the dissent. Both accept the principle that abortion should be treated like other medical procedures of comparable complexity and risk, except where there are health-related reasons to depart from such equality of treatment. In this respect, they both agree with the Neutrality Principle employed in the Establishment Clause approach.

Appropriate Judicial Skepticism

The Court's 5–4 split on the issue of required pathology reports appears to rest on the application, rather than on the acceptance, of the Neutrality Principle. This section points out that where the Establishment Clause is concerned, the Court not only requires neutrality but guards neutrality vigilantly. It requires that purposes alleged to justify deviations from neutrality be well articulated, be sincere (rather than a sham), and that alternate, neutral means of serving those purposes be impractical. In short, in Establishment Clause contexts, the Court is typically skeptical of state assertions of secular purposes that are not clearly expressed and apparently realistic. This skepticism imposes on the state something analogous to a burden of proof. Because Missouri had not shouldered this burden successfully, I argue, the dissenting four justices were correct. Missouri's pathology report requirement should have been declared unconstitutional. The section closes with a consideration of Missouri's requirements concerning written consents and recordkeeping. These, too, violate the Neutrality Principle because the state had not overcome the judicial skepticism that is appropriate where the exceptional treatment of abortion is concerned.

Regarding statutes that may contravene the Establishment Clause, the Court is typically skeptical of state assertions of secular public purposes. As we saw in Chapter 6, the Court was not convinced in

Abington School District v. Schempp (1963) that required readings from the Bible were justified by the state's announced secular purposes. The state maintained these purposes to be "the promotion of moral values, the contradiction to the materialistic trends of our times, the perpetuation of our institutions and the teaching of literature."[34] Because the establishment of religion was at issue, the Court adopted a skeptical attitude and rejected the adequacy of these alleged secular purposes.

The Court took the same skeptical stance toward a Kentucky statute requiring "the posting of a copy of the Ten Commandments, purchased with private contributions, on the wall of each public classroom in the State."[35] The Court noted: "The Commonwealth insists that the statute in question serves a secular legislative purpose." That purpose is supposedly explained on each copy in small print: "The secular application of the Ten Commandments is clearly seen in its adoption as the fundamental legal code of Western Civilization and the Common Law of the United States."[36] Referring to *Schempp*, the Court concluded: "Under the Court's rulings . . . such an 'avowed' secular purpose is not sufficient to avoid conflict with the First Amendment."[37]

The issue of secular purpose was raised again in *Wallace v. Jaffree* (1985). The Court there overturned a statute mandating that the public school day begin with a moment of silence "for meditation or voluntary prayer." The Court found the statute to lack a secular public purpose. In his dissent, Justice Rehnquist maintained that the secular purpose requirement "will condemn nothing so long as the legislature utters a secular purpose and says nothing about aiding religion."[38] Justice O'Connor disagreed. Concurring in the Court's judgment, she replied directly to Rehnquist's contention. "It is of course possible," she wrote, "that a legislature will enunciate a sham secular purpose for a statute. I have little doubt that our courts are capable of distinguishing a sham secular purpose from a sincere one."[39] Concurring separately in the same case, Justice Powell endorsed O'Connor's requirement that the state's "secular purpose . . . be 'sincere'; a law will not pass constitutional muster if the secular purpose articulated by the legislature is merely a 'sham.'"[40]

The creation science cases are additional examples of effective judicial skepticism, where the Establishment Clause is concerned, of a state's avowed secular purposes. In *Edward v. Aguillard* (1987), Justice Brennan wrote for a majority of seven, that "while the Court is normally deferential to a State's articulation of a secular purpose, it is required that the statement of such a purpose be sincere and not a sham."[41]

The Court rejected Louisiana's avowed secular purposes of providing a comprehensive scientific education and advancing academic freedom.

Consider again the disagreement in *Ashcroft* between the five justices who approved and the four who disapproved of Missouri's requirement that a pathologist examine tissues removed during abortions that take place in clinics. As we have seen, when the Court applies the Establishment Clause, it requires that states articulate a sincere secular purpose that is not a sham. As it happens, Missouri did not articulate any reason for treating abortions differently than it treats other minor surgeries performed in clinics. Justice Powell, writing for the majority, correctly noted that "medical opinion differs widely on [the] question"[42] of the need for a "pathologist's report on each and every specimen of tissue removed from abortion or for that matter from any other surgical procedure which involves the removal of tissue from the human body."[43]

The crux of the issue is that Powell cited no state rationale, or evidence at trial, to justify treating abortion differently in this regard from "any other surgical procedure which involves removal of tissue from the human body." On the contrary, the expert witness quoted by Powell explicitly endorsed treating abortion the same as these other surgical procedures. So to justify the different treatment required by Missouri's law, Powell offered his own speculation, based on newspaper stories about abortion clinics in a different state.

This sort of speculation does not accord with the Court's usual treatment of secular purpose in Establishment Clause contexts. The state must present a secular purpose, and the Court will not be extremely deferential. It will consider whether the avowed purpose is sincere or a sham. The same Establishment Clause approach should be applied to state regulations affecting abortions performed during the first twenty weeks of pregnancy. Missouri's exceptional treatment of abortion would appear to fail an Establishment Clause challenge. The state articulated no secular purpose for the exceptional treatment, and the Court had no evidence submitted to it to justify the exception. Purposes created on the spot by judicial speculation are not normally considered adequate to meet an Establishment Clause challenge. Using the Establishment Clause approach, Missouri's pathology report requirement is, on the evidence available to the Court, unconstitutional unless and until the requirement is made applicable equally to abortion and to "any other surgical procedure which involves removal of tissue from the human body."[44]

The same kind of analysis shows that the Court erred in *Danforth* (1976) when they accepted Missouri's written consent and recordkeeping requirements. As explained earlier in the chapter Missouri required a written consent before first-trimester abortions were performed. Missouri applied also to first-trimester abortions the requirement that confidential records be kept. These requirements were noted above as exceptions to the rule that the Court disallows state regulation of first-trimester abortions. They are noted here because, like the pathology reports reviewed in *Ashcroft*, these requirements contravene the principle of state neutrality in matters of religion (i.e., abortion).

Consider the written-consent requirement. Writing for the majority, Justice Blackmun acknowledged that with the exception of "persons committed to the Missouri State chest hospital, or to mental or correctional institutions,"[45] "no other Missouri statute . . . requires a patient's prior written consent to a surgical procedure."[46] Given the inherently religious nature of the abortion decision, the exceptional requirement of written consent for abortions (performed before the twenty-first week) should cause the Court to suspect an establishment of religion. They should suspect either a purpose or a primary effect related to religious beliefs about the personhood of young fetuses. So the Court should require the State to justify its exceptional treatment of abortion. But it did not do so. Instead, Blackmun wrote, "the decision to abort . . . is an important, and often a stressful one, and it is desirable and imperative that it be made with full knowledge of its nature and consequences."[47] He then generalized the point: "We could not say that a requirement imposed by the State that a prior written consent for any surgery would be unconstitutional. As a consequence, we see no constitutional defect in requiring it only for some types of surgery as, for example, an intracardiac procedure, or where the surgical risk is elevated above a specified mortality level, or, for that matter, for abortion."[48]

From the Establishment Clause perspective, Blackmun's reasoning here is flawed. Certainly the state could require prior written consent for *all* surgical procedures because surgery is, generally speaking, a serious matter, and the patient's consent is important. Alternatively, the state could require prior written consent only for especially risky procedures, such as "an intracardiac procedure, or where the surgical risk is elevated above a specified mortality level."[49] In this case the exceptional requirement of prior written consent would be clearly related to secular values. Given the importance in our secular value system of human life, health, and self-determination, it makes sense to require greater assurance of consent (self-determination) where human life and health are at greater risk. But abortions, even through the twentieth week of pregnancy, pose less risk to life and health than do most other surgical procedures. On what *secular* grounds, then, can an exception be made of abortion, so that prior written consent is required for abortion but not for other surgical procedures?

The fact, noted by Blackmun, that "the decision to abort . . . is an important, and often a stressful one" would constitute a secular rationale for making an exception of abortion only if the decision to abort were *exceptionally* important, *exceptionally* stressful, or both. Neither the state nor the Court has espoused this view. What is more, the view is not credible. Could one seriously claim that the decision to abort is more important or stressful than the decision of a woman with breast cancer who must choose one among three possible courses of treatment: radical mastectomy, simple mastectomy, and radiation therapy? The choice made by cardiac patients between bypass surgery and angioplasty would seem also to be at least as important and stressful as the decision to abort.

Thus the state and the Court have given no cogent reason for a requirement of prior written consent that is applied *exceptionally* to abortion. In view of the religious nature of beliefs about abortion, the state cannot without justification make an exception of abortion any more than it could, without secular justification, apply exceptional firecode regulations to churches of only one particular sect. Such unjustified exceptions violate the Establishment Clause. But, the state is still free to enact reasonable consent requirements and fire codes that apply uniformly or that have exceptions clearly justified on secular grounds.

Basically the same considerations apply to Missouri's recordkeeping requirement. "Recordkeeping of this kind, if not abused or overdone, can be useful to the State's interest in protecting the health of its female citizens."[50] But there is no showing by either the state or the Court that these benefits flow uniquely or especially from recordkeeping regarding abortions, and the state has no such requirements "with respect to other, and comparable, medical or surgical procedures."[51] Again, it contravenes the Establishment Clause to make an exception of abortion.

In sum, the Establishment Clause approach reveals that the Court erred in *Danforth* when it accepted Missouri's written consent and recordkeeping requirements, just as it did later in *Ashcroft* when it accepted that state's pathology-report requirement. At least until the twenty-first week of pregnancy, the decision whether to have an abortion is inextricably connected to religious beliefs concerning the humanity of young fetuses. The Establishment Clause requires state neutrality with regard to such religious beliefs. The exceptional treatment of abortion must therefore be justified by a sincere secular purpose that is not a sham. Missouri has not supplied convincing secular purposes for the written-consent, recordkeeping and pathology-report requirements.

Undue Burdens and Unconstitutional Endorsements

Justice O'Connor argued that these three requirements—related to written consent, recordkeeping, and pathology reports—are constitutional because they do not place an undue burden on the exercise of a woman's right to have an abortion. The right to have an abortion should, according to O'Connor, be protected "against state action 'drastically limiting the availability and safety of the desired service.'"[52] State imposed requirements "involving absolute obstacles or severe limitations on the abortion decision"[53] are thus unconstitutional precisely because they are unduly burdensome. O'Connor wrote: "In my view, this 'unduly burdensome' standard should be applied to . . . regulations throughout the entire pregnancy. . . . If the particular regulation does not 'unduly burde[n]' the fundamental rights, then our evaluation of that regulation is limited to our determination that the regulation rationally relates to a legitimate state purpose."[54] The present section shows that O'Connor's "unduly burdensome" standard is inconsistent with the Establishment Clause approach advocated here.

O'Connor would apply to legislation that is not "unduly burdensome" the relatively lax rational relationship standard of review. Under this standard of review, the Court finds legislation to be valid when it concludes that rational individuals could honestly believe that the legislation in question would further a goal (*any* goal) that the state is permitted to (attempt to) further. Using this standard, the Court is deferential to the legislators' views. It exercises judicial restraint. Most important in the present context, the Court does not require that the legislature articulate any goal at all. In the absence of a legitimate goal articulated by the legislature, the Court will supply a goal of its own, impute that goal to the legislature, and find the legislation in question constitutional because it is rationally related to furthering that goal.[55]

This is exactly what we saw Justice Powell do in *Ashcroft*. He upheld Missouri's pathology-report requirement by attributing to the state a special concern about mismanagement in abortion clinics. He then referred to newspaper articles concerning abortion clinics in a different state to justify the concern that he had just attributed to Missouri's legislators. O'Connor agreed with Powell's approach and conclusion.

She had already articulated the "unduly burdensome" standard in a companion case that was decided the same day as *Ashcroft*. She then wrote in her *Ashcroft* opinion, "I agree that the pathology report requirement . . . is constitutional because it imposes no undue burden on the limited right to undergo an abortion."[56] Where there is no undue burden, rational relationship is the appropriate test of constitutionality, according to O'Connor, and rational relationships exist as long as the Court can imagine a legitimate goal that the legislation might further.

I argued in the preceding section that where the Establishment Clause is concerned, the Court is generally less deferential. It requires that the state articulate a secular purpose; it requires that this purpose be sincere, rather than a sham; and it requires that alternate means, unrelated to religion, be substituted wherever possible for means that raise questions of religious establishment. The Establishment Clause approach to abortion-related legislation thus disallows the kind of deference that Powell and O'Connor showed to Missouri's legislators.

The present section contends that the Establishment Clause approach disallows completely O'Connor's "unduly burdensome" standard. Where the Establishment Clause is concerned, any invidious distinction is unconstitutional, no matter how minimal is the resulting inconvenience or burden. It is unconstitutional even if there is no burden at all. A one dollar tax levied only on Catholics would be unconstitutional, as would a state endorsement of Catholicism. The Court made this point in *Engel v. Vitale* (1962): "The Establishment Clause, unlike the Free Exercise Clause, does not depend on any showing of direct governmental compulsion and is violated by the enactment of laws which establish . . . religion whether those laws operate directly to coerce nonobserving individuals or not."[57] So even if Missouri's distinction between abortion and similar surgical procedures could be predicted to have no impact at all on women's access to abortion, it is unconstitutional because it deviates from state neutrality on a matter of religious significance. This consideration applies equally to the pathology-report, written-consent and recordkeeping requirements. When the state deviates from neutrality concerning a matter of religious significance, it implicitly (at least) endorses one religious view as preferable to another, and this is what the Establishment Clause forbids.

Obviously, if implicit endorsements are unconstitutional, explicit endorsements are more clearly so. This point was made by Justice Stevens in *Webster v. Reproductive Health Services*. Missouri (again!) enacted an abortion statute with a preamble that "sets forth 'findings' by the

Missouri legislature that '[t]he life of each human being begins at conception,' and that '[u]nborn children have protectable interests in life, health, and well-being.'"[58] The majority found this preamble acceptable because Missouri predicated none of its abortion restrictions on it. They reasoned that it could not interfere with anyone's abortion rights if it lacks all practical effect. From the Establishment Clause perspective, however, nothing could be more clearly unconstitutional than an official state "finding" that one religious belief is correct and opposing views are incorrect. So the Establishment Clause approach requires invalidating the statutory preamble considered in *Webster*. The preamble is an unconstitutional endorsement of a religious belief.

Conclusion

The availability of abortion would hardly be affected by the substitution of the Establishment Clause approach for the Court's approach to the issues discussed in the present chapter. Both approaches support state requirements designed to protect and improve the life chances of older fetuses. Where the two approaches differ, for example, concerning a statutory preamble and requirements regarding pathology reports, written consents, and recordkeeping, the practical availability of abortion is hardly affected by the difference of approach. The Court accepted the preamble to Missouri's statute precisely because no regulations were predicated on it. They accepted requirements regarding pathology reports, written consents, and recordkeeping on the explicit, and realistic, understanding that these requirements do not reduce significantly the practical availability of abortion. So the Establishment Clause rejection of these requirements, and of Missouri's preamble, implies no greater, or different, availability of abortion than that provided for by the Court.

The significant differences between the two approaches concern susceptibility to cogent objections. The Establishment Clause approach does not have problems that beset the Court's approach. The Court's trimester framework is not followed consistently by the Court; it leads to continual shifts in the stages of pregnancy at which state regulations of various sorts are allowed; it misallocates institutional responsibilities for keeping abreast of current medical practice; and it would become self-contradictory if certain technological developments were to occur. The Establishment Clause approach has none of these problems. In addition, it employs the Neutrality Principle, which provides consistent guidance regarding Missouri's preamble and state pathology-report, written-consent, and recordkeeping requirements.

The next chapter relates the Neutrality Principle to the public funding of abortion, and to requirements of information transfer, parental consent, and parental notification.

Abortion and Others

THIS CHAPTER APPLIES the Establishment Clause approach and the Neutrality Principle to regulations about public funding, information transfer, spousal consent, parental consent and parental notification. The Establishment Clause approach avoids the inconsistencies of the Court's approach but yields decisions that provide for (almost) the same availability of abortion services.

I first show that, like the Court's approach, the Establishment Clause approach allows the government to refuse funding for abortions, even when it pays for the costs incident to continued pregnancy and childbirth. But the Court reaches this conclusion only by assuming that the government may encourage the choice of childbirth over abortion. The next section shows that the Court abandons this assumption when information requirements are at issue. The resulting (apparent) inconsistency between the funding and information decisions bedevils a case concerning the information to be provided at publicly funded family planning clinics. The funding decisions suggest that this information may be designed to discourage abortions, whereas the information decisions suggest that it may not. The Establishment Clause approach provides more consistent guidance.

The next two sections discuss requirements that married women receive the consent of their husbands and that minors receive the consent of parents, or notify their parents, before abortions are performed. The Establishment Clause approach agrees with the Court's conclusion that married women and mature minors cannot be required to notify, or obtain the consent of, others. And the two approaches yield similar results regarding the availability of abortion to immature minors. But

while reasoning about consent, the Court rejects a notification requirement that it accepts while reasoning about notification. The Establishment Clause approach contains no such inconsistency.

Public Funding of Abortion

The Establishment Clause approach endorsed here may seem to be at
odds with all the Court's major decisions regarding the public funding
of abortion. The Court has maintained that municipalities, states, and
the federal government are permitted to make an exception of abortion
where public funding and support are concerned. The Court consistently upholds the government's right to discriminate against abortion
when it provides public funds for medical services. Initially, this may
seem to conflict with the government neutrality that the Establishment
Clause approach requires. In the first part of the present section I explain why this is not the case. The Establishment Clause approach
agrees with the Court's major conclusions in these cases. I then show
that the Court's own rationale commits it to the view that states may
discourage abortion in the interest of "protecting the potentiality of human life." But the section that follows shows that Court decisions about
information requirements rest on the view that states may *not* discourage abortion. I conclude that the Establishment Clause approach, being
more consistent, better justifies the Court's decisions about public funding and information requirements. Again, the Court reached reasonable
conclusions but lacked adequate rationales.

THE ESTABLISHMENT CLAUSE APPROACH TO PUBLIC
FUNDING

The general idea is this: The Establishment Clause approach treats the
decision to have an abortion (at least before the twenty-first week of
pregnancy) as a decision inextricably involving religious belief. Abortion differs in this regard from most other medical procedures. Their
value can be assessed on entirely secular grounds. Public funding is typically confined to matters of secular concern. The Establishment Clause
is usually interpreted to disallow the public funding of projects, such as
parochial school education, that are justified on religious grounds.
Where funding is disallowed, it certainly cannot be required. So if a
religious belief is integral to the decision to have an abortion, the government cannot be required to pay for abortions.

Some may object that abortion is no different in this regard than most other medical procedures, including medical interventions that foster healthy childbirth. Many in our society believe on religious grounds that human beings should reject all medical interventions. According to the objector, this religious belief ties all medical interventions, those fostering healthy childbirth no less than abortion, to religious belief. Accepting medical care of any kind implies the rejection of the religious belief that God alone is responsible for healing the sick. The objector concludes that because religious beliefs are involved equally in the acceptance of abortion as in the acceptance of other medical responses to pregnancy, the government cannot justifiably refuse to pay for abortions while paying for all medical costs of the same women when they choose childbirth.

The objector is mistaken. Religious beliefs are differently involved in abortion decisions than in other decisions about medical care, so the government can legitimately refuse to fund abortions while funding medical services that foster healthy childbirth. The difference is analogous to that explained in Chapter 4 between creation science, on the one hand, and the theory of biological evolution, on the other.

Creation science is religious on the *extended* epistemological standard for distinguishing religious from secular beliefs. The creation science belief that life on earth has existed for no more than several thousand years contradicts generally accepted secular beliefs. Creation science is considered a religious, rather than an erroneous secular, view because its major support comes from the Bible, which is a religious document. But the theory of biological evolution, which creation science opposes, remains secular. The opposition of the theory of evolution to a religious view does not make evolutionary theory an alternate religious view, according to the Courts. So the theory of biological evolution may be taught in public schools, and the state may not require that creation science be given equal treatment.

Analogous to creation science is the biblically based view that physical health is a dispensation from God. Medical interventions are therefore of no avail. Prayer is the only effective means of promoting healing. Like creation science, this general rejection of medical intervention in people's lives is religious according to the *extended* epistemological standard for distinguishing the religious from the secular. It is opposed to secular beliefs about the efficacy of medical care. This rejection of secular beliefs about medicine is considered religious because it is biblically based. Secular medical views remain secular despite their rejection by some people on religious grounds, just as evolutionary theory remains secular despite its rejection by some people on religious grounds. So, just as the government may financially support instruction in evolutionary theory, it may financially support medical care without that support being construed by courts as establishing religion.

Nontherapeutic abortions, however, are tied more closely to religious belief than is medical care generally. Nontherapeutic abortions are those that are not needed to preserve a pregnant woman's life or health. It is beyond the scope or need of the present inquiry to determine just how dangerous physically, mentally, or emotionally a pregnancy must be before abortion is considered therapeutic. It suffices here to say that nontherapeutic abortions are those that are not claimed to be medically required. So secular beliefs about the value of health and the efficacy of medical interventions in the promotion of health do not justify nontherapeutic abortions. Like many other things, then, including baseball, apple pie, and Chevrolets, nontherapeutic abortions are most often obtained because people want them (for various reasons of their own). The vast majority of those who have such abortions can be presumed to share our society's secular values about the preservation of human life. So their abortion decision logically commits them to the view that the unborn whose life is ended by the abortion is not a person.

But this is a religious belief. We saw in Chapter 6 that according to the *ordinary* epistemological standard, beliefs about the personhood of the unborn through twenty weeks of pregnancy are religious. Neither affirmation nor denial of the belief that young fetuses are persons contradicts secular views. Beliefs about the personhood of young fetuses are in this regard like beliefs about the existence of God. Neither affirmation nor denial contradicts secular views.

The state may justifiably fund activities predicated on secular beliefs while refusing to fund those predicated on religious beliefs. For example, the state provides funding for many educational activities. It may nevertheless refuse to fund the study of the Bible as literature when that study is so conducted as to assume or presuppose belief in the existence of God. Similarly, the state may fund medical care incident to childbirth just as it funds other sorts of medical care. It is not thereby committed to funding nontherapeutic abortions. Unlike ordinary prenatal and obstetric care, nontherapeutic abortions inextricably involve religious beliefs about the personhood of the unborn.

Through this reasoning the Establishment Clause approach reaches a conclusion essentially the same as the Court's. According to the Court, the government may refuse to fund abortions even when it is committed to paying for the medical costs associated with childbirth.

The Establishment Clause approach to public funding for abortion might seem to go further than merely not requiring the government to fund abortions. If abortion is a religious matter, it might seem that the Establishment Clause *forbids* public funding, just as it forbids the public funding of parochial schools. But this is not the case. The alternative to funding children's education in parochial schools is funding their education in public schools. Since, religious reasons apart, public schools are generally as good as parochial schools, the reasons for funding parochial schools are religious. Such funding, therefore, contravenes the Establishment Clause. The government would be spending money without a secular purpose.

Public expenditures on abortions are entirely different. The alternative to abortion is continued pregnancy and (usually) childbirth. During the first trimester, when the overwhelming majority of abortions take place, abortion is, by recent estimates, twenty-five times safer than continued pregnancy and childbirth.[1] It is twice as safe as receiving an injection of penicillin.[2] So a state could fund nontherapeutic abortions as a measure that serves the undeniably secular goal of protecting women's health.

It may seem paradoxical that *nontherapeutic* abortions could serve to protect women's health. Abortions are called nontherapeutic precisely when they are not medically necessary. The air of paradox dissipates when the medically necessary is distinguished from the medically advantageous. Abortion is not a medically necessary response to a normal pregancy. Normal pregnancy does not pose enough risk to a woman's health to justify abortion as necessary to preserve the life and health of pregnant women. Abortions in these circumstances are therefore nontherapeutic. Even normal pregnancy involves risk, however, as does abortion. Because the risks associated with early abortions are (generally) significantly less than those associated with continued pregnancy, early abortions are (generally) medically advantageous. So the state could fund nontherapeutic abortions as a means of reducing risk to women's health.

Saving government money is another secular purpose that could justify funding nontherapeutic abortions. If the government is committed to funding the medical care of certain women, including the medical care incident to pregnancy and childbirth, then it can save money by offering to pay for abortion services as well. These are generally much less expensive than is the medical care incident to continued pregnancy and birth.

Even though nontherapeutic abortions (performed before the

twenty-first week) inextricably involve religious beliefs about the personhood of the unborn, public funding of abortion is a constitutional means of protecting women's health and saving tax dollars because it passes the alternate means test. Abortion is the only alternative to continued pregnancy and (usually) childbirth. The advantage of reduced health risk and diminished costs that abortion affords over continued pregnancy cannot be secured by any other means. There is no way of securing these advantages through means that are less related to religious beliefs. So the public funding of abortions is constitutional.

At the same time, as we have seen, the religious nature of abortion relieves the government of any requirement that it fund abortions, even when it is committed to paying for the medical costs associated with childbirth. Funding can be denied for nontherapeutic abortions (performed before the twenty-first week) because, unlike most medical procedures, decisions about such abortions inextricably involve religious belief. Thus the Establishment Clause approach supports the Court's decisions to allow states, *Beal v. Doe* (1977)[3] and *Maher v. Roe* (1977),[4] and the federal government, *Harris v. McRae* (1980),[5] to fund medical care incident to pregnancy and childbirth while refusing to pay for abortions.

By the same reasoning, the Establishment Clause approach supports the Supreme Court decisions concerning the denial of public facilities and personnel for abortions. In *Poelker v. Roe* (1977)[6] the Court upheld the denial of municipal facilities for abortions, and in *Webster* (1989) the Court upheld the state's denial of state facilities and personnel for abortions. In both cases, the Court believed that safe abortions remained available, as a practical matter, to all women (who could pay for them). Assuming this was the case, the Establishment Clause approach supports these decisions. The government is free to direct public facilities and personnel, no less than public funds, away from a medical procedure that, unlike most others, inextricably involves religious belief. Yet, should the government wish to make its facilities and personnel available for abortions, it is free to do so. Secular goals related to costs and health would justify their decision.

Having explained in general terms the implications of the Establishment Clause approach regarding public support for abortions, I now explain the Court's reasoning about these matters.

THE COURT'S FUNDING RATIONALE

This part shows that the Court's reasoning about the denial of public support for abortion rests on two premises: (1) The state has an interest in "the potentiality of human life" at all stages of gestation; and (2) this interest justifies state actions designed to discourage abortions. The section that follows shows that after being used by the Court in 1977 and 1980, these premises were rejected by the Court itself in 1983 and 1986, only to be used again by the Court in 1989.

The Court decided in *Maher v. Roe* (1977) that Connecticut could deny public funding for abortions. The Court's majority and dissent agreed on the following: The state limited its Medicaid payments for first-trimester abortions to those that are "medically necessary." This impaired the ability of indigent women to secure abortions. It placed financial pressure on them to forgo the exercise of their fundamental right under *Roe v. Wade* to have first-trimester abortions, especially since the state would pay for the medical expenses incident to the alternative to abortion, continued pregnancy and childbirth.

The dissent maintained that the Connecticut regulation was unconstitutional. Justice Brennan wrote that "infringements of fundamental rights are not limited to outright denials of those rights. . . . The compelling-state-interest test is applicable not only to outright denials but also to restraints that make exercise of those rights more difficult".[7] He cited, among other cases, *Sherbert v. Verner* (1963), where the Court required the state to pay "unemployment compensation to a woman who for religious reasons could not work on Saturday."[8] The state "would have provided compensation if her unemployment had stemmed from a number of other nonreligious causes."[9] Failure to pay unemployment compensation in her case, then, placed unmistakable pressure on her to forgo the religious practice to which she had a fundamental right. According to Brennan, the Court upheld in *Verner* the principle that the state may not use financial pressure to influence people to forgo the exercise of their fundamental rights. Brennan concluded that where Medicaid payments for abortion are concerned, "the case for application of the principle actually is stronger than in *Verner* since appellees are all indigent and therefore even more vulnerable to the financial pressures imposed by the Connecticut regulation."[10]

Rejecting this reasoning, the majority pointed out that having a fundamental right to do something does not ordinarily entail a right to do it at public expense. For example, *Pierce v. Society of Sisters* (1925)[11] (reviewed in Chapter 1) established the right of parents to send their children to private schools. This does not, however, entail their right to do so at public expense. "It is one thing to say that a State may not prohibit maintenance of private schools and quite another to say that such schools must, as a matter of equal protection, receive state aid."[12] The state is entitled to use its taxing and spending policies to encourage the use of public schools, and it does not need to show a compelling interest to justify these policies. Similarly, Powell reasoned for the majority, "a State is not required to show a compelling interest for its policy choice to favor normal childbirth"[13] over abortion.

So far, it would seem, the majority is correct. The state does not need a compelling interest to justify its policy choices. Nevertheless, it does need *some* legitimate interest or purpose. No legislation or regulation is constitutional except when rationally related to a secular public purpose. For example, a state may justify its policy of encouraging attendance at public, rather than at private, schools by the greater ease of assuring the quality of public education or by the tendency of common educational experiences to foster mutual understanding in a heterogeneous population. What, then, is the public purpose that justifies funding policies that encourage normal childbirth over abortion?

This is where the reasoning of the majority is strained. What is the state's public purpose? Brennan raised pertinent issues in his dissent in *Beal v. Doe* (1977). *Beal* was a companion case to *Maher*. In *Beal* the Court upheld Pennsylvania's refusal to include nontherapeutic abortions among the services it provided under Title XIX of the Medicaid Assistance Program. In *Beal* the Court maintained that state funding discrimination against abortion complies with federal statutes; just as in *Maher* the justices maintained that this discrimination complies with the federal Constitution. The issue of the state's interest in discriminating against abortion is the same in these two cases, hence the relevance of Brennan's dissent in *Beal* to the issue in *Maher*.

Brennan argued that in both cases the denial of funding for abortion lacks a rational relationship to a public purpose when the state is committed to paying for medical care incident to pregnancy and childbirth. Brennan wrote in *Beal*: "The State cannot contend that it protects its fiscal interests in not funding elective abortions when it incurs far greater expense in paying for more costly medical services performed in carrying pregnancies to term, and, after birth, paying the increased welfare bill incurred to support the mother and child."[14] The purpose cannot be to protect the health of the women who are denied funding for first-trimester abortions, Brennan pointed out also, since these abortions are much safer than continued pregnancy and childbirth.[15]

Writing for the majority in *Maher*, Powell suggested a different secular purpose. He pointed out in a footnote that "a State may have legitimate demographic concerns about its rate of population growth. Such concerns are basic to the future of the State and in some circumstances could constitute a substantial reason for departure from a position of neutrality between abortion and childbirth."[16] This is true. "In some circumstances" there may be legitimate demographic concerns. No one has suggested, however, that Connecticut, one of the more densely populated states, is attempting by its regulation to increase its population. No other state policy, moreover, suggests that this is one of Connecticut's goals. So what is the legitimate purpose of denying Medicaid funding for abortions?

The only plausible purpose mentioned by the majority is drawn from the Court's opinion in *Roe v. Wade*. The Court there maintained that "the State has [an] important and legitimate interest in protecting the potentiality of human life" and that this interest "grows in substantiality as the woman approaches term."[17] Referring to this passage, the majority in *Beal* maintained that the State's interest in protecting the potentiality of human life "does not, at least until approximately the third trimester, become sufficiently compelling to justify unduly burdensome state interference with the woman's constitutionally protected privacy interest. But it is a significant state interest existing throughout the course of the woman's pregnancy."[18] The Court concluded in *Beal* that the state has "unquestionably strong and legitimate interest in encouraging normal childbirth."[19]

Referring with approval to these passages in *Roe* and *Beal*, the Court in *Maher* maintained: "The State unquestionably has 'a strong and legitimate interest in encouraging normal childbirth,'"[20] and "the subsidizing of costs incident to childbirth is a rational means of encouraging childbirth."[21] So the Court's view in *Maher* is that human fetuses ("the potentiality of human life") may legitimately be valued by the state. The value placed by the state on fetal life may increase during the course of pregnancy. Early in pregnancy, according to the Court, the state may not value fetal life so highly that it attributes rights to the fetus and denies women the right to have abortions. Nevertheless, because the state may, in the Court's view, place some value on even the youngest of the unborn, it may legitimately encourage childbirth by funding medical care incident to childbirth while not funding abortions.

In sum, the Court's decisions about public funding make sense by attributing to the Court the beliefs that the government has an interest from the time of conception in "the potentiality of human life" and that it may advance that interest through programs and policies that, by making childbirth the more attractive alternative, discourage abortion. Such programs and policies may include the allocation of funds by the state (upheld in *Maher*), the allocation of funds by the federal government (upheld in *Harris*), the denial of municipal facilities for abortions (upheld in *Poelker*), and the denial of state facilities and personnel (upheld in *Webster*).

The next section shows that in 1983 and 1986, after the major funding decisions, the Court held that states could not impose information requirements that discourage women from having abortions. But, as we have just seen, the Court held again in 1989 (in *Webster*) that states could discourage abortions through allocation of public facilities and public personnel. The Court's position is apparently inconsistent.

Information Requirements

The Court has in two major cases struck down information requirements. These were requirements that certain specific information be supplied to women before those women could legally consent to have an abortion. This section first explains the nature of the requirements, the reasons given by the Court for invalidating those requirements, and the apparent inconsistency between those reasons and the Court's reasoning in the funding cases. This (apparent) inconsistency is then shown to create difficulties when public funds are used to provide information about abortion. I conclude that the Establishment Clause approach justifies the Court's decisions about information requirements better than does the *Roe* framework.

THE COURT'S INCONSISTENT RATIONALE

Akron, Ohio, passed an ordinance that required "the physician to inform his patient that 'the unborn child is a human life from the moment of conception.'"[22] One subsection, which "begins with the dubious statement that abortion is a major surgical procedure and proceeds to describe numerous possible physical and psychological complications of abortion, is a parade of horribles intended to suggest that abortion is a particularly dangerous procedure."[23]

The Court objected to these requirements on two major grounds. First, the requirements intrude "upon the discretion of the pregnant woman's physician. This provision specifies a litany of information that the physician must recite to each woman regardless of whether in his judgment the information is relevant to her personal decision."[24] According to the Court, "it remains primarily the responsibility of the physician to ensure that appropriate information is conveyed to his patient, depending on her particular circumstances."[25] Second, the Court objected to the requirements because "much of the information required is designed not to inform the woman's consent but rather to persuade her to withhold it altogether."[26] This is not a legitimate goal of informed consent. "The validity of an informed consent requirement . . . rests on the State's interest in protecting the health of the pregnant woman."[27]

The Court took exception on exactly the same grounds in *Thornburgh v. American College of Obstetrics and Gynecology* (1986) to Pennsylvania's information requirements. In Pennsylvania women had to be informed that "medical assistance benefits may be available for prenatal care, childbirth and neonatal care and . . . 'that the father is liable to assist' in child support, 'even . . . where the father has offered to pay for the abortion.' The woman also must be informed that materials printed and supplied by the Commonwealth that describe the fetus and that list agencies offering alternatives to abortion are available for review."[28] According to the Court, these information requirements, like those invalidated in *Akron*, intrude on the doctor–patient relationship and seem designed to dissuade, rather than merely inform.

Dissenting in *Thornburgh*, Justice White undercut effectively the Court's justifications for overturning Pennsylvania's law. He agreed that the required information "may increase the woman's 'anxiety' about the procedure and even 'influence' her in her choice."[29] But, he accurately observed: "It is in the very nature of informed-consent provisions that they may produce some anxiety in the patient and influence her in her choice. This is in fact the reason for their existence, and— provided that the information required is accurate and nonmisleading— it is an entirely salutary reason."[30] White considered the information required by Pennsylvania, unlike that required by Akron, to be accurate and nonmisleading. So there is no problem if, by design or merely in effect, it dissuades women from having abortions. What is more, the Court's "decisions in *Maher, Beal,* and *Harris v. McRae* [the abortion funding cases] all indicate that the State may encourage women to make their choice in favor of childbirth rather than abortion, and the provision of accurate information regarding abortion and its alternatives is a reasonable and fair means of achieving that objective."[31]

White saw no merit either in the Court's concern that Pennsylvania's requirements intrude "on the discretion of the pregnant woman's physician."[32] It is a generally accepted role of the legislature to regulate "professions and . . . economic affairs generally."[33] For example, the Court had recently upheld a state requirement that "attorneys . . . disclose to their clients information concerning the risks of representing the client in a certain proceeding."[34] This disclosure requirement, applying to lawyers to protect their clients, was approved by the Court. So analogous requirements, applying to doctors, should similarly be approved. As White pointed out, "nothing in the Constitution indicates a preference for the liberty of doctors over that of lawyers."[35] So "the talk of 'infringement of professional responsibility' is mere window dressing for a holding that must stand or fall on other grounds."[36]

I believe that White is entirely correct, and that the "other grounds" are captured best by the Establishment Clause approach. As we saw in Chapter 7, that approach entails the Neutrality Principle. I now argue that the majority's decision makes sense as an application of that principle.

There are two aspects to Establishment Clause neutrality. The state must be neutral among different religions and religious beliefs, and the state must be neutral in its treatment of religion and nonreligion. The first of these requirements is sufficient to justify the majority's position in *Thornburgh*. The majority objected to the state's structuring the conversation preceding the abortion decision so as to dissuade people from consenting to abortions. Since the abortion decision involves religious beliefs, the state's regulation was like a state rule that rabbis inform prospective converts that Jesus claimed to provide the only path to salvation. The government must not try to influence individual choice on a matter inextricably involving religious belief. Establishment Clause neutrality requires that the government refrain from preferring one religious belief (about the humanity of the unborn) to another.

Also required by the Establishment Clause is neutrality between religion and nonreligion. As we saw earlier in this chapter, this neutrality is qualified by exceptions concerning financial support, where the state may treat nonreligion more favorably than religion. Also, as we saw in Chapter 5, there are exceptions concerning the free exercise of religion, where the state may, through "accommodation," treat religion more favorably than nonreligion. Neither of these exceptions applies to state information requirements. So the Neutrality Principle requires that states treat the abortion procedure like other medical procedures of comparable complexity and risk. The majority in *Thornburgh* pointed out that Pennsylvania had failed to do this. They remarked: "The Commonwealth does not, and surely would not, compel similar disclosure of every possible peril of necessary surgery or of simple vaccination."[37] Here it seems, the majority fault the state for its unequal treatment of abortion (a matter inextricably involving religious belief) and other medical procedures (which do not similarly involve religious beliefs).

Information requirements that tend to dissuade people from having abortions might be constitutional, the Court suggests, if they were part of a state concern that extended equally to other medical procedures.

The two requirements of Establishment Clause neutrality operate together. Thus it would be a breach of required neutrality if, without good reason, the government imposed exceptionally strict fire regulations on churches of a particular denomination (the first requirement) or on religious establishments generally (the second requirement). Analogously, it is illegitimate for Pennsylvania to impose information regulations that tend to dissuade people from consenting to abortions (the first requirement) and that differ from information regulations in non-abortion contexts (the second requirement).

The Establishment Clause understanding of the Court's position gains support from the consideration, noted by White, that the majority (including one of the same justices) allowed government funding decisions that "encourage women to make their choice in favor of childbirth rather than abortion."[38] We have seen that the Court justified its position by maintaining that the government has an interest in protecting "the potentiality of life." Why is this interest accepted in funding cases, but not in cases concerning information requirements? How can the (apparent) contradiction be resolved?

The resolution is through the Establishment Clause. The majority realized intuitively in *Maher* (the first funding case) that it was inappropriate for the Equal Protection Clause to dictate funding or non-funding for abortions. But they provided poor rationales for this result. Included among those rationales was the claim that the state could encourage women to choose childbirth rather than abortion. I earlier provided for the funding decisions an alternate Establishment Clause rationale that I believe to be more cogent. When this alternate rationale is substituted for the Court's, there is no need for the Court to accept the legitimacy of state attempts to influence women to choose childbirth over abortion.

This eliminates the inconsistency between the Court's rationales for its decisions about funding and information requirements. The rationales are consistent because they both rest on the Establishment Clause. The government may treat funding for abortion differently than it treats funding for other medical procedures because abortion, unlike other procedures, has a religious dimension. This kind of difference (between the religious and the nonreligious) is a legitimate consideration in funding contexts. But it is not a legitimate consideration in most other contexts, where the Establishment Clause requires government neutrality among various religions, as well as between religion and non-religion. So information requirements may not treat abortion in a special way or be designed to dissuade people from consenting to abortion. Thus the government may legitimately refuse to fund abortions or provide public facilities or personnel for abortions, but it may not use information requirements to dissuade women from having abortions. This consistent, Establishment Clause reasoning supports exactly what the Court decided.

PUBLICLY FUNDED FAMILY PLANNING CLINICS

The inconsistency in the Court's rationale concerning funding and information requirements is evident in a case concerning information restrictions applied to publicly funded family planning clinics. The case, *Rust v. Sullivan* (1991), arose as follows: Title X of the Public Health Service Act, which authorizes federal support for family planning, states that "none of the funds appropriated under this subchapter shall be used in programs where abortion is a method of family planning."[39] In 1988 the secretary of Health and Human Services issued new regulations to ensure that public funds did not support abortion. According to these new regulations, "the Title X project is expressly prohibited from referring a pregnant woman to an abortion provider, even upon specific request. One permissible response to such an inquiry is that 'the project does not consider abortion an appropriate method of family planning and therefore does not counsel or refer for abortion.'"[40] Pregnant women who come to the clinic are to be given "a list of available [health care] providers that promote the welfare of mother and unborn child."[41] That list may not include "health care providers whose principle business is the provision of abortions."[42] The new regulations also state that a "Title X project may not provide counseling concerning the use of abortion . . . or provide referral for abortion."[43]

The State of New York, and others, objected on several grounds to these new regulations. Among their complaints was the contention that the regulations unduly impaired the constitutional abortion rights of women served by Title X family planning clinics.

The Supreme Court's discussion of the regulations highlights the (apparent) inconsistency noted above between its treatment of funding issues and its treatment of information requirements. The majority in *Rust* cited *Maher* and *Harris*. They maintained that since Title X involves public funds, and the Supreme Court allows such funds to be used in ways that discourage abortion, the new regulations are constitutional. "The Government has merely chosen to fund one activity rather than another."[44] It is "a case of the Government refusing to fund activities, including speech, which are explicitly excluded from the scope of the project funded."[45] Again, in issuing these regulations, "the government . . . is . . . simply insisting that public funds be spent for the purposes for which they were authorized."[46] Permission for such discriminatory funding is found in the *Maher* doctrine that "the government may 'make a value judgment favoring childbirth over abortion, and . . . implement that judgment by the allocation of funds.'"[47]

The dissent cited *Akron* and *Thornburgh* and argued that "a woman's fundamental right to self-determination"[48] is abrogated here. "By suppressing medically pertinent information and injecting a restrictive ideological message unrelated to considerations of maternal health, the Government places formidable obstacles in the path of Title X clients' freedom of choice and thereby violates their Fifth Amendment rights. . . . The Title X client will reasonably construe" the newly required message that "abortion is not an 'appropriate method' of family planning" as "professional advice to forego her right to obtain an abortion."[49] Her decision will be misinformed and therefore not self-determined.

The situation is relevantly similar, the dissent argued, to those presented in *Akron* and *Thornburgh*, except in those cases *all* physicians were required to present information that may mislead pregnant women, whereas the requirement here applies only to those messages funded by the government. Justice Blackmun was not impressed by this difference: "The deprivation of liberty by the Government is no less substantial because if affects few rather than many. It cannot be that an otherwise unconstitutional infringement of choice is made lawful because it touches only some of the Nation's pregnant women and not all of them."[50]

As this summary suggests, both the majority and dissent have strong arguments. The arguments are strong because they rest on clear precedents. The arguments lead to opposite conclusions because the precedents are nearly contradictory. Little wonder that the Court split 5–4 in *Rust v. Sullivan*.

The Establishment Clause approach provides clearer guidance concerning the constitutionality of regulations prohibiting abortion counseling or referral at Title X family planning clinics. The Establishment Clause approach would find the regulations constitutional only if they maintained Establishment Clause neutrality regarding the inherently religious beliefs involved in abortion decisions.[51] Consider, for example, the requirement that client inquires about abortion be met with the statement: "The project does not consider abortion an appropriate method of family planning and therefore does not counsel or refer for abortion."[52] Is this neutral? Certainly not. Imagine an analogous requirement of teachers and counselors at publicly funded schools. The analogous requirement would be that when students ask about the existence of God, the efficacy of prayer, the need for salvation, and so forth, they be met with the statement: "The public school does not consider religion or religious belief an appropriate approach to life's problems and therefore does not counsel or refer for religious training." This would obviously be unconstitutional hostility, rather than constitutional neutrality, regarding religion. Thus, at least one part of the regulations at issue in *Rust v. Sullivan* is unconstitutional.

The issue of neutrality does appear in Blackmun's dissent. But the argument is unpersuasive because the government's lack of neutrality is related to the First Amendment's Free Speech Clause, rather than to the Establishment Clause. Blackmun wrote:

> While suppressing speech favorable to abortion with one hand, the Secretary compels anti-abortion speech with the other. . . . The Regulations pertaining to "advocacy" are even more explicitly viewpoint based. These provide: "A Title X project may not *encourage, promote, or advocate* abortion as a method of family planning." . . . The Regulations do not, however, proscribe or even regulate anti-abortion advocacy. These are clearly restrictions aimed at the suppression of "dangerous ideas,"[53]

and so violate the First Amendment's guarantee of free speech.

When the government's lack of neutrality is related to free speech, rather than to the establishment of religion, the majority has a cogent reply. "When Congress established a National Endowment for Democracy to encourage other countries to adopt democratic principles," wrote Chief Justice Rehnquist for the majority, "it was not required to fund a program to encourage competing lines of political philosophy such as Communism and Fascism."[54] Similarly, the government can fund a public health campaign against smoking cigarettes without providing equal funds for cigarette advertisements. In general, then, the government may discriminate among the messages whose dissemination it chooses to fund. So the majority has the better of the argument when, viewed as a matter of free speech, the government's funding is not neutral among different points of view.

But religious points of view are exceptional. The government is required by the Establishment Clause to be neutral among religious beliefs. Whereas it may fund activities designed to influence people's choices between democracy and communism, or smoking and not smoking, it cannot similarly fund activities designed to convince people to choose, say, Catholicism over Lutheranism, or deism over theism. The dissent is thus correct that the regulations are unconstitutional insofar as they tie funding to the content of one's speech about abortion. But the constitutional infirmity of the regulations rests not on the fact that speech is involved, but on the fact that the speech concerns a matter tied inextricably to religious belief. Again, the Establishment Clause approach securely guides deliberations about speech-related aspects of the government's regulations.

The constitutionality of other parts of the new regulations should be decided also by determining whether or not they maintain Establishment Clause neutrality between abortion and childbirth. It may be that some requirements in the new regulations are constitutional, while others are not. For example, the new regulations require that Title X facilities be physically separate from facilities where abortions are performed. Since we generally accept as neutral the requirement that public and parochial schools be in physically separate facilities, perhaps requiring the separation of Title X from abortion facilities is neutral and constitutional.[55]

Spousal and Parental Consent

The Court's decisions about consent requirements also accord/best with the Establishment Clause approach. This section reviews Court decisions regarding state requirements of spousal consent (for married women) and parental consent (for minors). First I show that both the *Roe* framework and the Establishment Clause approach provide sufficient grounds to justify the Court's position on spousal consent. Next I show that, using the *Roe* framework, the Court failed to justify adequately its position on parental consent. I then show that the Establishment Clause approach justifies adequately a position on parental consent resembling the Court's view by considering abortion (a) in its medical dimension and (b) in its religious dimension. In the section that follows I show additionally that the practical effect of applying the Establishment Clause approach is nearly identical to what the Court intended regarding both parental consent and parental notification.

SPOUSAL CONSENT

Both the Establishment Clause approach and the *Roe* trimester framework explain easily why spousal consent requirements are unconstitutional. The Court held in *Danforth* that the state could not, through a requirement of spousal consent, "delegate to a spouse a veto power which the state itself is absolutely and totally prohibited from exercising during the first trimester of pregnancy."[56] This agrees with the *Roe* framework. Thus, in striking down Missouri's spousal consent requirement, Blackmun wrote: "Clearly, since the State cannot regulate or proscribe abortion during the first stage, when the physician and his patient make that decision, the State cannot delegate authority to any particular person, even the spouse, to prevent abortion during the same period."[57]

This conclusion is supported equally by the Establishment Clause approach. If abortion is a matter tied inextricably to religious belief, allowing spousal veto of a woman's decision to have an abortion would amount to giving husbands power over the exercise of their wives' religious beliefs. It is obviously unconstitutional for a state to delegate to anyone the authority to make decisions on religious matters for his or her spouse. The religion guarantees protect the *individual's* religious conscience.

THE COURT'S FLAWED PARENTAL CONSENT RATIONALE

The majority in *Danforth* took the same position on Missouri's requirement that parental consent be secured before any nontherapeutic abortions are performed on unmarried minors. Blackmun wrote:

> Just as with the requirement of consent from the spouse, so here, the State does not have the constitutional authority to give a third party an absolute, and possibly arbitrary, veto over the decision of the physician and his patient to terminate the patient's pregnancy, regardless of the reason for withholding consent. Constitutional rights do not mature and come into being magically only when one attains the state-defined age of majority. Minors, as well as adults, are protected by the Constitution and possess constitutional rights.[58]

This reasoning is, in light of the *Roe* framework, much less persuasive than that concerning spousal consent. The *Roe* framework supports the right to terminate one's pregnancy as a matter of the right to privacy or liberty, and minors typically possess fewer such rights than do adults. Justice Stevens explained this clearly:

The State's interest in the welfare of its young citizens justifies a variety of protective measures. Because he may not foresee the consequences of his decision, a minor may not make an enforceable bargain. He may not lawfully work or travel where he pleases, or even attend exhibitions of constitutionally protected adult motion pictures. Persons below a certain age may not marry without parental consent . . . even when the young woman is already pregnant. The State's interest in protecting a young person from harm justifies the imposition of restraints on his or her freedom even though comparable restraints on adults would be constitutionally impermissible.[59]

So the fact that *Roe* establishes an adult's right to choose abortion does not imply that minors have the same constitutional right. The majority has presented no cogent argument for the view that where abortion is concerned, minors have the same rights as adults, even though they lack such rights in many other areas. If minors may not rent an apartment, live where they choose, or marry whom they wish without parental consent, then on what basis is the state denied the authority to require similar parental involvement in decisions about abortion? The majority presented no cogent justification.

Perhaps because they lacked such a justification, the Court qualified its position three years later. The Court would still not allow states to give parents the power to veto a minor's abortion decision. But they would allow less restrictive state requirements of parental consent. Parental consent requirements are constitutional when accompanied by provision for an expeditious, confidential, judicial bypass of parental consent. Judicial bypass procedures allow a minor to bypass the required parental consent upon convincing a judge either that she is mature enough to make her own abortion decision or that the abortion she seeks is in her own best interests.

These views were expressed by a plurality of four in *Bellotti v. Baird* (1979).[60] The Massachusetts statute considered in that case provided for appropriate judicial bypass, except that it did not require the judge to allow all minors found mature to make their own abortion decisions. The statute left open the possibility that a minor judged mature could be denied abortion through failure of a judge to approve her decision. The Supreme Court required that mature minors be allowed to make their own abortion decisions.

These views, maintained by four justices in *Bellotti II*, became the position of the majority in *Akron*[61] and *Ashcroft*[62] (1983). If the state requires parental consent for minors to have abortions, it must provide a timely opportunity for minors to receive judicial determination either that they are mature, or that the abortion is in their best interest. If the minor is found mature, then she must be granted permission to make her own decision regarding abortion.

The difficulty is that this mature-minor rule conflicts with ordinary constitutional limitations on state legislation regarding minors. States are ordinarily permitted to establish a chronological age as a precondition for people engaging in certain activities or making certain decisions for themselves. Stevens wrote in his *Danforth* dissent: "In all such situations chronological age has been the basis for imposition of a restraint on the minor's freedom of choice even though it is perfectly obvious that such a yardstick is imprecise and perhaps even unjust in particular cases."[63] Stevens observed in a later case: "If every minor with the wisdom of an adult has a constitutional right to be treated as an adult, a uniform minimum voting age is surely suspect. Instead of simply enforcing general rules promulgated by the legislature, perhaps the judiciary should grant hearings to all young persons desirous of establishing their status as mature."[64] Of course, the judiciary is not about to do any such thing. Where other decisions are concerned, they will continue to permit legislatures to establish criteria based on chronological age. Why is abortion any different? Employing the *Roe* framework, the majority lacks a convincing rationale.

THE ESTABLISHMENT CLAUSE APPROACH: MEDICAL DIMENSION

The Establishment Clause approach does better than the *Roe* framework. It justifies adequately a view of parental consent requirements that resembles the Court's position. Decisions about early nontherapeutic abortions are tied inextricably to religious beliefs about the personhood of the unborn. The Establishment Clause requires that state regulations regarding abortion have as neither their purpose nor their primary effect the promotion, endorsement, or encouragement of any such belief. The state meets its obligation of Establishment Clause neutrality only when its abortion regulations are similar to its regulations of comparable medical procedures or religious activities.

None of the state parental consent requirements reviewed by the Court met the demands of the Neutrality Principle. In each case, the state's treatment of abortion differed from its treatment of comparable medical interventions and religious activities. So the Establishment Clause approach justifies the Court's rejection in *Danforth* (1976) and

Bellotti II (1979) of state requirements that parental consent precede abortions performed on minors.

This part concentrates on the medical dimension of abortion. Abortion regulations are not neutral in their treatment of abortion as a medical procedure when abortion is treated differently from amniocentesis, cesarean delivery, or treatments for venereal disease or drug abuse. Reasons considered, and rejected, for treating abortion differently from these other medical interventions relate to medical complexity, medical risk, family integrity, parental authority, decisional importance, and emotional stress.

The Missouri law considered in *Danforth* failed to regulate abortion as that state regulates comparable medical procedures: "No other Missouri statute specifically requires the additional consent of a minor's parent for medical or surgical treatment, and . . . in Missouri a minor legally may consent to medical services for pregnancy (excluding abortion), venereal disease, and drug abuse."[65] The Court indicated here that Missouri regulated abortion more stringently than other medical procedures of comparable complexity and risk. Because the Court did not employ the Establishment Clause approach, it did not use this observation to construct a cogent argument that Missouri's law was unconstitutional. The cogent argument that the Court failed to present is the following: Parental consent was required before minors could have abortions, but not before they had such medically riskier procedures as amniocentesis and cesarean delivery. If the state had really been skeptical about the ability of minors, in consultation and cooperation with physicians, to make informed and reasonable decisions about health care, they would have required parental consent for other medical procedures of greater complexity and risk than abortions. The requirement of parental consent specifically and *only* for abortions deviates from Establishment Clause neutrality.

Instead of presenting this argument, the Court concentrated on considerations of family integrity and parental authority. It noted the contention that apart from considerations of medical safety, parental consent requirements serve the state interest in "safeguarding . . . the family unit and . . . parental authority."[66] But the Court was skeptical that requiring parental consent would serve either of these goals: "It is difficult . . . to conclude that providing a parent with absolute power to overrule a determination made by the physician and his minor patient to terminate the patient's pregnancy will serve to strengthen the family unit. Neither is it likely that such veto power will enhance parental authority or control."[67]

Here the Court substituted its judgment for the state's on cause–effect relationships between parental consent requirements (as cause) and strengthened family units and parental authority (as effects). Since it would appear that reasonable people could differ about the strength of such cause–effect relationships, the Court's argument is weak. The weak link is the assumption that, as a matter of fact, the state's parental consent requirement will not strengthen family units and parental authority. No one actually knows, so dogmatism is out of place. The Court's argument suffers from inappropriate dogmatism.

Regarding considerations of family integrity and parental authority, the Establishment Clause approach again does better than the Court. This approach employs the Neutrality Principle and compares a state's regulation of abortion with its regulation of other medical interventions. If, according to the state, required parental consent serves to strengthen the family unit and parental authority, why is it applied only to abortion? Until the state applies the parental consent requirement to other medical interventions on sensitive matters, establishes that such consent strengthens the family unit and parental authority only when applied to abortion, or presents other secular considerations to justify making an exception of abortion, the state's parental consent requirement contravenes the Establishment Clause. This is why it is unconstitutional. The Court need not substitute its judgment for the state's on uncertain matters of cause and effect. It need merely insist that the state be consistent in its judgments of cause and effect and in its evaluations of the relative importance of competing secular values.

Justice Stewart, concurring in *Danforth*, suggested that exceptional parental consent requirements may be justified where abortion is concerned because the abortion decision is very important, and the minor is subject to significant emotional stress. He wrote: "The State furthers a constitutionally permissible end by encouraging an unmarried pregnant minor to seek the help and advice of her parents in making the very important decision whether or not to bear a child. That is a grave decision, and a girl of tender years, under emotional stress, may be ill-equipped to make it without mature advice and emotional support."[68] In spite of these considerations of importance and emotional stress, Stewart agreed with the majority in *Danforth* that consent requirements that give parents an absolute veto over a minor's abortion are unconstitutional.

It is significant for our purposes that Stewart's comment was interpreted by Justice Powell in a later case as justifying the exceptional treatment of abortion.[69] But Powell was mistaken. Stewart's comment justified exceptional state measures reasonably designed to foster communication and consultation between parent and minor regarding *all* medical interventions that are especially important or emotionally stressful. Thus a state may justifiably have different requirements of parental involvement in minors' decisions regarding abortion than in their decisions regarding wart removal (which is presumably less important and stressful). This agrees with the Establishment Clause approach, and with Stewart's comment, because entirely secular concerns are served by encouraging parental involvement differentially in minors' decisions in proportion to the importance and emotional difficulty of those decisions. The state may similarly have different requirements of parental involvement in proportion to the complexity and risk of the medical procedures in question.

Missouri's law, however, could not be justified on any such basis. As already noted, Missouri required parental consent for abortions, but not for any other medical interventions related to pregnancy, childbirth, venereal disease, or drug abuse. Just as some of these interventions are (at least) equally complex and risky as abortion, some are (at least) as important and stressful. For example, most pregnant women who wish to have healthy babies consider important and stressful medical decisions bearing significantly on the health of their babies. These include decisions about amniocentesis, chemical inducement of labor, and cesarean delivery, to name but a few. Also important and stressful are decisions regarding the treatment of drug abuse. Since drug abuse can kill or permanently incapacitate, few decisions are more important than those related to treatment for drug abuse. And since many drugs are addictive, treatment that requires eventual abstinence is extraordinarily emotionally stressful. So, on the Establishment Clause approach, Missouri's exceptional parental consent requirement could not be justified by abortion decisions being more important or stressful than those (e.g., related to childbirth and drug abuse) that the state allows minors to make without parental consent.

This does not mean that the Establishment Clause approach disallows all parental consent requirements. On this approach, states may require parental consent before abortions are performed on minors. But in view of the Neutrality Principle, states may require such consent on medical grounds when, and only when, they require it for medical procedures that are in one or more relevant respects similar to abortion—those comparably risky or complex, those related similarly to parental authority or family integrity, or those comparably important or stressful.

It is unlikely that any state would enact parental consent requirements for abortion that satisfy the demands of the Neutrality Principle.
Predictably, some minors who are pregnant will want to conceal this
fact from their parents for as long as possible. A requirement of parental consent before such minors could have prenatal care might delay the
provision of care, jeopardizing the health of mother and child. Some
minors with venereal disease wish to conceal the disease from their parents. Again, a requirement that parents consent before treatment begins
may delay treatment significantly, jeopardizing the health of the minor
and others. Similarly, some minors with drug problems will be discour-
aged by a requirement of parental consent from seeking appropriate
treatment. In view of public concern, especially about drug abuse and
sexually transmitted diseases, it is unlikely that any state would require
parental consent before minors may receive treatment for these conditions. So it is unlikely that any state would enact parental consent requirements for abortion that are consistent with the Neutrality Principle.

THE ESTABLISHMENT CLAUSE APPROACH: RELIGIOUS DIMENSION

The Neutrality Principle is satisfied alternatively when, all other things
being equal, a state's abortion regulations are similar to its regulation of
other matters tied similarly to religious beliefs. Where minors are concerned, the Court has maintained, parental rights and duties "include
the inculcation of moral standards, religious beliefs, and elements of
good citizenship."[70] With this in mind, Justice Powell wrote: "Parental
notice and consent are qualifications that typically may be imposed by
the State on a minor's right to make important decisions. . . . [A] State
reasonably may . . . determine, as a general proposition, that such consultation is particularly desirable with respect to the abortion decision—one that for some people raises profound moral and religious
concerns."[71]

Powell indicated here his recognition of the abortion decision's religious dimension. Consistent with the Neutrality Principle, he compared
the rights and duties of parents regarding the abortion decisions of their
minor children with the rights and duties of parents regarding their
minor children's other religious beliefs and commitments.

Unquestionably, parents have the right to (attempt to) inculcate
their religious beliefs. But the Neutrality Principle requires that any legislation designed to facilitate parental influence over their minor chil-

dren's religious beliefs and preferences be neutral with regard to the contents of the religious beliefs and preferences in question. For example, it would be unconstitutional for a state to require parental consent before minors attend religion classes preparatory for conversion to Catholicism, but not before they attend classes preparatory for conversion to Lutheranism. By the same token, leaving aside the medical and emotional considerations already discussed in this section, a state could not require parental consent before abortions are performed on minors without requiring parental consent before minors engage in other pursuits that are similarly tied inextricably to religious beliefs, such as religious conversions or baptism. If the state bases a requirement of parental involvement in a minor's abortion decision on the religious dimension of that decision and the right of parents to inculcate religious beliefs, then it must require similar parental involvement in other decisions with a comparable or greater religious dimension. So unless and until the state makes written parental consent a precondition for a minor's religious conversion or baptism, it cannot make written parental consent a precondition for a minor's abortion.

Again, the Neutrality Principle featured in the Establishment Clause approach allows a state, under certain conditions, to require parental consent before an abortion is performed on a minor. But these conditions do not obtain in any state. No state requires written parental consent before minors can participate of their own volition in all activities inextricably tied to religious beliefs, including baptism and religious conversion.

Furthermore, if any state enacts legislation requiring parental consent before religious conversion or baptism is performed, that legislation would be challenged as violating minors' First Amendment rights to free exercise of religion.[72] Since this issue has never been litigated, it is impossible to predict the outcome. But there are reasons to believe that the Court would uphold a minor's right to religious self-determination.

Minors have fewer liberties than adults primarily to protect them, and others, from the bad consequences of decisions made or actions taken without adequate knowledge and rational deliberation. But the bad consequences in question are *secular* harms. For example, without parental consent, a minor may not marry, conclude a contract, or move away from home. The dangers inherent in such actions are secular. The potential harms include the following: for concluding contracts, indebtedness and exposure to lawsuits; for marriage, assumption of another's indebtedness and exposure to lawsuits; and for living where one chooses, physical assault or pollution-related health difficulties from living in areas of high crime or pollution. Our secular concepts include these as problems or disvalues.

Baptism and religious conversion typically involve no danger of secular harm. An incorrect decision may jeopardize one's reception of God's grace, one's resurrection at the Second Coming, and one's chances for eternal bliss in heaven, but it is not the law's business to protect anyone from such dangers as these. In other words, the kinds of considerations that normally justify limiting the self-determination of minors do not arise in contexts where the only dangers are those predicated on religious beliefs. So, if the issue were ever to arise, it could be argued that laws requiring parental consent before minors could of their own volition participate in ceremonies of baptism or religious conversion violate the minors' rights of free exercise of religion.

Yet if such laws were ever enacted, they might be defended as strengthening the family, vindicating parental rights to influence their children's religious training, enhancing parental authority generally, or all of these. But these points are currently moot because no state currently requires written (or any other form of) parental consent in these matters.

In sum, when abortion is considered in its religious dimension, state requirements of parental permission before abortions may be performed on minors violate the Neutrality Principle. Because states do not require such permission before religious conversion or baptism, their requirement of parental permission for abortion unconstitutionally discriminates among religious beliefs.

In conclusion, because decisions about early nontherapeutic abortions are tied inextricably to religious beliefs, legislation affecting the availability of abortion must satisfy the Neutrality Principle. So state requirements of parental consent before minors receive abortions must treat abortion similarly to comparable medical procedures, or they must treat abortion similarly to activities comparably tied to religious beliefs. No state's parental consent requirement meets either of these conditions.

Parental Notification

I now consider state requirements that parents be notified of their minors' abortion decisions. This section contains three parts. The first explains the implications of the Establishment Clause approach; the second exposes a glaring inconsistency in the Court's approach; and the third shows that despite their differences, these two approaches effectively allow to minors (almost) the same access to legal abortions *without parental consent or notification.*

IMPLICATIONS OF THE ESTABLISHMENT CLAUSE APPROACH

The implications of the Establishment Clause approach regarding parental notification requirements are clear and simple. The Neutrality Principle must be observed. States may not require parental notification before abortions are performed on minors if they do not require similar notification before comparable medical interventions or religious activities take place. The reasoning here parallels that in the preceding section concerning parental consent requirements. And as with parental consent, no parental notification statute considered so far by the Court conforms to the Neutrality Principle. So they are all unconstitutional.

Consider, for example, the statute reviewed by the Court in *Hodgson v. Minnesota* (1990). It required that both parents be notified at least forty-eight hours before an abortion is performed on a minor. According to the Minnesota Attorney General, the statute's "purposes are apparent from the statutory text and 'include the recognition and fostering of parent–child relationships, promoting counsel to a child in a difficult and traumatic choice, and providing notice to those who are naturally most concerned for the child's welfare.'"[73] The district court that reviewed the statute found additionally that required notification could improve health care provided to minors: "Parents can provide information concerning the minor's medical history of which the minor may not be aware. Parents can also supervise post-abortion care. In addition, parents can support the minor's psychological well-being and thus mitigate psychological sequelae that may attend the abortion procedure."[74] Finally: "The State . . . claims that the statute serves the interest of protecting parents' independent rights 'to shape the[ir] child[ren]'s values and lifestyle[s]' and 'to determine and strive for what they believe to be best for their children.'"[75]

The Establishment Clause approach recognizes the value in family communication. Surely the ideal is that pregnant minors voluntarily discuss their options with both parents, who provide helpful counsel, medical information, and emotional support. Justice Stevens pointed out in *Hodgson* that the Court shares this ideal. He wrote: "The Court . . . has never challenged a State's reasonable judgment that the decision should be made after notification to and consultation with a parent."[76] The Establishment Clause approach agrees.

Minnesota's parental notification requirement is unconstitutional nevertheless, on the Establishment Clause approach, because it makes an exception of abortion. As Justice Marshall pointed out, Minnesota "does not require parental notification where the minor seeks medical treatment for pregnancy, venereal disease, or alcohol and other drug abuse."[77] Since the purposes asserted to justify the parental notification requirement for abortion would be served equally, or in greater measure, by subjecting these other matters to the same requirement, Minnesota's statute violates the Neutrality Principle. Again, the reasoning is the same as that provided in the preceding section.

The statute's provision for judicial bypass of parental notification does not help, on the Establishment Clause approach, because the bypass provision does not address the fundamental weakness of the parental notification requirement, that is, its violation of the Neutrality Principle.

THE COURT'S INCONSISTENCY

By contrast to the consistency of the Establishment Clause approach, the Court's position is glaringly inconsistent. Four members of the Court judged in 1979 that parents notified of their children's impending abortions may effectively prevent the abortions to which these minors have a right. Two years later, the same four justices, ignoring the remonstrance of three colleagues, rejected this consideration as applied to the same class of minors.

In *Bellotti II* (1979), as we have seen, four members of the Court gave their views on a wide variety of issues pertaining to parental consent. One of their positions concerned parental notification as well. They maintained that a Massachusetts provision for a judicial bypass of parental consent was defective because it required that parents be notified as soon as the minor expresses an interest in being declared mature. The four justices seconded the district court's observation that "there are parents who would obstruct, and perhaps altogether prevent, the minor's right to go to court."[78] Writing for all four justices, Powell added:

> Many parents hold strong views on the subject of abortion, and young pregnant minors, especially those living at home, are particularly vulnerable to their parents' efforts to obstruct both an abortion and their access to court. It would be unrealistic, therefore, to assume that the mere existence of a legal right to seek relief in superior court provides an effective avenue of relief for some of those who need it the most.[79]

These thoughts seem realistic. One would assume, therefore, that at least four justices would object to any and all state requirements of parental notification regarding abortion. No such luck. Two years later, the Court considered Utah's requirement that parents be notified not, as in *Bellotti II*, before the minor has an opportunity to be judicially declared mature, but before the contemplated abortion actually takes place. All four justices reversed their position. They upheld Utah's requirement that parents be notified before an abortion is performed on a minor. The minor in question "was an unmarried 15-year-old girl living with her parents . . . and dependant on them for her support."[80] She would certainly seem to have been one of those minors, whom the four justices referred to in *Bellotti II*(1979), as "young . . . , living at home, [and] particularly vulnerable to their parents' efforts to obstruct . . . an abortion."[81] The justices offered no rationale to distinguish the situation presented by Utah's statute (1981) from that presented by Massachusetts two years earlier. Nor did they acknowledge having changed their minds, much less offer a rationale for changing their minds. They simply rejected a consideration still emphasized by three others on the Court that they had found dispositive two years earlier. This is a glaring inconsistency.

EQUIVALENT RESULTS

In spite of their differences, the Court's approach and the Establishment Clause approach give minors roughly equal access to legal abortion services. As we have seen, the Court insists consistently that statutes requiring parental consent or notification include bypass procedures that enable minors to get abortions legally without either parental consent or notification. The requirements of such procedures, explained initially by Powell in *Bellotti II*, were reiterated by Justice Kennedy in *Ohio v. Akron Center for Reproductive Health* (1990):

> First, the *Bellotti* plurality indicated that the procedure must allow the minor to show that she possesses the maturity and information to make her abortion decision, in consultation with her physician, without regard to her parents' wishes.
>
> Second, the *Bellotti* plurality indicated that the procedure must allow the minor to show that, even if she cannot make the abortion decision by herself, "the desired abortion would be in her best interests."
>
> Third, the *Bellotti* plurality indicated that the procedure must insure the minor's anonymity.
>
> Fourth, the *Bellotti* plurality indicated that the courts must conduct a

bypass procedure with expedition to allow the minor an effective opportunity to obtain the abortion.[82]

Such bypass procedures, which the Court continues to consider necessary in all statutes that require parental consent or notification, allow almost any minor who seeks an abortion, and can pay for it, to have one legally. Consider the requirement of parental consent. A minor who wishes to avoid obtaining such consent must be given the opportunity to show that she is mature enough to make the abortion decision without her parents' involvement or that, even if she is not mature enough to make the abortion decision on her own, "the desired abortion would be in her best interests." There is almost no room here for a rational denial of the minor's petition. If the judge finds the minor too immature to make her own abortion decision, it can hardly (except rarely) be in the *best interests* of an *immature minor* to complete her pregnancy and become a parent *against her will*. Yet it is *only the minor's best interests* that the judge is legally permitted to consider. Little wonder, then, that judges rarely deny such petitions.

Procedures to bypass state requirements of parental notification have similar results. Minnesota has a parental notification requirement, qualified by the necessary bypass procedure. Justice Stevens pointed out in *Hodgson v. Minnesota*: "During the period between August 1, 1981, and March 1, 1986, 3,573 judicial bypass petitions were filed in Minnesota courts. All but 15 were granted. The judges who adjudicated over 90 percent of the petitions testified; none of them identified any positive effects of the law."[83] The practical effects, then, of the Court's approach and the Establishment Clause are nearly identical. Both approaches allow virtually all minors to have the abortions they desire, and can pay for, without parental consent or notification. The Court reaches this result by mandating judicial bypass procedures. The Establishment Clause approach achieves the same result by applying the Establishment Clause neutrality to abortion.

Conclusion

The preceding chapter and the present one show that the Establishment Clause approach to the regulation of abortion differs fundamentally from the approach employed by the Court in *Roe* and subsequent cases. The two approaches rest on different constitutional guarantees. Consequently, while on the Court's approach a statute may unduly burden a fundamental right, on the Establishment Clause approach it violates the

Neutrality Principle by implicitly endorsing a religious belief. While on the Court's approach a statute may not correspond to accepted medical practice, on the Establishment Clause approach it fails to correspond to the *legislature's* practice of regulating medical procedures. (The state regulates abortion differently than it regulates other medical procedures of comparable complexity and risk, thereby, again, violating the Neutrality Principle.) While on the Court's approach funding may be denied to abortions because the state may encourage the choice of childbirth over abortion, on the Establishment Clause approach funding may be denied because the state may legitimately choose to refrain from supporting activities that are justified, in part, by religious beliefs. While the Court would not allow parents an absolute veto over their immature minor's abortion decision because the parents' choice may not be in the minor's best interest, the Establishment Clause approach would remove authority from parents unless and until the state gives parents equal authority over comparable medical or religious matters. Where the Court divided pregnancy into three trimesters, the Establishment Clause approach divides it into two parts. Where the Court is concerned about viability, the Establishment Clause approach is concerned about the essential physiological sameness of the unborn to a typical newborn.

In spite of these extensive differences in underlying rationale, the two approaches yield results with similar implications for the availability of abortion services. The approaches yield identical decisions concerning the funding of abortion services, requirements of spousal consent, requirements of parental consent and/or notification where mature minor's are concerned, and requirements that certain controversial information be supplied before abortions are performed.

Where the two approaches yield different decisions, the Court usually predicates its decision on the premise that the state requirement at issue does not affect significantly the availability of abortion services. Thus the Court approved state requirements regarding written consents, pathology reports, and recordkeeping, and allowed to stand a statutory preamble containing controversial "findings," on the premise that none of these provisions restricted significantly the availability of abortion services. On the Establishment Clause approach, these provisions would all have been declared unconstitutional. But since the Court's approval is conditioned by their understanding that abortion services are not thereby restricted significantly, the availability of abortion *intended* by the Court does not differ significantly from what it would be on the Establishment Clause approach. Another example of this is the Court's acceptance of parental notification before abortions are performed on minors. The Court predicated its decision on the premise that such notification will not enable parents to exercise a veto over their minor's plans. To ensure this result, the Court required bypass procedures. These procedures are so structured by the Court as to make abortion without parental consent or notification just about as available to minors as it would be on the Establishment Clause approach, which would invalidate requirements of parental notification. What is more, experience with bypass procedures supports the view that neither consent nor notification requirements reduce significantly the availability of legal abortions for minors.

Again, so far, nearly identical results obtain from the Court's viability standard and the standard, advocated here, of similarity to newborns. The Court chose viability when, as still today, a fetus is not viable until it is similar to newborns in just the ways I maintain to be sufficient for personhood.

The near identity of (intended) results suggests that in a wide variety of areas, judicial intuitions about the propriety of abortion's availability are satisfied by the Establishment Clause approach. On that score, in other words, the Court's approach and the Establishment Clause approach are (roughly) on a par. But in other respects the Establishment Clause approach is superior. It is better grounded in the Constitution; it allocates institutional responsibilities in ways that accord better with our political institutions, traditions, and ideals; it justifies its results without self-contradiction; and the results that it justifies are more stable. These matters are discussed in the concluding chapter.

Conclusion

F EW, IF ANY, THESES in controversial areas of constitutional law can be maintained with certainty, because few, if any, supporting arguments are impregnable and decisive. In the main, a thesis is accepted if it is self-consistent and accords better than its competitors with the words of the Constitution, authoritative interpretations of those words, our political institutions, our political ideals, and our moral aspirations (see the Introduction). Controversy may reign, however, because the Constitution is written in general terms, such as "liberty," "due process of law," and "unreasonable searches and seizures," which are susceptible of various interpretations. Accordingly, authoritative interpretations of those words often contradict one another.

What is more, political institutions, political ideals and moral aspirations all evolve in response to such factors as economic development, technological innovation, population growth and demographic change. So constitutional interpretations that conformed at one time to our political institutions, political ideals, and moral aspirations may at a later time clash with one, two, or all three of these. Such was the case, for example, with economic substantive due process (see Chapter 1).

In this environment of uncertainty and flux, the grandest claim that can reasonably be made for constitutional interpretations in controversial areas of the law is that they are on balance, all things considered, superior to the alternatives that have so far been proposed. I make this claim for the Establishment Clause approach to legislation regarding abortion.

Arguments supporting this claim occupy the bulk of the preceding chapters. This concluding chapter is limited to considering one view

245

that has not yet been addressed squarely in the present work, isolating the fundamental flaw in the *Roe* approach to abortion-related legislation, reiterating the rationale that justifies the Establishment Clause approach, and reviewing some advantages of that approach.

Justice Scalia's View

The view not yet addressed squarely in the present work is Justice Scalia's opinion that abortion is a political matter to be dealt with by state legislatures, not a matter of constitutional law to be dealt with by the courts. He wrote in *Webster v. Reproductive Health Services* (1989) that "the answers to most of the cruel questions posed [by abortion] are political and not juridical." So the Court should yield "sovereignty over a field where it has little proper business."[1] "[Our] retaining control, through *Roe*, of what I believe to be, and many of our citizens recognize to be, a political issue, continuously distorts the public perception of this Court."[2] Thus, as Justice Blackmun observed, "Scalia would overrule *Roe* . . . and would return to the States virtually unfettered authority to control the . . . decision whether to carry a fetus to term."[3]

Of course, I agree with Scalia's rejection of *Roe*. As I explained in Chapters 1, 2, and 7, I consider *Roe* to be in several respects fundamentally and fatally flawed. I offered an alternative that, I argue, is mandated by the Establishment Clause. That argument contains a reply to Scalia. To the extent that the Establishment Clause mandates answers to questions about abortion-related legislation, the issues remain juridical, not political.

I now present some additional reasons for rejecting Scalia's view that abortion's availability should be decided by state legislation. Pivotal to many issues regarding abortion is the status of the unborn. As Ronald Dworkin pointed out, if the unborn have a fundamental (constitutional) right to life, then no state would be entitled to deny it "equal protection of the laws." Legislation restricting severely the availability of abortion would be not only permitted but required by the Constitution.[4] If, in contrast, the unborn do not have a fundamental (constitutional) right to life, then legislation restricting severely the availability of abortion would be deprived of its most obvious purpose. Therefore, other purposes would have to be featured in the justification of such legislation. These purposes may be related to such matters as cost, medical safety, population growth, and (perhaps) punishment (of illicit sex).

It is certainly questionable whether such purposes as these could enable restrictive abortion laws to pass the minimal constitutional hurdle, applied to *all* legislation, of bearing a rational relationship to a legitimate purpose. But that issue is beside the present point. The point here is that a decision regarding the constitutional status of the unborn is a precondition to deciding which arguments are needed and relevant where abortion-related legislation is concerned. Before any further arguments can be evaluated properly, it must be determined when, if ever, the unborn have a fundamental (constitutional) right to life that is protected by the Due Process Clause.

This determination constitutes an interpretation of the Due Process Clause of the Fourteenth Amendment. The issue concerns the meaning of "person" as it appears in that amendment. Is the unborn at a given stage of prenatal development a person within the meaning of the Fourteenth Amendment, or is it not?

In sum, *all* laws must be constitutional to be valid, and whatever one's views about the legal or moral propriety of abortion, an interpretation of the Fourteenth Amendment must be considered fundamental to any review of the constitutionality of abortion-related legislation. Since in our system of government it is ultimately the Supreme Court's job to render such interpretations, Scalia is wrong. The issue is fundamentally juridical, not political. We do not allow state legislatures to have the final say on the meaning of the federal Constitution. Remitting entirely to the states issues surrounding abortion-related legislation is simply incompatible with our form of government.

Scalia was, perhaps, misled in this regard by associating a judicial determination of relevant issues with the decision in *Roe*. Having good reason to reject *Roe*, he may have thought he had equally good reason to reject a role for the Court. But, the essentially juridical nature of issues fundamental to any and all abortion-related legislation is independent of the merits of the Court's work in *Roe*. It is entirely independent, as well, of one's final opinion about the morality of abortion. Whether or not one believes an abortion at a certain stage of pregnancy to be *morally* permissible, its *legal* permissibility depends on the constitutionality of restrictive legislation. And, as we have seen, the determination of constitutionality requires judicial interpretation of the Fourteenth Amendment.

The Fundamental Flaw in Roe

Like Scalia, the majority in *Roe* and subsequent cases failed to deal appropriately with the issue of the unborn's humanity. This is the fundamental flaw in *Roe*. The majority focused attention, instead, on the right of the woman. This was a mistake on two major grounds. First, the right of the woman is poorly grounded in the Constitution. The general right of privacy is not contained in the Constitution and would not in any case apply unproblematically to abortion, which is a medical procedure and a commercial transaction (see Chapter 1). The general right to liberty is, of course, contained in the Constitution. But almost all legislation restricts people's liberty. Until some reason is articulated for making an exception of abortion, the general right to liberty cannot justify judicial attacks on abortion-related legislation without justifying similar attacks on any legislation of judicial choosing (again see Chapter 1). The specter of judicial sovereignty, which is inconsistent with our political institutions and political ideals, should restrain any substantive due process approach to abortion-related legislation.

The Court's focus on the woman's right was mistaken, also, because it dealt inadequately with the status of the unborn. As I have argued, constitutional issues cannot be clarified, much less resolved, before it is decided whether or not the unborn at a given stage of development is a person within the meaning of the Fourteenth Amendment. In effect, the Court decided in *Roe* that only beginning at about twenty-eight weeks may the state protect the fetus as a person. But the majority gave no justification for this line of division, or for any line of division, during prenatal development, though they seem to have been guided by the distinction between first and second potentiality (see "The Concept of Viability in Abortion Cases" in Chapter 2).

The majority further confused the issue of the unborn's status by suggesting in *Roe* and then maintaining explicitly in the funding cases (*Beal, Maher*, and *Harris*) that the state has an interest in younger fetuses. A sign of the Court's discomfort with acknowledging a state interest in "the potential of life" is their inconsistent recognition of that interest. It appears in funding cases, but disappears where it would seem equally relevant, in cases concerning State mandated information requirements (see Chapter 8).

The Rationale for the Establishment Clause Approach

There is good reason for this uncertainty about the status of the unborn. Before the twenty-first week, that status is a matter of religious belief (see Chapter 6). The Establishment Clause forbids the government, including courts and legislatures, from endorsing any religious belief. So legislation predicated on belief in the personhood of young fetuses is unconstitutional. This consideration justifies what I have called the Establishment Clause approach.

It is instructive to contrast the Fourteenth Amendment personhood of young fetuses with that of, for example, corporations. Extending legal protection to corporate "persons" may be justified by appeal to ordinary, legitimate public purposes. The legal protection of corporations (presumably) fosters economic development, employment, and the material well-being of those who are undoubtedly people. These justifications do not rest on any problematic metaphysical assertions about the nature of corporations themselves. Corporations are not accorded rights for their own sake. Because such instrumental considerations are absent where the unborn are concerned, the justification for protecting the unborn must be that they have rights of their own, intrinsic value, or inherent worth like ordinary people. But the unborn cannot plausibly be regarded as people for constitutional purposes except through analogies that employ entirely secular legal concepts, and such analogies apply only to fetuses twenty-one weeks or older.

Justice Stevens must be credited with the first Supreme Court recognition that government "findings" of personhood in younger fetuses constitute endorsements of religious belief.[5] With this recognition, the focus of constitutional debate shifts from Fourteenth Amendment equal protection to First Amendment establishment. It becomes clear at the same time why the *Roe* majority was reticent, equivocal, and then inconsistent in its treatment of the status of the unborn. That status cannot reasonably be settled by appeal to secular concepts alone. Viewed as a metaphysical issue, the humanity of the unborn is essentially a religious matter. The appropriate reaction to this realization is not to try to avoid the issue of the unborn's status, as the *Roe* majority did, but to relate that issue to the religion guarantees in the First Amendment.

Advantages of the Establishment Clause Approach

Issues raised by abortion-related legislation should be considered in the light of the Religion Clauses also because no alternative approach so far proposed is both self-consistent and consistent with Supreme Court decisions. The Court has introduced exceptions to its own trimester approach (see "The Trimester Framework and Its Exceptions" in Chapter 7). Justice O'Connor (see Chapter 7) has demonstrated ably the inherent weaknesses of the trimester approach, not the least of which is an allocation of institutional responsibilities that is both impractical and inconsistent with our form of government. In addition, the Court failed to justify adequately its decisions in the parental consent cases and is equivocal in its treatment of parental notification (see Chapter 8). As already noted, the Court's treatment of information requirements is inconsistent with its rationale in the funding cases (again, see Chapter 8).

The Establishment Clause approach, by contrast, suffers from none of the defects of *Roe* and subsequent decisions. First, because it is based on the Establishment Clause, it is firmly grounded in the explicit language of a specific provision of the Constitution. Second, the Establishment Clause approach to abortion-related legislation is consistent with the Court's other interpretations of the Establishment Clause. Thus it reflects some of our most cherished political ideals and moral aspirations: respect for individual self-determination, toleration of religious pluralism, and promotion of individualism in matters of conscience.

Lastly, most Supreme Court decisions about abortion-related legislation can be justified on the Establishment Clause approach. Equally important, where the Court reached a different result from the one suggested by the Establishment Clause approach, it did so on the understanding that the availability of abortion services would hardly be affected. In other words, the Court interprets the Constitution to require just about exactly the same availability of abortion services as would be constitutionally required by the Establishment Clause approach. But the Establishment Clause approach yields these results without obfuscation or self-contradiction and through a consideration of the fundamental issue that the Court attempted to ignore—the personhood of the fetus.

In sum, the Establishment Clause approach rests on the recognition that before the twenty-first week of pregnancy, the personhood of the unborn is a matter of religious belief. The resulting analysis of abortion-related legislation is self-consistent and accords better than any alternative so far proposed with the words of the Constitution, authoritative interpretations of those words, our political institutions, our political ideals, and our moral aspirations.

Notes

INTRODUCTION
1. *Roe v. Wade*, 410 U.S. 113 (1973).
2. *Doe v. Bolton*, 410 U.S. 179 (1973).
3. Douglas, Burger, Stewart, Powell, Marshall, and Brennan, who were part of the 7–2 majority.
4. *City of Akron v. Akron Center for Reproductive Health Services*, 462 U.S. 416, 459 (1983).
5. *Webster v. Reproductive Health Services*, 492 U.S. 490, 532 (1989).
6. *Thornburgh v. American College of Obstetricians and Gynecologists*, 476 U.S. 747, 786–788 (1986).
7. *Webster*, at 518.
8. *San Antonio School District v. Rodriguez*, 411 U.S. 1, 17 (1973).
9. See *McGowan v. Maryland* 366 U.S. 420, 425–426 (1961).
10. *Munn v. Illinois*, 94 U.S. 113, 134 (1877).
11. This is essentially the view of Justice Harlan Fiske Stone in *United States v. Carolene Products, Co.*, 304 U.S. 144, 152n. 4 (1938). I do not endorse this view in the present work. I include it here because it is one manner in which the Court sometimes reasons, and I am here describing significant "moves" characterizing the judicial "game" of constitutional interpretation. Most such "moves" are perfectly fair, but some I find to be illegitimate, for example, those used in the original rationale for *Roe v. Wade*. Other "moves" I find irrelevant to the present work. The "insular minorities" move in equal protection analysis is in this category, as explained in Chapter 2.
12. *Rodriguez*, at 16.
13. There may be an exception, however. Fortunately, it does not undermine any major contention of the present work. Five justices maintained in *Employment Division, Department of Human Resources of Oregon v. Smith*, 58 L.W. 4433 (1990) that the fundamental right to free exercise of religion could be

curtailed by generally applicable criminal statutes that are merely rationally related to a legitimate purpose. Oregon's law prohibiting "the knowing or intentional possession of a 'controlled substance'" included peyote among controlled substances and made no exception for the religious use of peyote. The Court held that since the statute concerns criminal conduct and was not aimed at denying anyone free exercise of religion, it is valid because it is rationally related to the goal of reducing drug abuse. The state need not show the law to be essential to meet a compelling public need. This opinion, Justice O'Connor pointed out for the remaining four justices, conflicts with the normal respect accorded fundamental rights in general and the right of free exercise in particular. Significant burdens on these rights are usually subject to strict scrutiny by the Court. In his confirmation hearing, Justice David Souter sided with O'Connor on this matter. In any case, the thesis of the present work rests primarily on an analysis of the Establishment Clause and on the rational relationship standard of review.

It is worth noting also the Court may have a standard of review between the extremes of requiring merely a rational relationship to public purpose and subjecting a statute to strict scrutiny. Justice Marshall presents several examples in his dissent in *Rodriguez*, 102–110. See also L. Tribe, *American Constitutional Law*, 2nd ed. (Mineola, N.Y.: Foundation Press, 1988), 1601–1625.

14. Robert Bork argued this in "Neutral Principles and Some First Amendment Problems," 47 *Indiana L. J.* 1 (1971).

15. This point is inspired by reading John Arthur, *The Unfinished Constitution* (Belmont, Calif.: Wadsworth, 1989), 5–6, 12–13.

16. October 17, 1788. Found in Arthur, *Unfinished Constitution*, 12.

17. A letter to John Taylor. Found in Arthur, *Unfinished Constitution*, 13.

18. For a good defense of a Liberal view, see Thomas Grey, "Do We Have an Unwritten Constitution?" 27 *Stan. L. Rev.* 703 (1975).

19. For a good critique of the Liberal view, see Sidney Hook, *The Paradoxes of Freedom* (Berkeley: University of California Press, 1964), especially Chap. 2. For a more recent treatment, see Robert Bork, *The Tempting of America* (New York: Free Press, 1990).

CHAPTER 1

1. *Lochner v. New York*, 198 U.S. 45, 56–57 (1905).

2. *Lochner*, at 72–73. Note also that there have been two justices in this century named John M. Harlan. The second one, whose opinions in cases concerning contraception are considered later in this chapter, was opposed to some of the views represented here by the first Justice Harlan.

3. *Nebbia v. New York*, 291 U.S. 502 (1934).

4. *Meyer v. Nebraska*, 262 U.S. 390, 390–391 (1923).

5. *Pierce v. Society of Sisters*, 268 U.S. 510, 534 (1925).

6. *Pierce*, at 535.

7. *Skinner v. Oklahoma*, 316 U.S. 535, 541 (1942).

8. *Skinner*, at 539.

9. Chief Justice Warren in *Loving v. Virginia*, 388 U.S. 1, 12 (1967), and Justice Stewart in *San Antonio School District v. Rodriguez*, 411 U.S. 1, 61n. 8 (1973).

10. Justice Marshall makes this point in *Rodriguez*, at 100.

11. *Griswold v. Connecticut*, 381 U.S. 479 (1965).

12. *Poe v. Ullman*, 367 U.S. 497 (1961).

13. *Poe*, at 542.

14. *Poe*, at 543.

15. *Griswold*, at 500.

16. *Griswold*, at 485–486.

17. *Griswold*, at 484.

18. *Griswold*, at 486.

19. *Griswold*, at 508.

20. *Griswold*, at 509.

21. *Griswold*, at 529.

22. Though in *Griswold* Stewart agreed with Black that the Constitution should be narrowly interpreted, he later changed his view and is quoted below as a champion in *Roe* of the inherently expansive doctrine of substantive due process.

23. *Eisenstadt v. Baird*, 405 U.S. 438 (1972).

24. *Eisenstadt*, at 453 (emphasis in original).

25. *Eisenstadt*, at 460.

26. Grounds were given as well for objecting to the statute's restrictions on distributors to married people (they must be physicians or registered pharmacists). That aspect of the case is not central, however, to the line of development culminating in *Roe v. Wade*.

27. *Roe v. Wade*, 410 U.S. 113, 152–153 (1973).

28. *Planned Parenthood of Central Missouri v. Danforth*, 428 U.S. 52, 68–71 (1976), concerns spousal consent and *Bellotti v. Baird*, 443 U.S. 622 (1979), concerns independence of minors from their parents where abortion is concerned.

29. *Roe*, at 172.

30. *Couch v. United States*, 409 U.S. 322 (1973).

31. *United States v. Dionisio*, 410 U.S. 1 (1973).

32. *Bowers v. Hardwick*, 478 U.S. 186 (1986).

33. Jed Rubenfeld, "The Right of Privacy," 102 *Harvard L. Rev.* 737, 745n. 47 (1989).

34. Some exceptions are made in the public interest. For example, states typically require the reporting of gunshot wounds and evidence of child abuse.

35. Rubenfeld, "Right of Privacy," 740.

36. Rubenfeld, "Right of Privacy," 788.

37. Rubenfeld, "Right of Privacy," 791.

38. Rubenfeld, "Right of Privacy," 794.

254 Notes to Chapter 1

39. Rubenfeld, "Right of Privacy," 794.

40. Rubenfeld, "Right of Privacy," 790.

41. Laurence Tribe, *Abortion: The Clash of Absolutes* (New York: Norton, 1990). Tribe justifies the draft as serving the compelling public need of national security, ignoring the fact that a peacetime draft is instituted instead of an all-volunteer force primarily to save the government money (literally at the expense of the draftees).

42. *Roe*, at 152.

43. *Roe*, at 152–153.

44. John Hart Ely, "The Wages of Crying Wolf: A Comment on *Roe v. Wade*," 82 *Yale Law Journal* 920, 948 (1973).

45. Ely, "Wages of Crying Wolf," 947 (emphasis in original).

46. *Roe*, at 168.

47. *Poe*, at 543.

48. The point is made with humor by Richard Posner, now a federal judge, in "The Uncertain Protection of Privacy in the Supreme Court," 173 *Sup. Ct. Rev.* 199 (1979).

49. See *Williamson v. Lee Optical* 348 U.S. 483 (1955).

50. This view is well articulated by Judge Learned Hand in *The Bill of Rights* (Cambridge: Harvard University Press, 1958), 50–51, and by Robert H. Bork in *The Tempting of America* (New York: The Free Press, 1990), 224–225.

51. But see Bernard Siegan, *Economic Liberties and the Constitution* (Chicago: University of Chicago Press, 1980), for the opposite inference.

52. See George Schedler, "Does the Threat of AIDS Create Difficulties for Lord Devlin's Critics?" *Journal of Social Philosophy* 20, no. 3 (Winter 1989).

53. *Griswold*, at 518.

54. *Griswold*, at 487. The inserted quote is from *Snyder v. Massachusetts*, 291 U.S. 97, 105 (1934).

55. *Griswold*, at 519.

56. *Griswold*, at 525, quoting from *Calder v. Bull*, 3 Dall. 386, 399 (1798).

57. *Griswold*, at 524.

58. *Griswold*, at 522.

59. *Loving v. Virginia*, 388 U.S. 1 (1967).

60. See *Reynolds v. United States*, 98 U.S. 145 (1879), for the constitutionality of antipolygamy statutes.

61. *Bowers*, at 216.

62. *Bowers*, at 213.

63. *Bowers*, at 216.

64. *Bowers*, at 194.

65. *Griswold*, at 521.

66. *Griswold*, at 523, quoting *Tyson v. Banton*, 273 U.S. 418, 446 (1927).

67. *Carey v. Population Services International*, 431 U.S. 768, 785 (1977).

68. *American Constitutional Law*, 2nd ed. (Mineola, N.Y: Foundation Press, 1988), 1352. Louis Henkin expresses a similar view in "Privacy and Autonomy," 74 *Colum. L. Rev.* 1410, 1424–1427 (1974).

69. Philip Heymann and Douglas Barzelay, "The Forest and the Trees: *Roe v. Wade* and Its Critics," 53 *B.U. L. Rev.* 765, 772 (1973). Robert Dixon, "The 'New' Substantive Due Process and the Democratic Ethic: A Prolegomenon," 1976 *B.Y.U. L. Rev.* 43, 84–85; Ira C. Luper, "Untangling the Strands of the Fourteenth Amendment," 77 *Mich. L.Rev.* 882, 1032–1033 (1979); Michael J. Perry, "Substantive Due Process Revisited: Reflections on (and Beyond) Recent Cases," 71 *Nw. U. L. Rev.* 417, 440–441 (1976); Richard Epstein, "Substantive Due Process by Any Other Name: The Abortion Cases," 1973 Sup. Ct. Rev. 159; Posner (1979); Ely (1973), 937–940; John H. Garvey, "Free Exercise and the Values of Religious Liberty," 18 *Conn. L. Rev.* 779, 780–781 (1986).
70. Tribe, *Abortion*, 87.
71. Tribe, *Abortion*, 87.
72. Tribe, *Abortion*, 88 (emphasis in original).
73. Tribe, *Abortion*, 90.
74. Tribe, *Abortion*, 92, from *Moore v. City of East Cleveland* 431 U.S. 494, 503 (1977) (plurality opinion)
75. Tribe, *Abortion*, 111.
76. Tribe *Abortion*, 111.

CHAPTER 2
1. *Row v. Wade*, 410 U.S. 113, 153 (1973).
2. *Roe*, at 155. References omitted. Emphasis added.
3. *Roe*, at 163.
4. *Roe*, at 163.
5. *Roe*, at 164–165.
6. *Roe*, at 159.
7. *Roe*, at 162.
8. *Roe*, at 163–164.
9. *Roe*, at 163.
10. *Roe*, at 160.
11. *Planned Parenthood of Central Missouri v. Danforth*, 428 U.S. 42, 63 (1976).
12. *Danforth*, at 63.
13. *Colautti v. Franklin*, 439 U.S. 379, 396 (1979).
14. *Colautti*, at 396n. 15.
15. *Colautti*, at 388.
16. *Roe v. Wade*, at 163.
17. *Akron v. Akron Center for Reproductive Health*, 462 U.S. 416, 461 (1983). Emphasis in the original.
18. *Thornburgh v. American College of Obstetricians and Gynecologists*, 476 U.S. 747, 794 (1986).
19. *Thornburgh*, at 795.
20. *Thornburgh*, at 793n. 2.
21. *Thornburgh*, at 792.
22. *Daniels v. Williams*, 474 U.S. 327, 334–335 (1986).

23. White and others identify conception with fertilization. This departure from medical terminology is so well entrenched in the legal literature that I will employ it myself.

24. *Thornburgh*, at 792.

25. *Thornburgh*, at 778.

26. *Thornburgh*, at 792.

27. *Webster v. Reproductive Health Services*, 492 U.S. 490, 501 (1989), referring to Mo. Rev. Stat. 1.205.1(1),(2) 1986.

28. S. 158 (1981). Quoted from J. Douglas Butler and David F. Walbert, eds., *Abortion, Medicine and the Law*, 3rd ed., (New York: Facts on File Publications, 1986), 439.

29. "Abortion," in Tom Regan, ed., *Matters of Life and Death*, 2nd ed., (New York: Random House, 1986), 290. Feinberg must be given credit for suggesting the basic thesis of the present work in this article, p. 291. I was unaware of Feinberg's treatment until after reading Justice Stevens's dissent in *Webster*, at 567–569, which suggests the same.

30. See *Roe*, at 157–158n. 54.

31. "Religion, Morality, and Abortion: A Constitutional Appraisal," 2 *Loyola U. (L.A.) L. Rev.* 1, 10. Cited by Douglas in *Doe v. Bolton*, 410 U.S. 179, 218.

32. *Doe*, at 218.

33. *Thornburgh*, at 795.

34. *Thornburgh*, at 795.

35. Nancy K. Rhoden, "Trimesters and Technology: Revamping *Roe v. Wade*," in John D. Arras and Nancy K. Rhoden, eds., *Ethical Issues in Modern Medicine*, 3rd. ed., (Mountain View, Calif.: Mayfield, 1989), 304.

36. *Roe*, at 160.

37. Rhoden, "Trimesters and Technology," 304.

38. *Akron*, at 456–458.

39. See Sylvia A. Law, "Rethinking Sex and the Constitution," 132 *Univ. of Pennsylvania L. Rev.* 955, 1023–1024n. 245 (1984).

40. *Thornburgh*, at 795.

41. "The Great Abortion Debate," *New York Review of Books*, June 29, 1989, 52. See also Feinberg, "Abortion," 273.

42. "Duties to Animals and Spirits," in *Lectures on Ethics*, trans. Louis Infield (New York: Harper & Row, 1963), 239.

43. *Thornburgh*, at 795.

44. *Roe*, at 150. Emphasis in the original.

45. See *Roe*, at 161.

46. *Roe*, at 162.

47. In the context of environmental ethics, where the well-being and value of the biosphere is in question, one cannot dogmatically maintain, as here, that all value must be value to a being that has rights. But considerations peculiar to such issues of environmental ethics concern intrinsic values, which are discussed in Chapter 6.

48. *Roe*, at 154.

49. *Thornburgh*, at 795.

50. *Thornburgh*, at 778.

51. Judith Jarvis Thomson, "A Defense of Abortion," in Arras and Rhoden, *Ethical Issues*, 265–275.

52. See Thomson, "A Defense of Abortion"; and Don Regan, "Rewriting *Roe v. Wade*," 77 Mich. L. Rev. 1569 (1979).

53. Law, "Rethinking Sex and the Constitution," 1017.

54. Law, "Rethinking Sex and the Constitution," 1019.

55. Law, "Rethinking Sex and the Constitution," 1020. Emphasis in the original.

56. Law, "Rethinking Sex and the Constitution," 1028.

57. Laurence Tribe, *American Constitutional Law*, 2nd ed. (Mineola, N.Y.: Foundation Press, 1988), 1355. Emphasis in the original. See also Laurence Tribe, *Abortion: The Clash of Absolutes* (New York: Norton, 1990), especially 98–99, 223–225, 227, and 230, where Tribe expresses views similar to those in *American Constitutional Law*.

58. Tribe, *American Constitutional Law*, 1357.

59. Tribe, *American Constitutional Law*, 1357.

60. Tribe, *American Constitutional Law*, 1357–1358. Emphasis in the original.

61. Tribe, *American Constitutional Law*, 1357.

62. Tribe, *American Constitutional Law*, 1359.

63. *Webster*, 492 U.S. 490 (1989).

64. *Thornburgh*, at 768–770.

65. This is essentially the view of Justice Stone in *United States v. Carolene Products Co.*, 304 U.S. 144, 152n. 4 (1938).

66. "The Wages of Crying Wolf: A Comment on *Roe v. Wade*," 82 Yale Law Journal 920, 935.

CHAPTER 3

1. Laurence Tribe, "Foreword: Toward a Model of Roles in the Due Process of Life and Law," 87 *Harv. L. Rev.* 1, 18 (1973).

2. Tribe, "Foreword," 19.

3. Tribe, "Foreword," 20.

4. Tribe, "Foreword," 23.

5. Tribe, "Foreword," 24–25.

6. Laurence Tribe, *American Constitutional Law*, 2nd ed. (Mineola, N.Y.: Foundation Press, 1988), 1349–1350.

7. *Harris v. McRae*, 448 U.S. 297 (1980).

8. *Thornburgh v. American College of Obstetricians and Gynecologists*, 476 U.S. 747, 779 (1986).

9. *Webster v. Reproductive Health Services*, 492 U.S. 490, 501 (1989).

10. *Webster*, at 568.

11. *Webster*, at 569.

12. *Webster*, at 504–506.
13. M. Meyers, ed., *The Mind of the Founder*, (Hanover, N.H.: University Press of New England, 1981).
14. *Everson v. Board of Education*, 330 U.S. 1, 63–72 (1947) (Rutledge dissenting).
15. *Everson*, at 8–11.
16. *Everson*, at 12.
17. See *Wallace v. Jaffree*, 472 U.S. 38, 96 (1985) (Rehnquist dissenting).
18. Massachusetts, in 1833, was the last to disestablish its state church.
19. Joseph Story, *Commentaries on the Constitution of the United States*, Vol. 2, 5th ed. (1891), 630–632; quoted by Rehnquist in *Wallace*, at 104–105.
20. Territorial legislation was subject to Federal jurisdiction before state legislation became subject to it through the Fourteenth Amendment.
21. *Davis v. Beason*, 133 U.S. 333, 346–347 (1890).
22. *Church of The Holy Trinity v. United States*, 143 U.S. 457, 468–469 (1892).
23. *Holy Trinity Church*, at 469.
24. *Holy Trinity Church*, at 470–471.
25. *Holy Trinity Church*, at 471.
26. *Walz v. Tax Commission*, 397 U.S. 664, 701–702 (1970).
27. *Chicago B. and Q. R.R. Co. v. Chicago*, 166 U.S. 226 (1897).
28. *Stromberg v. California*, 283 U.S. 359 (1931).
29. *Gitlow v. New York*, 268 U.S. 652 (1925).
30. *Abington School District v. Schempp*, 374 U.S. 203, 253 (1963) (Brennan dissenting).
31. *Abington*, at 253, contains an inserted quote from *Meyer v. Nebraska* 262 U.S. 390, 399 (1923).
32. *Hamilton v. Regents*, 293 U.S. 245, 258 and 265 (1934).
33. *Cantwell v. Connecticut*, 310 U.S. 296 (1940).
34. *Abington*, at 253–254.
35. *Everson*, 330 U.S. 1.
36. *Reynolds v. United States*, 98 U.S. 145 (1879).
37. *Reynolds*, at 164.
38. *Reynolds*, at 166.
39. *Reynolds*, at 167.
40. *Reynolds*, at 165.
41. *Cantwell*, at 303–304.
42. *Braunfeld v. Brown*, 366 U.S. 599 (1961).
43. *Braunfeld*, at 606.
44. *Sherbert v. Verner*, 374 U.S. 398, 399 (1963).
45. *Sherbert*, at 404.
46. *Thomas v. Review Board*, 450 U.S. 707 (1981).
47. *Hobbie v. Unemployment Appeals Commission*, 480 U.S. 136 (1987).
48. *United States v. Ballard*, 322 U.S. 78, 80 (1944).
49. *Ballard*, at 86.
50. *Ballard*, at 87.

51. *Ballard*, at 87.

52. *Everson*, at 16. Emphasis in original.

53. *Torcaso v. Watkins*, 367 U.S. 488, 489 (1961).

54. *Torcaso*, at 495n. 11.

55. *United States v. Seeger*, 380 U.S. 163 (1965).

56. *Seeger*, at 165.

57. *Seeger*, at 188–191.

58. *Seeger*, at 165–166.

59. *Seeger*, at 180–182.

60. *Seeger*, at 187, quoting from, and adding emphasis to, Paul Tillich, *The Shaking of the Foundations*, (New York: Scribner's, 1948), 57.

61. *Welsh v. United States*, 398 U.S. 333, 341 (1970).

62. *Welsh*, at 339.

63. *Welsh*, at 341.

64. *Welsh*, at 343.

65. *Welsh*, at 343.

66. *Welsh*, at 343.

67. *Welsh*, at 344.

68. *Torcaso*, at 489

69. *Lynch v. Donnelly*, 465 U.S. 668, 689 (1984) (O'Connor concurring).

70. *Lynch*, at 689 (O'Connor concurring).

71. *Thomas*, at 709.

72. *Thomas*, at 711.

73. *Thomas*, at 715–716.

74. *Thomas*, at 714.

75. *Thomas*, at 715.

76. *Thomas*, at 715.

77. *Thomas*, at 715.

78. *Bowen v. Roy*, 476 U.S. 693, 695 (1987).

79. *Bowen*, at 697.

80. *Bowen*, at 696.

81. Robert H. Bork, *The Tempting of America* (New York: Free Press, 1990).

82. Bork, *Tempting of America*, 168.

83. Bork, *Tempting of America*, 143.

84. Bork, *Tempting of America*, 144.

85. Bork, *Tempting of America*, 144.

86. Bork, *Tempting of America*, 144.

87. Bork, *Tempting of America*, 145.

88. Bork, *Tempting of America*, 168.

89. Bork, *Tempting of America*, 158.

90. Bork, *Tempting of America*, 158.

91. Bork, *Tempting of America*, 168.

92. *Plessy v. Ferguson*, 163 U.S. 537 (1896).

93. *Brown v. Board of Education*, 347 U.S. 483 (1954).

94. Bork, *Tempting of America*, 162–163.

95. Bork, *Tempting of America*, 149, referring to *Regents of the University of California v. Bakke*, 438 U.S. 265 (1978).
96. Bork, *Tempting of America*, 149.
97. Bork, *Tempting of America*, 149.
98. Bork, *Tempting of America*, 150.
99. John Hart Ely, *Democracy and Distrust* (Cambridge: Harvard University Press, 1980).
100. Bork, *Tempting of America*, 163.
101. Bork, *Tempting of America*, 163.
102. Bork, *Tempting of America*, 163.
103. Bork, *Tempting of America*, 81.
104. *Strauder v. West Virginia*, 100 U.S. 303 (1880).
105. Bork, *Tempting of America*, 182.
106. Bork, *Tempting of America*, 182. Emphasis supplied. Another leading proponent of "Originalism," Justice Scalia, apparently disagrees with Bork concerning levels of generality. In *Michael H. v. Gerald D.* Scalia maintains that the proper level of generality is "the most specific level at which a relevant tradition . . . can be identified." 491 U.S. 110, 128 n.6 (1989) (Plurality opinion) This would limit the application of the Fourteenth Amendment to issues involving violence against blacks and implies that the *Brown* decision was incorrect. For a good critique of Scalia's views about levels of generality, see Laurence Tribe, *Abortion: The Clash of Absolutes* (New York: Norton, 1990) 100–101.
107. *Thomas*, at 707.
108. *Thomas*, at 719.
109. *Thomas*, at 720–721. See also Bork, *Tempting of America*, 247–248.
110. *Engel v. Vitale*, 370 U.S. 421 (1962).
111. *Abington*, 374 U.S. 203.
112. *Grove v. Mead School District*, 752 F.2d 1528 (1985).
113. This was part of the rationale on the "creation science" side of the case in *Edwards v. Aguillard*, 482 U.S. 578 (1987).
114. *Grove*, at 1537.
115. *Grove*, at 1537.
116. *Grove*, at 1537.
117. *Grove*, at 1537.
118. *Grove*, at 1537.
119. *Everson*, at 32.
120. Tribe has in the 1988 edition of his book retracted his support for a dual definition analysis. See p. 1186.
121. Jesse Choper, "Defining 'Religion' in the First Amendment," 1982 *Univ. of Ill. L. Rev.* 579, 599.
122. Choper, "Defining 'Religion,'" 601.

CHAPTER 4

1. Jesse H. Choper, "Defining 'Religion' in the First Amendment," 1982 *Univ. of Ill. L. Rev.* 579.

2. Kent Greenawalt, "Religion as a Concept in Constitutional Law, 72 *Calif. L. Rev.* 753 (1984).

3. *Lemon v. Kurtzman*, 403 U.S. 602, 612 (1971). See also *Tilton v. Richardson*, 403 U.S. 672, 678 (1971).

4. *The Founding Church of Scientology v. United States*, 409 F.2d 1146, 1160 (1969). (References omitted.)

5. *Scientology*, at 1160.

6. *Thomas v. Review Board*, 450 U.S. 707 (1981).

7. *Bowen v. Roy*, 476 U.S. 693 (1987).

8. *Kolbeck v. Kramer*, 202 A.2d 889 (1964).

9. *United States v. Seeger*, 380 U.S. 163 (1965).

10. *Welsh v. United States*, 398 U.S. 333 (1970).

11. *Engel v. Vitale*, 370 U.S. 421, 424 (1962).

12. *Engel*, at 424.

13. *Engel*, at 424.

14. *Wallace v. Jaffree*, 472 U.S. 38, 40 (1985).

15. *Scientology*, at 1160.

16. *Malnak v. Yogi*, 440 F. Supp. 1284 (1977).

17. *Africa v. Commonwealth of Pennsylvania*, 662 F.2d 1025 (1981).

18. *Epperson v. Arkansas*, 393 U.S. 97 (1968).

19. *McLean v. Arkansas*, 529 F. Supp. 1255 (1982); *Edwards v. Aguillard*, 482 U.S. 578 (1987).

20. *Abington School District v. Schempp*, 374 U.S. 203, 224 (1963).

21. *Abington*, at 225.

22. *Allegheny County v. ACLU*, 492 U.S. 573, 597 (1989).

23. *McLean* (1982) and *Edwards* (1987).

24. See Grover Starling, *Managing the Public Sector* (Homewood, Ill: Dorsey Press, 1977), 336–337.

25. *Walz v. Tax Commission*, 397 U.S. 664, 687–689 (1970).

26. *Bob Jones University v. United States*, 461 U.S. 574, 595 (1983).

27. *Bob Jones University*, at 592.

28. *Abington*, at 303.

29. *Abington*, at 303.

30. *Walz*, at 676.

31. *Marsh v. Chambers*, 463 U.S. 783, 793 (1983).

32. *Torcaso v. Watkins*, 367 U.S. 488 (1961).

33. *Engel* at 424.

34. *Edwards*, at 599.

35. *Edwards*, at 599, quoting *Malnak*, at 1322.

36. *Scientology*, at 1160.

37. *Scientology*, at 1151. References omitted.

38. *Scientology*, at 1152. References omitted.

39. *Scientology*, at 1152.

40. *Scientology*, at 1161.

41. *Malnak*, at 1320.

42. *Bowen v. Roy*, 476 U.S. 693.
43. *United States v. Kauten*, 133 F.2d 703, 705 (1943).
44. *Board of Education v. Barnette*, 319 U.S. 624, 658–659 (1943) (Frankfurter dissenting).
45. *United States v. Ballard*, 322 U.S. 78, 86–87 (1944).
46. *Kauten*, at 705.
47. *Ballard*, at 86.

CHAPTER 5
1. *The Founding Church of Scientology v. United States*, 409 F.2nd 1146, 1152 (1969).
2. *McGowan v. Maryland*, 366 U.S. 420, 465–466 (1961).
3. *United States v. Kauten*, 133 F.2nd 703, 707 (1943).
4. *Kauten*, at 708.
5. *Gillette v. United States*, 401 U.S. 437, 439 (1971).
6. *Gillette*, at 455n. 21.
7. *Kauten*, at 7–8.
8. *United States v. Allen*, 760 F.2d 447, 449 (1983).
9. *Allen*, at 450.
10. *Allen*, at 450.
11. *Allegheny County v. ACLU*, 492 U.S. 573, 598 (1989).
12. *ACLU*, at 601.
13. *ACLU*, at 619.
14. *ACLU*, at 620.
15. *United States v. Ballard*, 322 U.S. 79 (1944).
16. *Ballard*, at 80.
17. *Ballard*, at 86.
18. *Ballard*, at 87.
19. *Thomas v. Review Board*, 450 U.S. 707 (1981).
20. *Bowen v. Roy*, 476 U.S. 693 (1987).
21. *Washington Ethical Society v. District of Columbia*, 249 F.2d 127, 128 (1957). See also *Fellowship of Humanity v. County of Alameda*, 315 P.2d 394 (1957).
22. *Washington Ethical Society*, at 129.
23. *Washington Ethical Society*, at 129.
24. *Scientology*, at 1160.
25. *Scientology*, at 1160–1161n. 51.
26. *Bob Jones University v. United States*, 461 U.S. 574 (1983).
27. *Grove v. Mead School District*, 753 F.2d 1528, 1537 (1985).
28. *Torcaso v. Watkins*, 367 U.S. 488, 495n. 11.
29. *Malnak v. Yogi*, 440 F. Supp. 1284 (1977).
30. *Africa v. Commonwealth of Pennsylvania*, 662 F.2nd 1025, at 1035–1036 (1981).
31. See *Sherbert v. Verner*, 374 U.S. 398 (1963).
32. *Board of Education v. Barnette*, 319 U.S. 624 (1943).

33. Exodus, Chapter 20, verses 4 and 5. See *Barnette*, at 629.
34. *Zorach v. Clauson*, 343 U.S. 306, 314 (1952).
35. *Zorach*, at 314.
36. *Abington School District v. Schempp*, 374 U.S. 203 (1963), at 295.
37. *Sherbert*, at 415–416.
38. *Walz v. Tax Commission*, 664, 669–670 (1970).
39. *Wallace v. Jaffree*, 472 U.S. 38 (1985), at 83.

CHAPTER 6

1. *Griswold v. Connecticut*, 381 U.S. 479, 485 (1965).
2. *Eisenstadt v. Baird*, 405 U.S. 438 (1972).
3. *Abington School District v. Schempp*, 374 U.S. 203, 205 (1963).
4. *Abington*, at 222.
5. *Abington*, at 223.
6. *Abington*, at 224.
7. *Abington*, at 222.
8. *Abington*, at 231.
9. *Abington*, at 222.
10. *Lemon v. Kurtzman*, 403 U.S. 602, 612–613 (1971). (References omitted.)
11. *Lynch v. Donnelly*, 465 U.S. 668, 688 (1984) (O'Connor concurring).
12. *Wallace v. Jaffree*, 472 U.S. 38, 79 (1985).
13. *Wallace*, at 76.
14. *Wallace*, at 83.
15. *Wallace*, at 83.
16. *Abington*, at 231.
17. *Griswold*, at 498 (Goldberg concurring) (References omitted.)
18. *Eisenstadt*, at 448.
19. *Eisenstadt*, at 449.
20. *Eisenstadt*, at 448.
21. *Eisenstadt*, at 448.
22. *Williamson v. Lee Optical*, 348 U.S. 483 (1955), referred to in *Eisenstadt*, at 448.
23. *Epperson v. Arkansas*, 393 U.S. 97 (1968); and *Edwards v. Aguillard*, 482 U.S. 578 (1987).
24. *Wallace*, at 83.
25. John Wisdom, "Gods," in John Hick, ed., *Classical and Contemporary Readings in the Philosophy of Religion* (Engelwood Cliffs, N.J.: Prentice-Hall, 1964), 417–418.
26. Wisdom, "Gods," 418.
27. Wisdom, "Gods," 418. Emphasis added.
28. Wisdom, "Gods," 418. Emphasis added.
29. E. Blechschmidt. "Human from the First," in Hilgers, Horan, and Mall, eds., *New Perspectives on Human Abortion* (Frederick, Md.: University Publishers of America, 1981), 7–8.

30. *Thornburgh v. American College of Obstetricians and Gynecologists*, 476 U.S. 747, 792 (1986).

31. Blechschmidt, "Human from the First," 12–13.

32. Robert E. Joyce, "When Does a Person Begin?" in Hilgers et al., *New Perspectives*, 348.

33. Joyce, "When Does a Person Begin?" 348.

34. A sleeping individual can be, at the same time, both a potential and an actual physician only because potentiality is taken in two different senses, first and second potentiality. A trained physician is actually a physician (relative to first potentiality) even when she is asleep. However, because she is asleep, she is a potential physician (relative to second potentiality).

35. Joel Feinberg, "Abortion," in Tom Regan, ed., *Matters of Life and Death*, 2nd ed. (New York: Random House, 1986), 261–262.

36. Gary B. Gertler, "Brain Birth: A Proposal for Defining When a Fetus Is Entitled to Human Life Status," 59 *Southern California L. Rev.* 1061, 1066 (1986).

37. Wanda Franz, "Fetal Development: A Novel Application of Piaget's Theory of Cognitive Development," in Hilgers et al., *New Perspectives*, 42.

38. *Thornburgh*, at 778 (1986) (Stevens concurring).

39. *Thornburgh*, at 795 (White dissenting).

40. See Feinberg, "Abortion," 270–271; Mary Anne Warren, "The Moral and Legal Status of Abortion," *The Monist* 57 (1973); Stanley I. Benn, "Abortion, Infanticide, and Respect for Persons," in J. Feinberg, ed., *The Problem of Abortion* (Belmont, Calif.: Wadsworth, 1973).

41. Kent Greenawalt, *Religious Convictions and Political Choice* (New York: Oxford University Press, 1989), 12.

42. Greenawalt, *Religions Convictions*, 136.

43. Greenawalt, *Religions Convictions*, 137.

44. Greenawalt, *Religions Convictions*, 189.

45. Greenawalt, *Religions Convictions*, 187.

46. Greenawalt, *Religions Convictions*, 187.

47. Greenawalt, *Religions Convictions*, 155.

48. Greenawalt, *Religions Convictions*, 121.

49. Greenawalt, *Religions Convictions*, 121.

50. Greenawalt, *Religions Convictions*, 137.

51. Greenawalt, *Religions Convictions*, 127.

52. Greenawalt, *Religions Convictions*, 188.

CHAPTER 7

1. *Roe v. Wade*, 410 U.S. 113, 164 (1973).

2. *Roe*, at 164.

3. *Roe*, at 164–165.

4. *Roe*, at 149.

5. *Connecticut v. Menillo*, 423 U.S. 9, 11 (1975).

6. *Planned Parenthood of Missouri v. Danforth*, 428 U.S. 52, 65 (1976).

7. *Danforth*, at 67.

8. *Danforth*, at 80.

9. *Danforth*, at 81.

10. *Roe*, at 163.

11. *Roe*, at 163.

12. *Akron v. Akron Center for Reproductive Health*, 462 U.S. 416, 436 (1983).

13. *Akron*, at 431.

14. *Akron*, at 434.

15. *Roe*, at 163.

16. *Roe*, at 165.

17. *Akron*, at 458 (O'Connor dissenting). Significant changes in the point of viability are currently speculative. But dramatic medical advances are sometimes difficult to predict, and the trimester framework is susceptible of being reduced to absurdity by the first significant change in the point of viability. O'Connor is justified in considering this a weakness of that framework.

18. *Akron*, at 456 (O'Connor dissenting). Emphasis in original.

19. *Akron*, at 460 (O'Connor dissenting).

20. *Akron*, at 461 (O'Connor dissenting). Emphasis in original.

21. *Roe*, at 146–148.

22. *Lemon v. Kurtzman*, 403 U.S. 602, 612–613 (1971).

23. For these latter two changes, see *Danforth*, at 75–79.

24. *Planned Parenthood Association v. Ashcroft*, 462 U.S. 476, 483 (1983).

25. *Ashcroft*, at 484–485.

26. *Doe v. Bolton*, 410 U.S. 179, 193 (1973).

27. *Doe*, at 194. (References omitted.)

28. *Doe*, at 192.

29. *Doe*, at 199.

30. *Thornburgh v. American College of Obstetrics and Gynecology*, 476 U.S. 747, 764 (1986). See Chapter 8 for a fuller account of this issue.

31. *Ashcroft*, at 488 (Powell's opinion).

32. *Ashcroft*, at 497 (Blackmun dissenting).

33. *Ashcroft*, at 488n. 12.

34. *Abington School District v. Schempp*, 374 U.S. 203, 223 (1963).

35. *Stone v. Graham*, 449 U.S. 39 (per curiam).

36. *Stone v. Graham*, at 41.

37. *Stone v. Graham*, at 41.

38. *Wallace v. Jaffree*, 472 U.S.38,108 (1985).

39. *Wallace*, at 75.

40. *Wallace*, at 64.

41. *Edwards v. Aguillard*, 482 U.S. 578, 586–587 (1987).

42. *Ashcroft*, at 489.

43. *Ashcroft*, at 489 (quoting the testimony of expert witness at district court, Dr. Keitges).

44. *Ashcroft*, at 489.

266 Notes to Chapter 7

45. *Danforth*, at 66n. 6. (References omitted.)
46. *Danforth*, at 66–67.
47. *Danforth*, at 67.
48. *Danforth*, at 67.
49. *Danforth*, at 67.
50. *Danforth*, at 81.
51. *Danforth*, at 80–81.
52. *Akron*, at 464 (O'Connor dissenting).
53. *Akron*, at 464 (O'Connor dissenting).
54. *Akron*, at 453 (O'Connor dissenting).
55. The classic illustration is contained in *Williamson v. Lee Optical*, 348 U.S. 483 (1955).
56. *Ashcroft*, at 505 (O'Connor concurring in part).
57. *Engel v. Vitale*, 370 U.S. 421, 430 (1962).
58. *Webster v. Reproductive Health Services*, 492 U.S. 490, 501 (1989).

CHAPTER 8
1. *Ragsdale v. Turnock*, 842 F.2d 1358, 1385n. 12 (1988).
2. Appellee brief submitted to the Supreme Court in *Ragsdale v. Turnock*, 8.
3. *Beal v. Doe*, 432 U.S. 428 (1977)
4. *Maher v. Roe*, 432 U.S. 464 (1977).
5. *Harris v. McRae*, 448 U.S. 297 (1980).
6. *Poelker v. Roe*, 432 U.S. 519 (per curiam) (1977).
7. *Maher*, at 487 (Brennan dissenting).
8. *Maher*, at 488–489 (Brennan dissenting).
9. *Maher*, at 489 (Brennan dissenting).
10. *Maher*, at 489 (Brennan dissenting).
11. *Pierce v. Society of Sisters*, 268 U.S. 510 (1925).
12. *Norwood v. Harrison*, 413 U.S. 455, 462 (1973).
13. *Maher*, at 474.
14. *Beal*, at 453 (Brennan dissenting).
15. *Beal*, at 453–454 (Brennan dissenting).
16. *Maher*, at 478n. 11.
17. *Roe*, at 162–163, quoted in *Beal* at 446 and referred to in *Maher* at 478.
18. *Beal*, at 446.
19. *Beal*, at 446.
20. *Maher*, at 478
21. *Maher*, at 479.
22. *Akron v. Center for Reproductive Health*, 462 U.S. 416 (1983), at 444.
23. *Akron*, at 444–445.
24. *Akron*, at 445.
25. *Akron*, at 443.
26. *Akron*, at 444.
27. *Akron*, at 443.

28. *Thornburgh v. American College of Obstetricians and Gynecologists*, 476 U.S. 747 (1986), at 761.

29. *Thornburgh*, at 801 (White dissenting).

30. *Thornburgh*, at 801 (White dissenting).

31. *Thornburgh*, at 801–802 (White dissenting).

32. *Thornburgh*, at 762 (quoted at 802 by White dissenting).

33. *Thornburgh*, at 802 (White dissenting).

34. *Thornburgh*, at 803 (White dissenting).

35. *Thornburgh*, at 802 (White dissenting).

36. *Thornburgh*, at 804 (White dissenting).

37. *Thornburgh*, at 764.

38. *Thornburgh*, at 801 (White dissenting). The Justice in question was Powell.

39. *Rust v. Sullivan*, 59 L.W. 4451, 4453 (1991).

40. *Rust*, at 4453.

41. *Rust*, at 4453.

42. *Rust*, at 4453.

43. *Rust*, at 4453.

44. *Rust*, at 4457.

45. *Rust*, at 4457.

46. *Rust*, at 4457.

47. *Rust*, at 4456, quoting *Maher*, at 474.

48. *Rust*, at 4463 (Blackmun writing also for Marshall and Stevens).

49. *Rust*, at 4463.

50. *Rust*, at 4464.

51. The religious beliefs referred to here are beliefs that are religious according to the *ordinary* epistemological standard.

52. *Rust*, at 4453.

53. *Rust*, at 4461, emphasis supplied by Blackmun.

54. *Rust*, at 4457, citation omitted.

55. But it may fail some other test. For example, it may not constitute a reasonable implementation of the Public Health Service Act. Such issues of statutory interpretation are outside the scope of the present study.

56. *Planned Parenthood of Central Missouri v. Danforth*, 428 U.S. 52, 69 (1976), quoting from 392 F. Supp., at 1375.

57. *Danforth*, at 69.

58. *Danforth*, at 74.

59. *Danforth*, at 102 (Stevens dissenting).

60. *Bellotti v. Baird*, 443 U.S. 622, 643–644 (1979). The four justices were Powell, Burger, Stewart, and Rehnquist. As the second case with the name *Bellotti v. Baird*, this case is called *Bellotti II*.

61. *Akron*, at 439–440.

62. *Planned Parenthood Association v. Ashcroft*, 462 U.S. 476 (1983), at 490–493.

63. *Danforth*, at 104–105 (Stevens dissenting).

8 **Notes to Chapter 8**

64. *H.L. v. Matheson*, 450 U.S. 398, 425n. 2 (Stevens concurring in judgment).
65. *Danforth*, at 73.
66. *Danforth*, at 75.
67. *Danforth*, at 75.
68. *Danforth*, at 91.
69. *Bellotti II*, at 640.
70. *Wisconsin v. Yoder*, 406 U.S. 205, 223 (1972) (Burger for the majority). Quoted by Powell in *Bellotti II*, at 638 (Plurality opinion).
71. *Bellotti II*, at 640.
72. See *Yoder*, at 244–245 (Douglas dissenting in part).
73. *Hodgson v. Minnesota*, 58 L.W. 4957, 4960 (1990) (Stevens for the majority).
74. *Hodgson*, at 4960.
75. *Hodgson*, at 4971 (Marhall, dissenting in part).
76. *Hodgson*, at 4964.
77. *Hodgson*, at 4971.
78. *Bellotti II*, at 647, quoting from *Baird III*, 450 F. Supp., at 1001.
79. *Bellotti II*, 647.
80. *H.L. v. Matheson*, at 400.
81. *Bellotti II*, at 647.
82. *Ohio v. Akron Center for Reproductive Health* 58 L.W. 4982 (1990) (Kennedy for majority). References omitted.
83. *Hodgson*, at 4963.

CONCLUSION
1. *Webster v. Reproductive Health Services*, 492 U.S. 490, 532 (1989) (Scalia concurring in part and concurring in the judgment).
2. *Webster*, at 535.
3. *Webster*, at 537–538 (Blackmun concurring in part and dissenting in part).
4. Ronald Dworkin, "The Great Abortion Debate," *New York Review of Books*, June 29, 1989, 50.
5. *Thornburgh v. American College of Obstetricians and Gynecologists*, 476 U.S. 747, 749 (1986); and *Webster*, at 566–569. See also Chapter 3.

Glossary of Terms

The following are specialized terms and the meanings associated with them in the present work. In some cases there are additional meanings or associations that can be found in a law, or other, dictionary.

ACCOMMODATION ANALYSIS.   Reconciles the FREE EXERCISE CLAUSE requirement that religious claims be given special treatment with the ESTABLISHMENT CLAUSE requirement of neutrality between religion and nonreligion. Maintains that implicit in the Establishment Clause is the duty to accommodate free exercise.

ALTERNATE MEANS TEST.   The government may not use religious means to accomplish secular goals if alternate secular means are readily available and sufficient.

BYPASS PROCEDURES.   Judicial proceedings that enable minors who would otherwise have to notify or obtain consent from parents before having an abortion to avoid parental involvement. The judge must be convinced that the minor is mature enough to make her own abortion decision or that the abortion is in her own best interests.

CONSCIENTIOUS OBJECTION.   Refusal on grounds of religious principle to participate in war.

CONSEQUENTIALISM.   Moral reasoning that judges actions and omissions not by what is inherent in those actions or omissions, but by the further effects produced.

CONSERVATIVE VIEW (of constitutional interpretation).   The meaning of the Constitution today is (for the most part) the meaning understood by those who ratified it.

COUNTERFACTUAL CONDITION.   A state of affairs that does not obtain in fact but that could have obtained, for example, my presence at the office. I am not there in fact but I could have been there at this time (had I decided to stay at work).

CREATION SCIENCE.   The theory that the earth is only several thousand years old, that all living species assumed their present form at roughly the same time, and that no species has ever evolved from or into a different species.

DIANETICS.   *See* SCIENTOLOGY.

DICTUM.   A judicial pronouncement in a legal decision not essential or integral to the decision's legal justification.

DUE PROCESS OF LAW.   Required in the United States by the FIFTH and FOURTEENTH AMENDMENT injunctions against depriving anyone "of life, liberty, or property, without due process of law."

ECONOMIC SUBSTANTIVE DUE PROCESS.   The view that the Due Process Clause of the FOURTEENTH AMENDMENT requires all commercial regulations that interfere with property rights or economic self-determination be essential to meet a compelling public need. Property rights and economic freedom are fundamental (constitutional) rights.

EIGHTH AMENDMENT.   Known primarily for its prohibition of "cruel and unusual punishments."

EMBRYO.   A fertilized human ovum (egg) from the time of implantation on the uterine wall (a week after fertilization) until about seven weeks after fertilization.

EPISTEMOLOGICAL STANDARD.   A standard for distinguishing religious from secular beliefs. Religious beliefs are those that cannot be established through cogent arguments employing only secular beliefs as premises.

EPISTEMOLOGY.   That branch of philosophy dealing with how we know, and how we could have come to know, what we claim to know.

EQUAL PROTECTION OF THE LAWS.   A guarantee in the FOURTEENTH AMENDMENT. No state may "deny to any person within its jurisdiction the equal protection of the laws."

ESTABLISHMENT CLAUSE.   Part of the FIRST AMENDMENT, where Congress is disallowed legislation "respecting an establishment of religion."

ESTABLISHMENT CLAUSE APPROACH.   The approach to abortion-related legislation based on the view that the personhood of fetuses twenty weeks or younger is a religious matter about which the government must remain neutral.

ETHICAL CULTURE.   An organization, tax exempt as religious, that does not include belief in the existence of God or any other specifically religious beliefs among its tenets.

FETUS.   A fertilized human ovum (egg) seven or more weeks after fertilization, but before birth.

FIFTH AMENDMENT.   Guarantees DUE PROCESS OF LAW and compensation for property taken, and disallows double jeopardy and forced self-incrimination in criminal matters.

FIRST AMENDMENT.   Guarantees freedoms of religion, speech, press, assembly and petition.

FOURTEENTH AMENDMENT. Noted especially for requiring states to accord people DUE PROCESS OF LAW and EQUAL PROTECTION OF THE LAWS.

FOURTH AMENDMENT. Disallows unreasonable searches and seizures.

FREE EXERCISE CLAUSE. A clause of the FIRST AMENDMENT guaranteeing free exercise of religion.

INCORPORATION OF THE BILL OF RIGHTS. The application of most guarantees in the Bill of Rights to state legislation. The rights are considered aspects of the liberty guaranteed in the Due Process Clause of the FOURTEENTH AMENDMENT.

INHERENT WORTH. *See* INTRINSIC VALUE.

INSTRUMENTAL VALUE. The value that something has because it promotes the existence of something else of value.

INTRINSIC VALUE. The value that something has just for what it is in itself. Other things being equal, the world is a better place merely for the existence of whatever has positive intrinsic value.

JEHOVAH'S WITNESS. A religion that includes pacifism among its tenets.

JUDICIAL BYPASS. *See* BYPASS PROCEDURES.

JUDICIAL RESTRAINT. Reluctance of members of the judiciary to substitute their judgment for that of elected representatives concerning the wisdom or probable efficacy of legislation.

LIBERAL VIEW (of constitutional interpretation). The belief that the Constitution should be interpreted to protect individual rights of great moral importance regardless of whether or not those rights are enumerated in the document.

MODERATE VIEW (of constitutional interpretation). The Constitution should be interpreted to guarantee only those rights specifically enumerated, and emphasis should be placed on relatively specific, rather than more general rights (e.g., free speech rather than liberty). The meaning of these rights evolve, so their current meaning is not necessarily what the Framers intended or ratifiers understood. The guarantees in The Bill of Rights should (generally) be applied to the states through incorporation of the Bill of Rights into the FOURTEENTH AMENDMENT.

NATURAL LAW. Universally applicable principles of ethics that include among their requirements respect for individual rights.

NEUTRALITY PRINCIPLE. An implication of the ESTABLISHMENT CLAUSE. The government should not favor either religion or nonreligion, nor should it favor some religions over others.

NINTH AMENDMENT. People retain rights in addition to those enumerated in the Constitution.

ORIGINAL UNDERSTANDING VIEW. Robert Bork's term for his Conservative-to-Moderate view of constitutional interpretation. *See* CONSERVATIVE VIEW and MODERATE VIEW.

RATIO. The part of a judicial opinion that explains the reasoning essential to justify the decision reached in the case.

RATIONAL RELATIONSHIP STANDARD OF REVIEW. Courts accept as valid laws that a reasonable person might think efficacious in promoting a legitimate public purpose.

RELIGION CLAUSES.   The ESTABLISHMENT CLAUSE and the FREE EXERCISE CLAUSE of the FIRST AMENDMENT.

RELIGIOUS BELIEF.   Opinion that cannot be established through cogent arguments that employ only secular beliefs as premises.

SCIENTOLOGY.   A belief system that is religious. The group is not tax exempt as a religious organization because it is profit making.

SECULAR BELIEF.   A belief or practice that is fundamental to a society's way of life. According to the Supreme Court, secular beliefs about matters of fact are considered, in principle, provable by appeal to evidence and argumentation. Secular beliefs about values are not.

SEVENTH DAY ADVENTISTS.   A religion that proscribes work on Saturday.

STARE DECISIS.   The judicial practice of basing current decisions on the rules and principles enunciated or implied in prior decisions.

STRICT SCRUTINY.   The judicial practice of invalidating legislation whose classifications and requirements are not, in the judge's opinions, essential to meet a compelling public need. Used principally where legislation curtails fundamental rights or employs suspect classifications.

SUBSTANTIVE DUE PROCESS.   The view that the Due Process Clause of the FOURTEENTH AMENDMENT guarantees to individuals specific rights nowhere mentioned specifically in the Constitution.

SUSPECT CLASSIFICATIONS.   Classifications by religion, race, or national origin. More controversially, all classifications that disadvantage significantly "insular minorities," that is, groups that cannot protect their collective interests through normal political processes. Legislation employing suspect classifications is subject to strict scrutiny by the courts.

THIRD AMENDMENT.   During peacetime, homeowners may not be required to house soldiers.

TRANSCENDENTAL MEDITATION.   A technique of meditation that courts found too religious for inclusion in public school curricula.

TRIMESTER FRAMEWORK.   From *Roe v. Wade*. Conceptual division of pregnancy into three phases of roughly equal length. During the first of these, the government may not regulate abortions. During the second, it may regulate abortion in the interests of maternal health. During the third, it may regulate, and even proscribe, abortion in the interest of fetal survival, as long as the mother's life or health is not thereby jeopardized.

VIABILITY.   The stage of maturation at which a fetus can be removed from its mother and have a 2 or 5 or 10 percent chance of developing, albeit with artificial aid, into a normally healthy child. This was in 1973 at about twenty-eight weeks after fertilization and corresponded to the onset of the third trimester. It may now be at twenty-five or twenty-six weeks.

WRIT OF CERTIORARI.   Judicial agreement to hear a case. Four justices of the Supreme Court must agree before a case is put on the Court's docket.

ZYGOTE.   A human ovum (egg) from the time of fertilization to that of implantation on the uterine wall, about a week later.

Annotated Table of Cases

All cases referred to or cited in the text are listed below. Except for those of marginal significance for the thesis of the present work, the cases are followed by brief statements of the principal issue(s), holding(s), and/or pronouncement(s) that make these cases noteworthy in the present context.

Abington School District v. Schempp, 374 U.S. 203 (1963). State requirement that either passages from the Bible or the Lord's Prayer be read at the start of each school day was held to violate the Establishment Clause.

ACLU. See Allegheny County v. ACLU.

Africa v. Commonwealth of Pennsylvania, 662 F.2d 1025 (1981). Revolutionary organization MOVE held not to be a religion under the Free Exercise Clause.

Aguillard. See Edwards v. Aguillard.

Akron. See Ohio v. Akron Center for Reproductive Health or *Akron v. Akron Center for Reproductive Health.*

Akron v. Akron Center for Reproductive Health, 462 U.S. 416 (1983). Invalidates state requirements that (1) dilatation-and-evacuation abortions take place in hospitals; (2) all minors under the age of fifteen obtain parental approval for abortion; (3) physicians only may inform patients of risks; (4) an inflexible waiting period be maintained between consent and abortion; and (5) certain information, designed to dissuade a woman from having an abortion, be supplied before consent is obtained.

Alameda. See Fellowship of Humanity v. County of Alameda.

Allegheny County v. ACLU, 492 U.S. 573 (1989). Creche alone on public property violates Establishment Clause neutrality, but holiday display on public property that includes more than one religion's symbols and celebrates liberty is constitutional.

Allen. See United States v. Allen.

273

Clauson. See *Zorach v. Clauson.*

Colautti v. Franklin, 439 U.S. 379 (1979). State requirements that viable or possibly viable fetuses removed during abortion receive medical care must be clear about the responsibility for determining possible viability. The standard of care required for such fetuses must be clear as well.

Commonwealth of Pennsylvania. See *Africa v. Commonwealth of Pennsylvania.*

Connecticut. See *Cantwell v. Connecticut* or *Griswold v. Connecticut* or *Connecticut v. Menillo.*

Connecticut v. Menillo, 423 U.S. 9 (1975). States may require that abortions be performed only by licensed physicians.

Couch v. United States, 409 U.S. 322 (1973). There is no right of privacy regarding tax records given to one's accountant.

Danforth. See *Planned Parenthood of Central Missouri v. Danforth.*

Daniels v. Williams, 474 U.S. 327 (1986).

Davis v. Beason, 133 U.S. 333 (1890). Government may remove the right to vote and to hold public office from anyone who practices, or advocates the practice of, polygamy.

Dionisio. See *United States v. Dionisio.*

District of Columbia. See *Washington Ethical Society v. District of Columbia.*

Doe. See *Beal v. Doe* or *Doe v. Bolton.*

Doe v. Bolton, 410 U.S. 179 (1973). Companion case to *Roe v. Wade.* States may not have unjustified residential, medical, hospital, or board approval requirements that apply only to abortion and reduce its availability.

Donnelly. See *Lynch v. Donnelly.*

East Cleveland. See *Moore v. City of East Cleveland.*

Edwards v. Aguillard, 482 U.S. 578 (1987). State may not require that creation science be taught whenever the theory of evolution is taught.

Eisenstadt v. Baird, 405 U.S. 438 (1972). State may not restrict the access of unmarried people to contraceptives, since unmarried people, too, have a right of privacy.

Engel v. Vitale, 370 U.S. 421 (1962). State may not require that an official nonsectarian prayer be recited in public schools.

Employment Division, Department of Human Resources of Oregon v. Smith, 58 L.W. 4433 (1990). The state may deny unemployment compensation to those fired for violating a drug law, even though the violation occurred as part of a religious ceremony. Free exercise of religion is not violated by the drug law in question if the law is rationally related to a public purpose.

Epperson v. Arkansas, 393 U.S. 97 (1968). State law prohibiting instruction in the theory of evolution violates the Establishment Clause.

Everson v. Board of Education, 330 U.S. 1 (1947). State may provide at public expense transportation to and from all nonprofit private schools, including those with religious affiliation. This case is the first to maintain clearly that, through incorporation into the Fourteenth Amendment, the Establishment Clause applies to the states.

Fellowship of Humanity v. County of Alameda, 315 P.2d 394 (1957). An or-

because the statute was not enforced. The case is known for Justice Harlan's dissent, which foreshadowed his opinion in *Griswold v. Connecticut.*

Poelker v. Roe, 432 U.S. 519 (1977). A city providing services for childbirth at public hospitals need not provide services for nontherapeutic abortions as well.

Population Services International. See *Carey v. Population Services International.*

Ragsdale v. Turnock, 842 F.2d 1358 (1988).

Regents. See *Hamilton v. Regents*, or *Regents of the University of California v. Bakke*

Regents of the University of California v. Bakke, 438 U.S. 265 (1978).

Review Board. See *Thomas v. Review Board.*

Reynolds v. United States, 98 U.S. 145 (1879). The government may prohibit polygamy even though some people consider polygamy a religious duty. Free Exercise encompasses beliefs, not actions.

Richardson. See *Tilton v. Richardson.*

Rodriguez. See *San Antonio School District v. Rodriguez.*

Roe. See *Roe v. Wade* or *Maher v. Roe* or *Poelker v. Roe.*

Roe v. Wade, 410 U.S. 113 (1973). A woman's right of privacy encompasses her decision to have an abortion. Trimester framework established.

Roy. See *Bowen v. Roy.*

Rust v. Sullivan, 59 L.W. 4451 (1991). Supreme Court gave approval to information regulations applying to publicly funded Title X family planning clinics. The government may use its funds to discourage abortion.

San Antonio School District v. Rodriguez, 411 U.S. 1 (1973). Method for financing public schools in Texas is constitutional, even though inequitable, because poor people are not a suspect class, so strict scrutiny is not employed. Case known in part for its discussion of strict scrutiny, rational relationship, and intermediate standards of review.

Schempp. See *Abington School District v. Schempp.*

Scientology. See *Founding Church of Scientology v. United States.*

Seeger. See *United States v. Seeger.*

Sherbert v. Verner, 374 U.S. 398 (1963). State may not refuse unemployment benefits to someone fired from work because, pursuant to religious belief, she refused to work on Saturday.

Skinner v. Oklahoma, 316 U.S. 535 (1942). State may not prescribe sterilization as a punishment for repeated "felonies involving moral turpitude." Statute violates the Equal Protection Clause. Case known for contention that the ability to procreate is a fundamental right.

Smith. See *Employment Division, Department of Human Resources v. Smith.*

Snyder v. Massachusetts, 291 U.S. 97, 105 (1934).

Society of Sisters. See *Pierce v. Society of Sisters.*

Stone v. Graham, 449 U.S. 39 (1980). State may not require the posting of the Ten Commandments in public schools.

Strauder v. West Virginia, 100 U.S. 303 (1880). Equal protection is violated when a state excludes by law blacks from jury service and an all white jury condemns a black man to death. Case known for applying equal protection to all racial and ethnic classifications in such cases.

Stromberg v. California, 283 U.S. 359 (1931). Incorporates First Amendment free speech into Fourteenth Amendment due process.

Sullivan. See *Rust v. Sullivan*.

Tax Commission. See *Walz v. Tax Commission*.

Thomas v. Review Board, 450 U.S. 707 (1981). Person who quit work because working on gun turrets violated his pacifist religious beliefs is entitled to unemployment compensation by the state. Denial of compensation improperly burdens his right to free exercise of religion.

Thornburgh v. American College of Obstetricians and Gynecologists, 476 U.S. 747 (1986). State may not require physicians to convey certain information before abortions when the information is designed to dissuade women from having abortions.

Tilton v. Richardson, 403 U.S. 672 (1971). State may allocate public funds for the construction of higher education facilities at church-affiliated colleges and universities when these facilities are devoted entirely to secular purposes for at least twenty years.

Torcaso v. Watkins, 367 U.S. 488 (1961). State may not require that a declaration of belief in the existence of God be a condition of holding public office. Justice Black maintained that nontheistic belief systems, including Secular Humanism, are religious.

Turnock. See *Ragsdale v. Turnock*.

Tyson v. Banton, 273 U.S. 418, 446 (1927).

Ullman. See *Poe v. Ullman*.

Unemployment Appeals Commission. See *Hobbie v. Unemployment Appeals Commission*.

United States v. Allen, 760 F.2d 447 (1983). Nuclearism is a political view about the importance of nuclear weapons in national defense, not a religion.

United States v. Ballard, 322 U.S. 78 (1944). The truth of religious claims cannot be judged in a court of law. People may believe what they cannot prove.

United States v. Carolene Products Co., 304 U.S. 144 (1938). Known for Justice Stone's decision that classifications are suspect when they affect disproportionately and negatively members of "insular minorities" who are unable to protect themselves through normal political processes.

United States v. Dionisio, 410 U.S. 1 (1973). A grand jury can require that someone make a vocal recording to be used as a kind of vocal fingerprint.

United States v. Kauten, 133 F.2d 703 (1943). The government is not required to grant to selective conscientious objectors the same exemption that it grants to other conscientious objectors. "Religious belief" arises from a sense of the inadequacy of reason and results in "a general scruple" against military service.

United States v. Seeger, 380 U.S. 163 (1965). People whose pacifist beliefs are of "ultimate concern" are conscientious objectors "by religious training and belief" whether or not they believe in the existence of God. Ultimate concerns are essentially religious.

Verner. See *Sherbert v. Verner.*

Virginia. See *Loving v. Virginia.*

Vitale. See *Engel v. Vitale.*

Wallace v. Jaffree, 472 U.S. 38 (1985). States unconstitutionally establish religion when they require in public schools a moment of silence for "meditation or prayer."

Walz v. Tax Commission, 397 U.S. 664 (1970). Tax exemptions for religious organizations do not constitute establishment of religion.

Washington Ethical Society v. District of Columbia, 244 F.2d 127 (1957). An Ethical Society may claim tax exempt status as a religious organization notwithstanding the absence from its official tenets of belief in the existence of God.

Watkins. See *Torcaso v. Watkins.*

Webster v. Reproductive Health Services, 492 U.S. 490 (1989). State may include "findings" in statutory preamble that human life begins at conception. They may disallow public facilities and public personnel for elective abortions. State may require tests, where appropriate in medical judgment, to determine the viability of fetuses believed to be at least twenty weeks old. *Roe*'s trimester framework is too rigid, and states may protect potential life before viability.

Welsh v. United States, 398 U.S. 333 (1970). An objection to military service is conscientious objection by reason of religious training and belief, even if the objector does not characterize his belief as religious and does not relate his belief to a Supreme Being, as long as the belief is, like traditional religious beliefs, a deeply held moral scruple against participating in war of any kind.

West Virginia. See *Strauder v. West Virginia* or *Board of Education v. Barnette.*

Williams. See *Daniels v. Williams.*

Williamson v. Lee Optical, 348 U.S. 483 (1955). State may allow optometrists and opthalmologists to fit lenses to a face while not allowing opticians to do the same, as long as there is a rational relationship to a public purpose. Case known for its explanation of the weak rational relationship test.

Wisconsin v. Yoder, 406 U.S. 205 (1972). State may not require Amish parents to send children to school past the age of fourteen. Case known for emphasizing parents' rights regarding their children's upbringing, especially as an aspect of the parents' free exercise of religion.

Yoder. See *Wisconsin v. Yoder.*

Yogi. See *Malnak v. Yogi.*

Zorach v. Clauson, 343 U.S. 306 (1952). Public schools do not establish religion when they release some students from school to permit them to receive religious instruction elsewhere while other students remain in the public school. Case known for Justice Douglas's using accommodation language and distinguishing neutrality from hostility to religion.

Bibliography

Arthur, John. *The Unfinished Constitution.* Belmont, Calif. Wadsworth, 1989.

Benn, Stanley I. "Abortion, Infanticide, and Respect for Persons." In *The Problem of Abortion,* edited by J. Feinberg. Belmont, Calif. Wadsworth, 1973.

Blechschmidt, E. "Human from the First." In *New Perspectives on Human Abortion,* edited by Thomas W. Hilgers, Dennis J. Horan, and David Mall. Frederick, Md.: University Publishers of America, 1981.

Bork, Robert H. "Neutral Principles and Some First Amendment Problems." 47 *Indiana L. J.* 1 (1971).

———. *The Tempting of America.* New York: Free Press, 1990.

Butler, Douglas, and David F. Walbert, eds. *Abortion, Medicine, and the Law.* 3rd ed. New York: Facts on File Publications, 1986.

Choper, Jesse H. "Defining 'Religion' in the First Amendment." 1982 *Univ. of Ill. L. Rev.* 579–613.

Clark, Tom C. "Religion, Morality, and Abortion: A Constitutional Appraisal." *Loyola U. (L.A.) L. Rev.* 1 (1969).

Dixon, Robert. "The 'New' Substantive Due Process and the Democratic Ethic: A Prolegomenon." 1976 *B.Y.U. L. Rev.* 43.

Dworkin, Ronald. "The Great Abortion Debate." *New York Review of Books,* June 29, 1989, 49.

Ely, John Hart. "The Wages of Crying Wolf: A Comment on *Roe v. Wade.*" 82 *Yale L. J.* 920 (1973).

———. *Democracy and Distrust.* Cambridge: Harvard University Press, 1980.

Epstein, Richard. "Substantive Due Process by Any Other Name: The Abortion Cases." 1973 *Sup. Ct. Rev.* 159.

Feinberg, Joel. "Abortion." In *Matters of Life and Death,* edited by Tom Regan. 2nd ed. New York: Random House, 1986.

Franz, Wanda. "Fetal Development: A Novel Application of Piaget's Theory of

Cognitive Development." In *New Perspective on Human Abortion*, Frederick, Md.: University Publication of America, 1981.

Garvey, John H. "Free Exercise and the Values of Religious Liberty." 18 *Conn. L. Rev.* 779 (1986).

Gertler, Gary B. "Brain Birth: A Proposal for Defining When a Fetus is Entitled to Human Life Status." 59 *Southern Calif. L. Rev.* 1061–1078, 1986.

Greenawalt, Kent. "Religion as a Concept in Constitutional Law." 72 *Calif. L. Rev.* 753–816 (1984).

———. *Religious Convictions and Political Choice*. New York: Oxford University Press, 1989.

Grey, Thomas. "Do We Have an Unwritten Constitution?" 27 *Stanford L. Rev.* 703–718 (1975).

Hand, Learned. *The Bill of Rights*. Cambridge: Harvard University Press, 1958.

Henkin, Louis. "Privacy and Autonomy." 74 *Colum. L. Rev.* 1410–1433 (1974).

Heymann, Philip, and Douglas Barzelay. "The Forest and the Trees: *Roe v. Wade* and Its Critics." 53 *Boston Univ. L. Rev.* 765.

Hilgers, Thomas W., Dennis J. Horan, and David Mall, eds. *New Perspectives on Human Abortion*. Frederick, Md.: University Publishers of America, 1981.

Hook, Sidney. *The Paradoxes of Freedom*. Berkeley, Calif.: University of California Press, 1964.

Joyce, Robert E. "When Does a Person Begin?" In *New Perspectives on Abortion*, edited by Thomas W. Hilgers, Dennis J. Horan, and David Mall. Frederick, Md.: University Publishers of America, 1981.

Kant, Immanual. *Lectures on Ethics,*. trans. by Louis Infield. New York: Harper & Row, 1963.

Law, Sylvia A. "Rethinking Sex and the Constitution." 132 *Univ. of Penn. L. Rev.* 955–1040 (1984).

Lupu, Ira C. "Untangling the Strands of the Fourteenth Amendment," 77 *Mich. L. Rev.* 982.

Madison, James. *The Mind of the Founder*, edited by Marvin Meyers. Hanover, N.H.: University Press of New England, 1981.

Perry, Michael J. "Substantive Due Process Revisited: Reflections on (and Beyond) Recent Cases." 71 *NW. U. L. Rev.* 417–469 (1976).

Posner, Richard. "The Uncertain Protection of Privacy in the Supreme Court." 1979 *Supp. Ct. Rev.* 173.

Regan, Don. "Rewriting *Roe v. Wade*." 77 *Mich. L. Rev.* 1569–1646 (1979).

Rhoden, Nancy K. "Trimesters and Technology: Revamping *Roe v. Wade*." In *Ethical Issues in Modern Medicine*, edited by John D. Arras and Nancy K. Rhoden. 3rd ed. Mountain View, Calif.: Mayfield, 1989.

Rubenfeld, Jed. "The Right of Privacy." 102 *Harvard L. Rev.* 737 (1989).

Schedler, George. "Does the Threat of AIDS Create Difficulties for Lord Devlin's Critics?" *Journal of Social Philosophy* 20 (Winter 1989): 33–45.

Siegan, Bernard. *Economic Liberties and the Constitution*. Chicago: University of Chicago Press, 1980.

Starling, Grover. *Managing the Public Sector*. Homewood, Ill.: Dorsey Press, 1977.

Story, Joseph. *Commentaries on the Constitution of the United States*, vol. 2, 5th ed. (1891).

Tillich, Paul. *The Shaking of the Foundations*. New York: Scribners, 1948.

Thomson, Judith Jarvis. "A Defense of Abortion." In *Ethical Issues in Modern Medicine*, edited by John D. Arras and Nancy K. Rhoden. 3rd ed. Mountain View, Calif.: Mayfield, 1989.

Tribe, Laurence. *American Constitutional Law*. Mineola, N.Y.: Foundation Press, 1978.

———. *American Constitutional Law*. 2nd ed. Mineola, N.Y.: Foundation Press, 1988.

———. *Abortion: The Clash of Absolutes*. New York: Norton, 1990.

———. "Foreword: Toward a Model of Roles in the Due Process of Life and Law." 87 *Harvard L. Rev.* 1 (1973).

Warren, Mary Anne. "On the Moral and Legal Status of Abortion." *The Monist* 57 (1973): 43–61.

Wisdom, John. "Gods." In *Classical and Contemporary Readings in the Philosophy of Religion*, edited by John Hick. Engelwood Cliffs, N.J.: Prentice-Hall, 1964.

Index

Abington School District v. Schempp (1963), 86, 117, 129, 158, 163, 205

Abortion: consent of parents, 230–240; consent of spouse, 229–230; and equal protection, 4; fundamental right to, 8; and Liberal view, 11–12; medical risks of, 192–193, 196, 202–203, 217; and Neutrality Principle, 201–204; nontherapeutic, 216–217; notification of parents, 238–242; pathology report requirements, 203–204, 206, 208–209; and privacy, 30–38; public funding of, 214–221; and record-keeping requirements, 208–209; and religious convictions, 170–176, 179, 184–186; and stare decisis, 1–2; and strict scrutiny, 8; and written consent requirements, 206–209

Accomodation analysis, 157–160

ACLU. See Allegheny County v. ACLU

Adams, John, 11–12

Affirmative action, 98

Africa v. Commonwealth of Pennsylvania (1981), 118, 154

Aguillard. See Edwards v. Aguillard

Akron. See Akron v. Akron Center for Reproductive Health; Ohio v. Akron Center for Reproductive Health

Akron v. Akron Center for Reproductive Health (1983), 1, 56, 194, 231–232

Alameda. See Fellowship of Humanity v. County of Alameda

Allegheny County v. ACLU (1989), 118, 145–146

Allen. See United States v. Allen

Alternate means test, 164, 200–201; and public funding of abortion, 218

American Bar Association, 197

American College of Obstetrics and Gynecology (ACOG), 194

Animals: cruelty to, 42, 68; and religious convictions, 186–189

Aristotle, 55, 173

Arkansas. See Epperson v. Arkansas; McLean v. Arkansas

Arthur, John, 252nn. 15–16

Ashcroft. See Planned Parenthood Association v. Ashcroft

Bakke. See Regents of the University of California v. Bakke

Baird. See Bellotti v. Baird; Eisenstadt v. Baird

Ballard. See United States v. Ballard

Banton. See Tyson v. Banton

Baptism, and secular harm, 182

Barnette. See Board of Education v. Barnette

Barzelay, Douglas, 255n. 69

Beal v. Doe (1977), 218, 220–221, 223

Beason. See Davis v. Beason

Belotti v. Baird (1979), 231, 233, 240–241

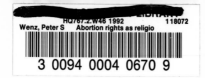